"I just wanted to thank you for writing the wonderful book *Resumes For Dummies*. I am changing careers in the near future (as soon as I find a job) and this book is helping me out immensely in rewriting my resume. I have used numerous resources in identifying my resume needs and find this book to be the best — the most useful tool. Thanks again."

— Mohammed Fares, Rockville, Md.

"*Resumes For Dummies* is an all-purpose, content-filled resume book that has enough humor to focus your interest on what is a very serious matter: you as a marketable product. One chapter (Chapter 3) stood out for me. It clarifies the use of hooks — when to use an objective and when to use a skills summary, citing advantages and disadvantages of each. I also liked the detailed chart on updating your resume for scanning technology and for sending it online. A very timely read!"

— Patricia S. Pigg, Florissant, Mo.

"I love *Resumes For Dummies*! It's my job search bible."

— Bonnie J. Mclurg, Mayfield, Ohio

"I really did love *Job Interviews For Dummies*. It was the first book that actually taught me how to answer specific questions. It was VERY valuable in my job search process. I have a lot of experience, but was always lacking in interview skills. (I would get really nervous before and during the interview, and would bomb it because of this.) I can see why this book won the year's best career book award."

— Susan Postma, Burnaby, British Columbia

"After a disappointing job search, I picked up *Job Interviews For Dummies*. In two days, I read the first eight chapters, went to the interview, and my answers flowed very smoothly — I showed confidence when meeting with three key people individually for three hours. The next day I had an offer for the pay I wanted plus stock options. I am overjoyed — your book was a tremendous help. Thanks for writing the book the way you did."

— Ali Khan, Fairfax, Va.

"I wish to thank Joyce Lain Kennedy for writing the books *Job Interviews For Dummies* and *Cover Letters For Dummies*. I relied solely on the two books in my attempt at a career move.

I have been driving a truck for eight years and just recently finished night school with a Magna Cum Laude BS degree in accounting. Every job interview and cover letter was tailored by Joyce.

"I'm now a portfolio accountant with an investment company in Andover, Massachusetts. I have begun my dream career thanks to you and your effective material."

[second letter]

"Joyce's book saved me again. I had been interviewing for the past couple of months to take my career to the next level. After an interview that went awry, I dug out *Job Interviews For Dummies* and crammed all the pertinent chapters the night before the next big interview for a job I really wanted. The interview the next day with the director of human resources went PERFECTLY. For each forthcoming interview, I read this book again the night before interviews with the supervisor, manager, and director of the department. I began working at my present great job a month ago, thanks to Joyce and her book.

I was so excited about the results that I let two coworkers at my previous employer borrow it before their interviews. They both received offers after those interviews. I'm touting the praises of Joyce's book all over Boston, and it's having a great effect."

> — Mark W. Emmith, Newburyport, Mass.

"There are lots of books on how to create a sharp resume. I would recommend *Resumes For Dummies* by Joyce Lain Kennedy. . . "

> — Werner Koepf (Web posting — How I found my job: www.physics.ohio-state.edu/~koepf)

"Two books I found helpful in writing my resume were: *Resumes For Dummies* by Joyce Lain Kennedy and . . . [A resume book for scientists and engineers]"

> — Chris Pippenger (Web posting — Civilian Transition Resources [military to civilian jobs]: www.geocities.com/~cga86/civ.html)

Cover Letters

FOR

DUMMIES®

2ND EDITION

Cover Letters

FOR DUMMIES®

2ND EDITION

by Joyce Lain Kennedy

WILEY

Wiley Publishing, Inc.

Cover Letters For Dummies,® 2nd Edition

Published by
Wiley Publishing, Inc.
111 River Street
Hoboken, NJ 07030
www.wiley.com

Copyright © 2000 by Wiley Publishing, Inc., Indianapolis, Indiana

Published simultaneously in Canada

Library of Congress Cataloging-in-Publication Data:

Library of Congress Control Number: 99-69711

ISBN: 0-7645-5224-4

Manufactured in the United States of America

15 14 13 12 11 10

2O/QU/QU/QT/IN

About the Author

Joyce Lain Kennedy is the author of the *Los Angeles Times* Syndicate's column **CAREERS**, now in its 32nd year and appearing in more than 100 newspapers.

Her twice-weekly column is carried in the *St. Louis Post-Dispatch, The L.A. Times,* the *Dallas Morning News,* the *Seattle Times,* the *Louisville Courier Journal, Tulsa World,* and more.

Recognized as America's favorite careers journalist, Kennedy has received more than three million reader letters. In her column, she has answered in excess of 4,200 queries from readers.

Kennedy's wise counsel about job and career development addresses universal problems experienced by most working people — problems ranging from dealing with demotion to celebrating or coping with defining career moments. First to report on many new technologies and trends, Kennedy advises job seekers to relearn many strategies and tactics to prosper in a distinctly new job market.

She is the author or co-author of eight books, including *Joyce Lain Kennedy's Career Book* (VGM Career Horizons) and *Electronic Job Search Revolution, Electronic Resume Revolution,* and *Hook Up, Get Hired! The Internet Job Search Revolution* (the last three published by John Wiley). The last three books are groundbreaking works for the new technology that's bringing people and jobs together. With Dr. Herm Davis, she wrote *College Financial Aid For Dummies.*

Cover Letters For Dummies is one of a trio of job market books by Kennedy published under the wildly popular *For Dummies* imprint: *Resumes For Dummies, Cover Letters For Dummies,* and *Job Interviews For Dummies.*

Writing from Carlsbad, California, a San Diego suburb, the dean of careers columnists is a graduate of Washington University in St. Louis. Her e-mail address is jlk@sunfeatures.com.

Author's Acknowledgments

A million sunny smiles to

James M. Lemke, HR Staffing and Systems consultant, Redondo Beach, California (`jmlemke@aol.com`). Once again, Jim has proved himself to be number one at "He who knows the answers."

Kelly Ewing, project editor of this edition, Indianapolis, Indiana. Working online with Kelly is a genuine pleasure.

Karen Hansen, acquisitions editor of this edition, Chicago, Illinois. Karen steps up to the plate and hits one out of the park when challenges arise.

Lisa Roule, acquisitions coordinator, Chicago, Illinois. Lisa, your production support is tops.

Walter Tamulis, Sun Features Inc., Carlsbad, California, my technical associate. Wally knows weighty ways around the Web.

Society for Human Resource Management (SHRM) in Alexandria, Virginia. Special thanks to **Allison Branick** and **Kathy Compton** for facilitating the SHRM survey in Chapter 1. Allison and Kathy, I appreciate you.

Employment Management Association (EMA) in Alexandria, Virginia. Special thanks to **Rebecca Hastings** for coordinating contributors to Chapter 20. Rebecca, you made it easy.

John Lucht, The Lucht Consultancy, New York. John's consults are golden nuggets, and this book is enriched by his help. He is the author of the classic *Rites of Passage at $100,000+: The Insider's Lifetime Guide to Executive Job-Changing*.

Michael R. Forrest, CEO of JobOptions, Cleveland, Ohio, whose knowledge of DotCom recruiting is awesome. Thanks, Michael.

Publisher's Acknowledgments

We're proud of this book; please send us your comments through our online registration form located at www.dummies.com/register.

Some of the people who helped bring this book to market include the following:

Acquisitions, Editorial, and Media Development

Project Editor: Kelly Ewing

   (Previous Edition: Kathleen M. Cox)

Acquisitions Editor: Karen Hansen

Acquisitions Coordinator: Lisa Roule

General Reviewer: James M. Lemke HR Staffing and Systems consultant

Editorial Director: Kristin A. Cocks

Editorial Administrator: Michelle Hacker

Production

Project Coordinator: Regina Snyder

Layout and Graphics: Joe Bucki, Matt Coleman, Barry Offringa, Tracy K. Oliver, Jill Piscitelli, Brent Savage, Jacque Schneider, Erin Zeltner

Proofreaders: Laura Albert, Corey Bowen, Arielle Carole Mennelle, John Greenough, Toni Settle, Charles Spencer

Indexer: Ann Norcross

Publishing and Editorial for Consumer Dummies

   Diane Graves Steele, Vice President and Publisher, Consumer Dummies

   Joyce Pepple, Acquisitions Director, Consumer Dummies

   Kristin A. Cocks, Product Development Director, Consumer Dummies

   Michael Spring, Vice President and Publisher, Travel

   Brice Gosnell, Publishing Director, Travel

   Suzanne Jannetta, Editorial Director, Travel

Publishing for Technology Dummies

   Richard Swadley, Vice President and Executive Group Publisher

   Andy Cummings, Vice President and Publisher

Composition Services

   Gerry Fahey, Vice President of Production Services

   Debbie Stailey, Director of Composition Services

Contents at a Glance

Cartoons at a Glance

By Rich Tennant

page 7

page 53

"Do you think being able to play N64, Dreamcast, and Playstation could be considered transferable skills?"

page 91

"Some of these cover letters include too much personal detail. This one has a centerfold."

page 121

page 165

page 219

Fax: 978-546-7747
E-mail: richtennant@the5thwave.com
World Wide Web: www.the5thwave.com

Table of Contents

Introduction

I'll let you in on a little secret: Revising books is not an author's favorite pastime. When the first edition of this book came out in 1996, I thought, "Oh, good. Cover letters — a topic I won't have to revise for ten years. Do this book right the first time, and it'll serve readers well for a l-o-o-ng time. Letters are letters." Yeah, right. What was I thinking?

Only four years later, I stand wised-up: The New Economy is here with its riches of information and services that leave behind an age of manufacturing and steel. Technology-driven, the New Economy is flipping traditional job market concepts on their heads, and that includes the perception of what constitutes a cover letter — and how it should be used.

As I said in the first edition, every resume needs a bodyguard. That's a cover letter's role. But now there's a newcomer — the e-mail cover note. Think of it this way: If the cover letter is a big, muscular, formidable racehorse, the e-mail cover note is a fleet-footed pony.

Horse or pony, the purposes of cover communications are to

- ✔ Nail the reviewer's interest
- ✔ Tell the reviewer what you can do in the future (the resume reports what you have done in the past)
- ✔ Focus on the employer (the resume focuses on you)
- ✔ Showcase your wonderful personality
- ✔ Nudge follow-up action (scheduling of a job interview) by telling the reviewer you'll be in contact for an appointment; or if that's not possible in a digital exchange, encourage the reviewer to contact you

The New Economy is rapidly expanding, and unemployment rates are in the basement. Unfortunately, the longest boom in three decades isn't pulling everyone along, particularly workers on the shady side of 40, people with disabilities, moms who've been out of the workplace for more than a couple of years, and workers whose skills are obsolete. (The insights this book offers may empower you to take back your place in the paycheck crowd.)

But at this writing, we're in a seller's market, which is great for most of you professionals, managers, technicals, and administrators — experienced hands or job-market newcomers! Seize opportunities to land the very best job you can while the sun shines.

Use the RedHot letter or RedHot note to prove that you're a RedHot candidate whom reviewers had better whoosh into their office to interview before someone else grabs you.

What Is a RedHot Cover Letter?

A RedHot cover letter is

- ✔ Hot-wired to a target job
- ✔ So intriguing that a reader makes room in a busy schedule to meet you
- ✔ An electrifying personal advertising tool that short-circuits the competition

A RedHot cover letter is not

- ✔ Bland and indifferent
- ✔ Littered with frozen, dry facts
- ✔ What the hiring manager's kid uses for scratch paper

Okay, so you're still a little skeptical. *RedHot* may sound slightly devilish, like you've got something up your sleeve. You do: your skills, accomplishments, and experience — which you can use to achieve future great work. Your RedHot cover letter sparks the reader's interest as a hot-poker introduction to your FirstRate resume. The cover letter is your chance to personalize your resume. Here's where you make yourself into a living, breathing human being and set your accomplishments aglow. Drawing from your FirstRate resume — and it had better be FirstRate, or your cover letter may as well go to the employer solo — you spice up your data by paralleling your qualifications to those on the employer's hot list.

But to Whom Do You Write?

Write to everyone with whom you interact. Write in answer to printed job ads and online job postings, as well as to recruiters whom you hope will carry your banner. Write networking letters to acquaintances or old friends you haven't talked to in years. Write initiating (direct application) letters to employers you've sourced as good places to work.

Cover letter is an umbrella term encompassing a whole new slew of employment communications. Just as you write to different people, your individual letters highlight different aspects of your career needs in a job search.

What's in This Book

Part I, Cover Letters in the New Economy, clues you in on changing rules in the New Economy, rules that deeply impact the way work gets done and the way you are finding the work to do. You discover the results of an exclusive new cover letter study among members of the Society for Human Resource Management (SHRM) — folks who can impact your future. You find out how and where to use the new e-mail cover notes.

Part II, RedHot Cover Letters That Say You're Hot, tells why you need a cover letter, the types of cover letters, the myths that surround them, and how to break out of writer's block.

Part III, Working Out What Sizzles, presents a skills finder to help you identify where your skills fit in today's workplace and guides you through a number of self-assessment worksheets. (These worksheets are helpful in creating your resume as well.)

Part IV, Writing RedHot Cover Letters, helps you jump through the cover letter-writing hoops. This part shows how your letter should look and sound, with tips on language, content, and image. You'll get ideas on writing a dazzling opening line. And you'll work through a RedHot Cover Letter checklist to make sure that the best you lives in your letter.

Part V, RedHot Cover Letters: What They Look Like, shows you models from which to learn. Each is a candidate for reformulation as an e-mail cover note.

Part VI, The Part of Tens, sums up surefire tips for working with recruiters, answering job ads, avoiding the salary question, handling negative references, and creating letters that even a computer can love.

And some problem words and ways to use them correctly are included in the **Appendix,** so you can avoid making embarrassing mistakes that could literally cost you a job.

Icons Used in This Book

One helpful feature of the *...For Dummies* series is the liberal use of cute pictures called icons that draw your attention to information too hot to ignore. These are the icons used in this book and what they signify.

These powder-keg tips will make your cover letter burn all the rest.

Pay attention to this icon so you don't come across as a clueless beginner, even if you are one.

This icon highlights tips for the individual who's been around the business block but whose experience may need to be fired up.

This icon notes the fundamental facts of cover letter preparation and job hunting. When you need to get down to basics, this is it.

Look here for smokin' advice from whizzes in the job-finding business.

This icon spotlights differences of opinion in the art of cover letter writing.

This icon highlights tips to target online opportunities and issues.

This dinosaur icon chomps away at job-killing goofs; ignore these warnings and you may be eaten alive.

A Time for RedHot Cover Letters

If you're still in doubt about the power of cover letters, consider this example supplied by Jim Lemke, a staffing and systems consultant who is the technical reviewer for this book. Lemke, a former manager of employment at Walt Disney Imagineering, shares this delightful cover letter story:

At Disney, a job letter arrived from a young man with a simple message:

> *I want to work for Walt Disney. I am creative. My resume proves it.*

The human resource department at Disney sent back a standard software-generated response acknowledging the receipt of the resume and stating that his resume would be scanned into a database. If a suitable job opening arose, he would be contacted.

A second letter arrived from the young man. It said:

> *I don't think you understand. I really, really, really, really, really want to work for Walt Disney.*

Disney's human resource job computers sent out a second message promising to keep his resume.

Soon a third communication from the young man arrived. It was a ransom note, with letters cut from a newspaper. One ear from a mouseketeer hat was pinned to the note:

> *You still don't get it. I've got the mouse. I want a job.*

Yes, the young man got the job. The key is that Disney hired him for his creative mind. Don't try this ploy at Bank of America, but also remember that a cover letter gives you your chance to really shine. A well-written cover letter can help make your ideal job a reality. So start writing.

Part I

Cover Letters in the New Economy

The 5th Wave   By Rich Tennant

BARBARA KNOWS PACKAGING GETS COVER LETTERS READ

YOU MAY ALREADY BE A WINNER!

In this part . . .

*I*n the United States, our main business isn't making industrial products anymore — it's become information and services, a huge change causing economists and businesspeople to talk about the New Economy. Much of the New Economy is technology-driven — especially information technology, such as the Web and wireless telephones. This new paradigm is becoming pervasive, powerful, and ingrained in the workplace. The New Economy deeply impacts the way work gets done and the way you are finding the work to do.

This part clues you in on the changing rules — such as the new online cover notes — for creating cover communications as integral parts of the self-marketing materials you need to thrive in the New Economy.

Chapter 1

What Employers Are Telling Us

In This Chapter

▶ The world is between economies

▶ Thriving in an era of transition

▶ 582 employment professionals discuss cover letters today in a new survey by the **Society for Human Resource Management**

A re you looking for a job in the early 21st century? Like Mom said, "Look both ways before crossing the street."

Turning back in time, you'll see the traditional search process fueled by paper cover letters and resumes; looking forward, you'll spot the digitally altered hunt as millions of people jump on the Internet bandwagon. We live in a time of historical transition, moving from a paper norm to DotCom innovation. But we're not all the way there yet.

So where does the changeover leave the cover letter and the resume, the two self-marketing stalwarts in the job search? "What now, brown cow?" you ask yourself. "Should I go cyber or stick with paper?"

If you're in a high-tech industry, the answer obviously falls on the cyber-side — go straight to Chapter 2. But, for the rest of us, especially at companies with fewer than 1,000 employees, the majority of employers and job seekers continue to meet each other in customary channels and to use familiar paper-based tools.

When will cyber-search come to all? Web-based recruiting is tornadoing through the American recruitment industry, and cyber-search will be totally mainstream before the decade is out. For now, your best bet is to take a bicentric approach to finding work, merging traditional and innovative methods. Look both ways. Do a crossover job search.

The key question in this book is How do I conceptualize, create, and distribute my cover letter, a tool too good to leave behind in an era of transition? HR (human resource) staffing and systems consultant James M. Lemke, the technical reviewer of this book, offers the right answer:

> *The issue is not which media I use to communicate my availability, but how do I organize my information to get a job interview?*

The question of paper or cyber-resources is reflective of the larger trend influencing your search issues; the larger trend is the movement from an Industrial Economy to what is being called the New Economy.

Signs of the New Economy

Coming on the heels of a 300-year-old industrial economy based on hard resources like coal, steel, and oil, as well as on manufacturing and human muscle, a services- and knowledge-based economy is leaping out of the chute in the United States. The New Economy is choking some occupations (traditional retailer, travel agent, mutual fund broker) and oxygenating others (e-commerce manager, Web developer, wireless engineer).

The New Economy is technology driven, particularly information technology. (Think of all those IT jobs you see advertised.) The hallmark of the New Economy is faster growth and lower inflation.

With the United States leading the way by spinning the longest and most spectacular boom in three decades, the rest of the world is starting to adopt the benefits of a technology driven expansion. Even when the boom goes poof, as one day it must, there will be no turning back to the old way of finding work; the toothpaste is out of the tube.

How the New Economy Impacts the Job Market

The American boom has fathered a full-employment economy, encouraging huge numbers of people to change jobs when they please. (The Bureau of Labor Statistics says that the average time people are spending in a job is under four years.) Computers are facilitating job changing as workers go online at home — or in their workplace — to find new opportunities.

E-mail responding is the heavy favorite. Everyone loves e-mail! There's no sign of diminishing interest as the novelty wears off. (Don't use your office computer unless you don't care if you get caught job shopping on company time.)

If you doubt that the use of e-mail communication in the job market will continue to bounce off the scale, researchers at Jupiter Communications say that the exploding availability of free Internet access means that the number of Internet households in the U.S. will jump from 45 million today to 68 million in 2003.

By another measure — individuals rather than households — a Neilsen/NetRating survey figures the online universe now exceeds 120 million Americans. (Worldwide, other studies show more than 200 million global viewers.)

Although the conversion to cyberspace-rooted cover letters and resumes is well underway, smaller firms continue to rely on manual methods. The following recent survey offers many clues to how employers view cover letters today.

Inside a Hiring Professional's Head

With more than 135,000 professional and student members throughout the world, the Society for Human Resource Management (SHRM) is the leading voice of the human resource profession.

The SHRM Foundation, a nonprofit organization of multiple purposes, includes among its charges a mandate to support applied research aimed at helping its members stay current with the latest developments and trends.

A SHRM professional emphasis group, The Employment Management Association (EMA) — with more than 5,600 members — is the top professional association for employment management practitioners and service providers who are concerned with staffing issues and trends.

In late 1999, I had the pleasure of participating in a *SHRM Survey on Cover Letters and Resumes*. The survey was faxed to randomly selected members of the EMA; 582 human resource professionals responded.

Starting with the highlights, the following SHRM survey data details concerning cover letters were written by SHRM's Allison Branick and are printed here by permission of the Society for Human Resource Management.

- ✔ Most resumes are accompanied by cover letters.
- ✔ Cover letters are typically read in less than one minute.
- ✔ HR professionals are split on cover letter quality.
- ✔ Typos can kill candidates' chances.
- ✔ HR professionals favor personalized cover letters.

> ✔ Most resumes (and cover letters) come via postal mail or fax . . . but e-mail is preferred.
>
> ✔ Importance of cover letters versus resumes: Respondents are split.

Most resumes are accompanied by cover letters

On average, two out of three resumes (67 percent) received by human resource departments today are accompanied by cover letters, according to survey respondents. One out of every three resumes arrives as a stand-alone document.

So what happens to resumes that arrive without cover letters? Are they still considered for vacant positions within organizations? When asked what their organizations do with such unaccompanied resumes, 70 percent of respondents report that the resumes are always considered for vacant positions, suggesting that missing cover letters are not an issue. However, 28 percent of respondents say they consider resumes only sometimes if they arrive without cover letters, and 2 percent of respondents never consider resumes that come alone.

Cover letters are typically read in less than one minute

More than eight out of ten HR professionals spend less than one minute on average reading a cover letter. According to survey results, 83 percent of respondents report that the average length of time they or a member of their staff spend reading a cover letter sent by a job applicant is one minute or less. About 15 percent of respondents spend more than one minute reading each cover letter.

Survey data shows that the larger the organization is, the less time the HR professionals tend to spend reading the cover letters they receive for vacant positions. For example, respondents from larger organizations (52 percent), or those with 250 or more employees, are more likely to spend between 1 and 30 seconds reading the cover letters they receive than are respondents from smaller organizations (39 percent), or those with fewer than 250 employees. Conversely, HR professionals from smaller organizations (42 percent) are slightly more likely than those from larger employers (34 percent) to spend between 31 and 60 seconds reading cover letters. This data suggests that larger organizations may have more job vacancies at any given time than smaller employers, thus are receiving more cover letters and resumes and have less time to spend reading each cover letter.

Demographics of the SHRM survey

Three-quarters of SHRM respondents work for companies of fewer than 1,000 employees, and nearly half for companies that employ 250 or fewer employees. Bear in mind that the majority of job openings in the United States occur in smaller companies. Here are the demographics for the companies that completed the survey:

Total number of employees

29%	Fewer than 100 employees	11%	1,001 to 2,500 employees
19%	100 to 250 employees	4%	2,501 to 5,000 employees
15%	251 to 500 employees	4%	More than 5,000 employees
12%	501 to 1,000 employees	5%	No answer

Type of organization

23%	Business and professional services	2%	Education
20%	Manufacturing	2%	Government
13%	Finance/Insurance/Real estate	2%	High-tech/Computers
9%	Nonprofit	2%	Publishing
6%	Health services	2%	Utilities
5%	Telecommunications	10%	Other
3%	Retail	2%	No answer

HR professionals split on cover letter quality

When asked to rate in general terms the overall quality of the cover letters they receive today, nearly half (48 percent) of the survey respondents rate the quality as good, while the same percentage (48 percent) of respondents rate the quality as fair. Two percent of respondents believe cover letters are of excellent quality today, while 2 percent think today's cover letters are of poor quality.

Cover letter quality has remained unchanged in recent years, however. Six out of ten respondents (61 percent) report that over the past three years the quality of the cover letters their organizations have received has stayed about the same. Nearly one out of five respondents (18 percent) feel the quality has decreased, while approximately one out of ten (9 percent) feel cover letter quality has increased in recent years. The remaining respondents are unsure.

So what happens if HR professionals receive cover letters that are of poor quality? Is the entire package — resume and all — discarded, or is the quality of the cover letter simply overlooked? More than three out of four HR professionals (77 percent) report that when they receive a cover letter of poor quality, they read the resume, but still keep in mind that the cover letter was of poor quality. Fourteen percent of survey respondents say that when they receive a cover letter of poor quality, the candidate is eliminated as a possibility for the position to which they have applied. Only 8 percent of the survey respondents say they read the resume and disregard the fact that it was accompanied by a cover letter of poor quality. Thus, most HR professionals take into consideration the quality of a cover letter — in some cases it could actually make or break a candidate's chances.

Typos can kill candidates' chances

According to HR professionals, errors found in cover letters can have an impact on candidates' chances of being considered for vacant positions (see Figure 1-1). More than three out of four survey respondents (76 percent) say that typos or grammatical errors found in cover letters would cause them to remove the applicant from the pool of possible candidates. Six out of ten respondents (61 percent) say the same thing about cover letters addressed to the wrong company.

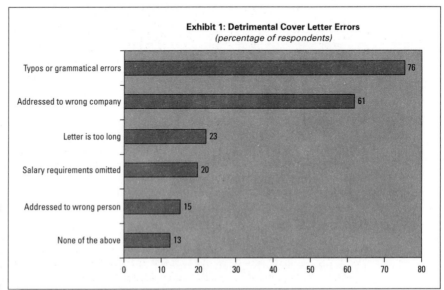

Exhibit 1: Detrimental Cover Letter Errors
(percentage of respondents)

Typos or grammatical errors	76
Addressed to wrong company	61
Letter is too long	23
Salary requirements omitted	20
Addressed to wrong person	15
None of the above	13

Figure 1-1:
Key reasons
cover
letters fail.

Letters that are too long (more than one page) cause applicants to be removed from consideration at 23 percent of respondents' organizations. Omitting salary requirements in the letter when they are specifically requested in the job listing is detrimental to an application at 20 percent of respondents' organizations. Fifteen percent of respondents report that addressing the cover letter to the wrong person will eliminate the application from the pool of possible candidates. Interestingly, 13 percent of respondents say that none of the possible cover letter foibles listed in the survey would cause their organizations to remove the candidate from the applicant pool.

HR professionals favor personalized cover letters

Survey respondents were asked how personalized cover letters, rather than generic ones, are viewed. Nearly seven out of ten respondents (69 percent) view personalized cover letters positively, and approximately three out of ten (29 percent) view them neutrally. Personalized cover letters are viewed negatively by only 1 percent of HR professionals, according to survey results.

Importance of cover letters versus resumes: Respondents are split

More than half of the survey respondents (54 percent) believe that cover letters are less important than resumes. However, more than four out of ten respondents (43 percent) believe cover letters are just as important as resumes. In addition, cover letters are deemed more important than resumes by 3 percent of respondents.

Even though many of the survey respondents report that cover letters are not as important as resumes, the majority keep the letters on file. Ninety-five percent of respondents report that their organizations keep the cover letter they receive as part of an applicant's file. Five percent of responding organizations, on the other hand, do not.

E-mail is preferred

Although survey results show that fewer than one in five resumes are submitted via e-mail, one-third of HR professionals (34 percent) prefer to receive them via e-mail, according to survey results (see Figure 1-2). Approximately three out of ten respondents (31 percent) choose regular mail as their delivery method of preference. Fax is favored by 25 percent of respondents, particularly those from smaller organizations, 7 percent favor Web-based delivery formats (HTML resumes), and 2 percent like hand-delivered resumes.

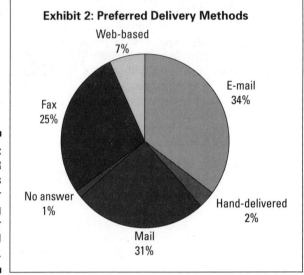

Figure 1-2:
How HR
professionals
favor
receiving
your cover
letter and
resume.

Tilt Toward Tomorrow

The general consensus is that there *is* no general consensus on recruiting viewpoints in this era of transition. There are no absolutes in a job search, which explains why various career advisers offer what may be conflicting advice.

For instance, although 70 percent of SHRM respondents say that they'll consider stand-alone resumes, we can't know how well stand-alones fare as hiring decisions are made.

Moreover, 30 percent (28 percent+ 2 percent) say that omitting a cover letter is risky. Are you willing to risk writing off a third of your prospects?

As you take a bicentric approach and look in both directions before starting a job search — back toward paper and forward toward cyber-search — keep staffing expert Jim Lemke's point in mind and ask yourself:

> *The issue is not which media I use to communicate my availability, but how do I organize my information to get a job interview?*

Most of this book contains solid, classic information you can use as is or adapt to a cyber-search. The next two chapters show you how to take advantage of the Web- and e-mail-based process: Click. Write. Address. Send.

Chapter 2

Your DotCom Cover Note

*T*echnology's transforming power is giving a lift to everything — including the wider-than-ever world of cover letters. Rather than evaporating in an e-mail era, cover communications are more widespread than ever as they accompany millions of resumes flying across the Web each day.

But there's a sea change in the looks and length of cover communications: cover letters look plainer and more informal than their paper predecessors. And they are much shorter.

E-mail cover letters are so much shorter, in fact, that we are calling them **cover notes.**

The fact is that resume reviewers sag under the sheer volume of resumes flooding in because they're so easy to send online. Twenty years ago, a company recruiter typically had perhaps 40 open requisitions (job openings to fill) at one time; today that number may be as high as 150. They have to just keep punching stuff through day in and day out. You can understand why contemporary reviewers want their cover communications short and sweet, highlighting the beef right away.

What happens when a cover letter's too long? Reviewers do a fast scroll to the resume it accompanies. If they don't see reasons to linger, their itchy trigger fingers reach for the delete button, and it's adios amigo for the whole package, cover letter and resume alike.

Although there will be occasions when you are invited to send a full-blown cover letter online as a prettied-up attachment, nine out of ten times I advise you to send a short cover note.

Answers to New Kinds of Questions

Ray Kurzweil and other futurists catch our attention with predictions like this one:

> By 2009, computers will be embedded in our clothes. By 2019, they'll be hidden in our bodies. By 2099, human and machine intelligence will have merged.

Whether you do or don't believe that the merger of man and machine will occur in the 21st century, you'll have to agree that innovation is racing at blinding speed. We have one foot in the old postindustrial era and the other in a new digital age — a transition that is affecting cover letters along with everything else.

In question-and-answer format, here are details about creating the effective cover notes that work best in cyberspace.

What is the number one thing to remember about writing a RedHot e-mail cover note?

Content is the real master of the universe. Concentrate on content, not on chasing after fancy formatting or polishing high-gloss e-mail looks. Construct your e-mail cover note in ASCII text — and paste your resume right after your letter. Anything fancier is an exception.

What is ASCII?

Pronounced ASKee, ASCII is American Standard Code for Information Interchange. It is also called "text" or "plain text" because it is the text language that computer software programs use to communicate with each other. ASCII is UGHlee and not easy to read unless you have 10-year-old eyes and no sense of style. But online distribution requirements and conventions mean we're stuck with ASCII, at least for the time being.

Does my ASCII cover note have style limitations?

Is a cubicle a padded cell without a door? "Limitations" is ASCII's middle name. Moreover, your e-cover note/resume duo has to pass muster in computerized resume tracking systems.

Here are the conventions to respect when using ASCII:

✔ Put each item of your contact information flush left on a separate line:

- name
- e-mail address

- telephone number

- residential address

Computers process this style more easily; the worst thing you can do is scramble your contact information and end up lost in (cyber) space.

✔ Use asterisks or em dashes, not bullets (solid or hollow).

✔ Skip the bold typeface, underlining, or graphics.

✔ Don't use *emoticons* — symbols to replace body language; for instance, :-) is an emoticon of a person smiling.

✔ Avoid columns of information (like newspaper columns) requiring continuity of text.

Here are the conventions for sending Word documents in attachments:

✔ Save and send your cover note and resume in what is likely to be the lowest common denominator program — such as Word 5. Even if you have the latest and greatest word-processing program, such as Word 2000, use Version 5. The reason is that companies tend to be about two years behind your personal software. And software typically can read older versions, but older versions cannot read newer versions.

✔ The data in attachments are likely to be scanned into a resume tracking system. The system is more liberal than sending data online over the Internet. Underscoring is okay as long as it isn't too closely spaced to the text.

✔ All the above limitations apply, except you can use solid bullets. Placement of your contact information is less restrictive — as long as adequate white space separates items that appear on the same line.

What about content tips?

The subject line of your e-mail sparks a reading of your cover note, which sparks a reading of your resume. Power each one with a sales message that causes the reviewer to keep on scrolling.

Think of your subject line as a magazine story headline attracting attention (BS computer science/5 yrs xp/will relo); think of your cover note as the summary of what the article promises; think of your resume as the main article.

In the cover note, use names of mutual friends, list matching skills to job requirements, and try for fresh, eye-catching phrasing, unless you're applying for seriously serious work like button-down banking or brain surgeon jobs.

But don't go overboard on being informal, casual, or chummy when you're communicating with a stranger.

Why not use handsome word-processed letters in attachments?

Recruiting systems and databases are designed for maximum efficiency — recruiters say they're drowning in resumes and are reading as fast as they can. They don't encourage the extra work required to open attachments, especially those that come in unsolicited. Recruiters usually work in a PC world and don't welcome time lost converting attachments from Mac senders. Additionally, even if they're running Dracula-slaying virus protection, they worry about viruses lurking in attachments.

There are two times when you should use a Word document (or equivalent) in a cover letter attachment:

- ✔ When the recipient — employer or recruiter — invites you to do so.

- ✔ When your visual presentation and urge to tell a more complete message is so compelling you couldn't sleep if you jammed everything into a short ASCII e-mail. Sometimes you just need to get more bounce than ASCII delivers, especially if your many talents are difficult to capsulize. In truth, ASCII benefits recruiters and systems, not job seekers.

 In those cases, send two attachments, one for your cover letter and the second for your resume. In the e-mail message to which they are attached, simply say: "Two Word documents are attached — my cover letter and my resume. Please review. I'd appreciate it if you'd get back to me. Thank you." The technical reviewer for this book, HR staffing and systems consultant Jim Lemke, says this terse approach "puts pressure on recruiters to open and look at attachments."

Examples of attachment cover letters are shown in Chapters 14 and 15.

Why not use HTML?

HTML, a markup language used to jazz up Web pages with video and sound, is usually reserved for resumes typically used by technology whizzes, designers, and contractors. Most people should avoid it because not all e-mail systems can read it.

HTML resumes tend to be supplements to, not replacements for, the traditional electronic resume. Contact may begin with an ASCII cover note enhanced with a hyperlink suggesting the reviewer click to the linked HTML Web site where viewers can see a variety of work samples illustrated portfolio style.

Reviewers who aren't fighting the clock may prize a chance to dig deeply into a candidate's abilities. California author and online instructor Rebecca Smith is an HTML expert; learn more about its format on her Web site, `www.eresumes.com`

What does an e-mail cover note look like?

Subject: Strong HR candidate/10 yrs/BS-HR Mgt.

FROM:

Victoria Downey
victoriadowney@earthlink.com
(812) 123-4567
9876 Treasure Isle Way
Redondo Beach, CA 999999

Dear Marshall Rodriguez:

After researching HR consulting firms in the LA area, I feel sure I have the experience (both client site and virtual consulting) and education (bachelor's in HR management) to make a strong contribution to your organization. I'd like to work with you if you like the skills you see in my resume.

I will e-mail you on Monday to see when it might be convenient for us to meet.

Sincerely, Victoria Downey

----------------------------------[begin resume]------------------------------

Subject: Managerial CPA/credit, taxes, valuation/rock solid

Daniel R. Pollock
drpollock54@yahoo.com
987-133-4455
91234 Perth St.
Louisville, KY 67676

Dear Wendy Lee:

As a Certified Public Accountant with PC and systems skills to match, I'm interested in moving into e-commerce. For the past four years, I've worked in credit analysis, tax assessment reporting, and valuation analysis on Wall Street; I was a manager of accounting professionals the last 18 months. My resume overviews how I can help.

As a resume is limited in the information it conveys, why don't we meet in person? If you need additional facts before arranging an interview, call me at 987-133-4455. Otherwise, I'll e-mail you next week to confirm your interest.

Yours truly,

Dan Pollock.

------------------------------------[begin resume]-------------------------------

Subject: Fundraiser/SE Journal,8-23-XX/Over-goal record

Leticia Sunguia
(760) 849-9487
lsunguia@juno.com.
895 Wisteria Way
Brooklyn, NY 15974

Dear Samantha Browich:

As a highly motivated and energetic person who is ready to move up the next level, I was delighted to see your advertisement for a senior development specialist for Wallaby College. I am an experienced foot soldier in the fundraising ranks; exceeded my goals by 12% and 18% in the last two annual campaigns.

Please contact me by phone or by e-mail. After looking me over, if you want to chat, let's do it!

Sincerely yours, Leticia Sunguia

(Place resume here)

How do I send an e-mail cover note?

If you already know how to cut, paste, and format your resume into an ASCII text e-mail, skip these instructions. But if you're like most of us, you might like a little reminder.

Use the following steps to create one unified communication — that is, your DotCom ASCII cover note, into which you paste your resume. This guide is planned for Microsoft Word on a Windows system using Netscape Messenger. But, with a few modifications, these steps will work with other software (such as WordPerfect) or e-mail systems (such as Microsoft Outlook or Eudora; Juno only works in ASCII).

From MS Word on Windows and Netscape:

1. **Open or create your resume in your word-processing program.**

   Set your margins to display 6.5 inches of text. Use a font that is not proportional (Courier 12) to give you 65 characters per line. Save your resume as a "text only" file with "line breaks." If you use hard carriage returns at the end of paragraphs, save as "text only" without line breaks.

2. **Choose Edit⇨Select All.**

3. **Choose Edit⇨Copy.**

4. **Minimize (or close) your word processor.**

5. **Start your e-mail program (Messenger).**

6. **Click New Message to start a new message.**

7. **Fill in the e-mail address window and type a subject.**

8. **Click the upper-left corner of the blank body-of-message space — as though you were beginning to type an e-mail.**

9. **Choose Edit⇨Paste.**

10. **Look at your screen; replace all unsupported characters that did not convert with their ASCII equivalent.**

    That is, use asterisks or hyphens for bullet points or other emphasizers. Also check your line wrapping — no sloppy zigzags. Be sure your paragraphs are lined up evenly.

11. **Once you're satisfied with the way your unified e-mail note and resume look, send your document as a test e-mail to yourself.**

12. **If your e-mail looks the way you intended, send it to the recipient.**

How do I send my resume as an attachment?

You will rarely send your cover letter as an attachment to an e-mail message.

But it is not uncommon to send both a unified document in ASCII and also append a resume in a nicely formatted, word-processed attachment. Here's how you add an attachment to your e-mail.

1. **Click the Attach button in your e-mail program.**

2. **Find your resume file wherever you have saved it on your hard drive and double-click it.**

3. **Send your message.**

Should I include a scanned signature?

The vast majority of digital cover notes are submitted in ASCII text and don't need an electronic replica of your signature.

But if you're a tech sophisticate or design professional or contractor who does a cover letter in an MS Word (or equivalent) attachment, a signature replica is a nice touch.

You probably already know how to do it, perhaps using a program such as Signature-mail (www.signature-mail.com). But just in case you don't know how to throw in a replica signature for pizzazz, here is the homemade method for electronic signature capture.

1. **Write your signature using a thick black marker on an 8.5 x 11-inch white page.**

2. **Scan it at the highest possible resolution (600 x 600, 300 x 300).**

3. **Save the scanned document as a graphic file with a .jpg, .tif, or .gif, extension.**

4. **Use a graphics program — for example, MS Paint, MS Image Composer, Kodak Image, and so on — to dress it up and adjust the size.**

5. **Paste the signature into your word-processed document where you would normally sign.**

Should I put contact information on my note or resume?

In the past, you were advised to put your contact information — name, address, telephone, fax, and e-mail address — on each document, in case the documents were separated and lost or filed in different databases. Here's a rethinking of that conventional wisdom:

✔ **One unified e-mail:** If you are sending a unified e-mail with cover note and resume bonded together, put your contact information on your cover note. Just put your name on your resume. The reason: The single unified e-mail will be stored together in the same database; they are joined at the hip. Resume-reading systems (computers) like to see contact information at the top of a document, not search below for it. *Remember: All resume data extraction systems read from the top down.*

✔ **Attachments:** If you are using attachments, the old wisdom survives. Attachments usually aren't separated from the main e-mail communication, but depending upon a recruiter's office routine, they could go flying in different directions. Put your contact information on the top of each attachment.

Does it work to send the equivalent of the paper broadcast letter in an e-mail version?

Paper broadcast letters are self-marketing materials that are postal mailed by the thousands to a carefully targeted list of potential employers. Many career advisers consider them wasteful junk mail, except when mailing them to recruiters to jumpstart a job search.

But Robert Bronstein, CEO of Pro/File Research (`BronsteinR@aol.com`), has impressive broadcast-letter results for clients that refute that blanket condemnation, saying the trick is in the list selection. Concerning an e-mail job solicitation blitz, Bronstein says the jury's still out. Here are some of his conclusions as the 21st century begins:

✔ E-mail is cheaper and quicker than postal mail, growing rapidly and producing similar results in many circumstances, particularly with executive recruiters and venture capital firms.

✔ Recruiters like e-mail because they can punch a button and shoot your materials to clients with ease.

✔ Do not conduct an e-mail campaign to employers. Unless a company has advertised an HR (human resources) address, you have no assurance that your campaign will get to the right people.

Should I call to see if my cover note and resume arrived?

Modern applicant systems tend to have an automatic response feature that sends you an e-mail saying, "We received your resume." Don't read encouragement or anything else into this message except that the recipient says, "We got it."

To contact the employer asking "Did you get my resume?" after receiving the automated message of receipt probably won't reflect well on your judgment. The reviewer may think "idiot" or "doesn't read his e-mail."

If you do get back in touch after an automated message, think of a better tact, such as "Have you made a decision yet?"

But supposing you don't get an automated acknowledgement of your cover note and resume? Before calling people to confirm they have received your e-mail, nudge them electronically. Here's a sample follow-up campaign:

1. *[Send this message]* I hope you've had a chance to review my resume (sent 9/3/XX), which shows my experience and education in convention management. I'll be glad to fill in any blanks — what else would you like to know?" Avoid closed-end messages — Did you receive my resume? — that make it too easy for the recipient to send back a one-word answer, "Yes."

2. *[If thundering silence is your answer, try again.]* Since my last note, I've uncovered two recent articles about your organization that make me even more certain that my communications skills and bilingual competencies would be valuable in your operations department. If you haven't seen the articles [identify by name], I'll be happy to pass them along if that would be useful.

3. *[Still no answer, try again.]* Since we haven't been able to make contact, I'll check back with you next week — unless another time would be better. How many times should you try to make contact? Until you get an e-conversation going, or until the recruiter/employer irately tells you to buzz off.

Do e-mail overtures work? Sometimes they do, but success may not arrive overnight. A newly graduated MBA found a job as product manager for an Internet site through e-mail. He says he got to know the brass at the site by "doing the e-mail slow dance" for nine months before the offer came. Even then, the MBA, who describes e-mail as "less threatening than a phone call," had to call and say it was time for the hiring manager to step up and make an offer.

Is there anyone to whom I should not send a cover note or letter?

Do not send a cover message when you are cybershipping your resume off to a resume database, such as those found on Monster.com or CareerMosaic.

On e-notes, do I need a salutation? Complimentary close?

Yes, you should use a salutation and complimentary close in your e-cover notes. (See Chapter 11.) But e-mail is an informal medium, and you should skip the inside address and titles. On first contact, use the recipient's first and last name — "Dear Karen Gross:" and then begin your note. Make every effort to get a human name, but where it is simply not available, "Dear Recruiter" or "Dear Employer" may have to do.

What would be some good ways to open or close a cover note?

One hundred samples of cover note content follow. Half are *openers,* and half are *closers.* You can create many variations by assembling openers and closers in different combinations.

50 E-Mail Cover Openers

Here are 50 sample approaches to opening your cover note that you can use for patterns. You can mix and match them with the 50 cover closers that follow.

Cashing in on referrals

These openers mention a name or connection that will attract the reader's attention and almost guarantee the message will be read.

- ✔ Jackie Sevigny suggested I send you my resume, believing that we might find mutual value in trusting my abilities to your leadership. The resume summarizes my credentials. In addition, my B.B.A. in accounting has given me a strong grasp of financial applications.

- ✔ At a meeting of the North County HR Society yesterday, Virginia Byrd gave me your name and recommended I contact you ASAP. As a newly graduated dental hygienist, I was thrilled to be referred to a leading dentist for consideration as an addition to your staff. I am proficient in general prophylaxis, charting, patient education, ultrasonic scaling, and other dental office skills.

- ✔ Judge Kevin Gown of the 9th Circuit Court of Appeals, for whom I clerked, recommends me to you for inclusion in your law firm. Judge Marvin Applegate of San Diego Superior Courts seconds that recommendation. My resume follows.

- ✔ Fern Goldwyn's daughter tells me Fern is retiring from your firm as a law office administrator and thought I might make a good successor. I have recently completed a paralegal certificate program from [name of educational institution]. Additionally, I soon will receive my associate degree in information technology, which would carry my value to you much beyond the use of Lexis and similar database programs.

- ✔ In the course of talking with Dr. Kenneth B. Hoyt of Kansas State University, I learned about the program

"Counseling for High Skills." It is exciting — the first real scientific measure of what happens to the 75 percent of high school graduates who do not complete four years of college. If you anticipate enlarging your group to foster this program, please consider me as a project leader, based on my considerable background in subbaccalaureate education. I have taken the liberty of attaching a virus-checked attachment of my CV.

✔ Lynn O'Shaunessy certainly throws good parties. I enjoyed talking to you at Lynn's and responding to your suggestion. Here is my resume (virus-checked attachment in Word). Since our talk, I've thought about what you said about upcoming openings at your firm, and, yes, I'm definitely interested.

✔ Sally Segundo tells me you're in the market for a dependable and conscientious subcontractor to manage your tenant improvement projects. I am fully insured, can do virtually all types of construction, including electrical, carpentry, painting, and specialized wall finishes. I know building materials, am familiar with costing procedures, and can supply solid references verifying on-time, on-budget finishes. My resume explains more about how I can be a valuable addition to your construction program.

✔ Dr. Brian Brown, your dentist, says you'll be happier spending time with me than with him. Aside from that lame joke, I do have managerial skills you may be able to make good use of. After running my own business for 15 years, I like the idea of working with younger people who could use someone with a broad range of financial and operations management experience to keep a small firm operating in the black. My resume follows in text and also as a MS Word document attachment.

Responding to published job openings

When you spot a job advertised in print or online, try a variation of one of these openers. Paired with the right closer, you'll be noteworthy.

✔ As I sat down to read my 49th issue of *Training* magazine, I also spotted your newspaper advertised position. Bingo! You asked for a multitasker and plate-spinner with a proven track record of project management. Count me in. I can put a checkmark beside each requirement you list — as my resume confirms.

✔ Reading the NationJobNetwork database paid off; although I'm employed, I've been looking for the right opportunity to work with your company, and last night I found it! The requirements of your position #7777 for a regional distribution manager fit me like a glove, from my BA in economics to my fleet maintenance experience.

✔ My day lit up when I saw your opening for a software architect in the *Post-Dispatch* on 11/23. My C++, object-oriented design, and 32-bit environment are a good start on the skills you require. As my resume shows, I'm a close match.

✔ Your February 19th job ad in the *Morning News* to recruit a capable, self-motivated representative for customer service describes a position for which I am well credentialed. My record of increased and varied responsibilities in a hot-box of an environment has prepared me for solving problems and juggling multiple assignments.

✔ Please consider me for your advertised (4/15 *Union Tribune*) position of office administrator. As assistant office administrator, I have successfully introduced systems, processes, and techniques to boost productivity, increase efficiency, and promote satisfaction from support staff.

✔ RE: Executive Assistant, August 10 issue of the *Sentinel Journal*: My resume follows. I am an experienced EA to senior management, offering proficient computer and online skills, as well as time management, organization, scheduling, prioritizing, and gatekeeping strengths, as well as a reputation for loyalty and confidentiality.

✔ Your position for an administrative manager advertised in the July 12 issue of *HealthCosts* caught my attention. This sounds like a fine opportunity relating to my career goals, which include responsibility for overseeing department operations and staff, as well as quality assurance and organizational development.

✔ I read your December 12th ad in the *Times* for a plant manager in the electronics industry with a great deal of interest. This position strongly appeals to me, prompting the submission of my credentials for your review. It appears that my background and experience are a great match for your needs, including knowledge of hazardous waste disposal.

✔ I enclose my resume in response to your March 9th *Journal* advertisement for a loan officer position with your credit union. This appears to be a substantial career opportunity. My resume will attest to my credentials for this position, including designing a successful e-loan program.

✔ Your recent advertisement in the *Accounting Insider* for an entry-level accountant caught my attention. This seems to be exactly the kind of position for which I have prepared and appears to require the skills [identify a few] and experience I acquired in my previous co-op work assignments. My resume follows for your review.

✔ Your request for a contract arbitrator, which I found on the sports page of the *Globe* yesterday, took me by surprise. I just didn't expect to see the subject of civilized arbitration juxtaposed with a picture of the Rams trashing the Raiders. However, I recovered quickly enough to provide the following brief outline of my arbitration management background. A more comprehensive view is available on my Web site: arbitrationfairness.com (hyperlinked).

✔ I am responding with enormous interest to your recent job ad in the *Courier* for [identify position]. My qualifications, as outlined in the following resume, appear to be a terrific match with the requirements listed for this position. I offer [name several skills] that should meet your challenging position with abilities to spare.

✔ JobOptions posted your attractive offer #7777, which is located in Portland. My wife and I are relocating to Portland because of her recent agreement to become the administrator of St. Elsewhere's Hospital. We'll be in place by June 15. I relocate with a reputation in the [identify industry] as a product manager who can be counted on to play an integral part in increasing shareholder value and launching new products on schedule. Some specific achievements are described in my resume, which follows.

✔ [talent auction response for consultant] Building efficient marketplaces is my expertise. Throughout my 18-year retail site and retail software industry career, I can document measurable savings as profiled in my resume. Top references.

✔ My attached resume is an uncommon match for the science [identify] position advertised on your Web site. My professional and educational background cover [identify matching requirements with your qualifications].

✔ After reading your online job posting for an EXPRESS DELIVERY FACILITY OPERATIONS COORDINATOR, my qualifications would like to introduce themselves to your requirements. I will leave the U.S. Marine Corps in two months after a ten-year assignment [identify persuasive civilian matching points — such as overseeing high-volume unloading operations and redistributing urgent materials]. These duties demanded team leadership skills, strong communications ability and careful time management. My ASCII resume is supplemented with a Word attachment — just a quick click away.

✔ Spotting your BrainBuzz listing, 2-1, for a content developer to direct a new media Internet company's communities division was a symbiotic discovery: We go together like writing and business development prowess, and project management and strong technical skills — all of which you want and I have. What would appeal to communities of Network Engineers, Developers, and Java users? Try me: I read minds. Can I draft a proposed content program for your evaluation? Enthusiasm? Mentally, my train has already left the station headed your way. I am instructing BrainBuzz to send you my resume.

✔ Found on FreeAgent: Your requirement for a part-time medical reporter stopped my browsing cold. My present part-time position on a weekly newspaper doesn't make full use of my interest in health issues or writing skills, which I began to hone as an undergraduate English major five years ago. Your ad mentioned telecommuting; as a resident of the health-facility-rich Chicago area, I am well positioned to supply you with factual, crisp, timely articles. My resume follows.

✔ When I saw your ad for a [identify position], I realized I may be an ideal match for [identify company]. You indicate you need someone with outstanding [identify skills]. I own those skills, and I am the toughest taskmaster I know. In addition to technical proficiency, I'm told that my interpersonal and team-working strengths rank me among choice candidates.

✔ The following letter (not really a resume — that's too crass) responds to your uninspired, graphics-free Web site posting for a start-up Webmaster who isn't cubicle-adverse, who doesn't mind a job that pays great for 40 hours but not so great for 70 hours, and who has a creative bent way over. You're being contacted by your future Webmaster now! (Check out my page: savvydesign.com.) Okay, I'll work for peanuts plus stock options and a Michael Ovitz-style severance package because if your company flushes and I've already cut lose my project clients, I'll be hosed. As to my awards, I may already be a winner of the Magazine SuperSales Sweepstakes.

Making direct applications

Asking to be considered for employment when you don't know that a job opening exists is proactive and usually happens as a result of research.

- ✔ As a sales manager, I've beat my numbers 99.9 percent of the time. What about that last tenth of a percent? I tried, failed, learned something, and never missed again. For me, it's time to move up. My resume suggests what I can do for you.

- ✔ Holding a master of nursing degree since June, I qualify as a pediatric nurse practitioner and seek a collaborative role with a pediatric surgeon. Since my services are reimbursable by insurance companies, I could be a profit center for you.

- ✔ Although I work for one of your competitors, Tektronic has always been at the top of my short list of employers. And I hope the clock is striking the opportunity hour for me to be at the top of your short list. My technical skills include UNIX Shell Script (sh, ksh, csh) and BASIC; a healthy handful of others are in my resume.

- ✔ IT is a field in which I have five years of serious experience — internship, volunteerism, and unchecked enthusiasm for everything digital. Plus, I have an A.S. degree in computer science. In addition to Java, Linux, and Microsoft certification, my other skills are noted on my resume.

- ✔ Although others have rated my past accomplishments as an administrative assistant impressive, I don't stand pat but move enthusiastically into new challenges. I'm an experienced Internet researcher and can maintain basic Web sites.

- ✔ From Day One of my project management experience, I've been known for bringing the jobs in on time and on budget. Treating contractors, subs, and craftworkers as "customers" is my trademark. My following resume explains why you and I should explore project assignments.

- ✔ While checking over your Web site, I see that not only do my skills [identify a couple] fit your enterprise, but our priorities and values [identify them] are a good pairing.

- ✔ If you seek a well-rounded management professional with experienced knowledge of the rental car industry, my following resume will be of interest. I can leverage for your benefit more than 15 years in operations, staffing, supervision, and purchasing.

✔ As my resume shows, I have had superior progression in operations management with a top consumer products company. In my current position as group plant manager (five plants), my cost reduction programs resulted in $4.5 million savings over two years. I'm looking for an e-opportunity, and your company looks like a winner.

✔ After spending the last ten years as president and CEO of Catalog Creations Unlimited, I'm anxious to take on new challenges. I've turned around three companies, with no less improvement than 25% ROI. I'm open to travel, relocation.

✔ Are you interested in seeing your sales figures climb the charts before the end of the year? I can make that happen for Jackson Computer Repair Service Contracts, Inc. New in town, I can start building your business as soon as you give the word.

✔ Thank you for taking the time to speak with me this morning. As you requested, my resume is presented in an MS Word document attachment. After we talked, I went even deeper into your company's stockholder investment program and feel doubly confident that my skills are right on target with your needs for a new investor relations manager.

✔ After researching weight-loss enterprises in the Chicago area, I believe I offer the attributes that bring client satisfaction in your organization. As a weight-loss coach I have training in [identify activities]. My communications skills are well developed with people of diverse backgrounds. Oh yes, I personally shed 35 pounds, which gives me the sensitivity to be part of an effective support team.

✔ TO: 21st Century Human Services; Please route to HR: A select number of nonprofit organizations are being e-mailed my resume as I seek an entry-level service representative position. I will receive a bachelor's degree in social work within three months with a GPA above 3.0, plus two successful internships. As of September 1, I will serve where needed: domestically or internationally.

✔ Please consider this note of introduction to my resume as an expression of my interest in exploring professional sales opportunities in your long-term care insurance organization. A former minister, I hope to apply my interpersonal skills and financial services license in a transition to help people protect themselves against the catastrophic costs of long-term care so that they can live out their lives in dignity.

✔ Forecast: My passion, Texas teaching credential, and year of substitute teaching mean I will be teaching math soon. I hope it will be in your school district [identify by name]. After having trained as a civil engineer and working in that profession for 13 years, I discovered my true calling two years ago when tutoring a neighbor's child in math. I really like opening young minds.

✔ At the job fair (9-30) designed for low-tech people in high-tech fields, I obtained your card when I said I would like a receptionist position at your company and asked about training opportunities. I told you I take work seriously, and you asked me to send you a resume. Here it is. Thank you for considering me for employment.

✔ A proven and satisfyingly employed marketer, I'm one of those passive job candidates employers lust after. Things changed after reading in Business magazine how your company is seizing the e-moment and leveraging new content-manipulation tools in different ways, I'm onboard to explore opportunities with you leaders. Since I'm coming in cold, my resume follows — confidential please. A Microsoft Word version is attached in case that's the way you like it. Thank you for your reading investment.

✔ Do you have an opening for an IS operations manager with two years' civilian experience who consistently maintains a 99 percent systems uptime rate? I have a bachelor's degree in computer science and Navy computer experience. My resume expands on my skill sets.

✔ Just because I'm about to graduate in electrical engineering, I'm not expecting to be spoon-fed a great job — despite the platoon of campus recruiters setting up interviewing shop here. My 3.6 GPA from a respected university [identify your alma mater if it's nationally ranked or regionally regarded, otherwise stick with generic language] suggests my technological competence. My aim: to work for the best company in the wireless industry, and my research shows you win. Your people aren't here recruiting.

Reaching out to (third-party) recruiters

By any name — headhunter, executive recruiter, technical recruiter — these outside talent scouts can give your career a big boost.

✔ [to recruiter] Following this note, please find my text resume for your review against any of your client's requirements for a tax attorney. A formatted copy also is attached in WordPerfect 8. If you don't have an active assignment, please retain my resume in your database for future requirements. Thanks.

✔ [to a recruiter] RE: PHARMACY MANAGER. Responding to your request, here's my ASCII resume outlining qualifications for managerial post, preferably in a local retail rather than an online pharmacy. My salary history: $55,500 to $85,000. I am looking for a base of $90,000 minimum. Although I would prefer not uprooting, for the right offer, I will consider relocation anywhere in the West or Southwest. In case your client prefers a more orderly presentation, my resume is also attached in a Word file. Thanks for your consideration.

50 E-Mail Cover Closers

Here are 50 sample closing statements you can use for patterns in your e-mail. You can mix and match them with the 50 cover openers in the preceding section.

Hoping to hear from you

These closers end on a warm and friendly tone, but aren't too pushy. They merely say, "I hope you'll get in touch with me for the job."

✔ Can we explore an employment acquisition: me?

✔ Until we meet, thanks for your consideration.

✔ Although I'm employed and saw no position advertised on your Web site, I'm willing to wait for the right spot at your company. When the time comes, I'd like to meet and talk about what I can bring to your table.

✔ My resume shows I have a proven sales track record; an interview will show I have natural sales ability. I would do a top-flight job for your company. I look forward to meeting you.

✔ I'm enthusiastic about providing you with a close-up of my professional value. Until we meet, thank you for your consideration.

✔ My resume follows. Can we schedule an interview?

✔ Based on these highlights and abilities outlined in my resume, I am certain I'm a strong match for your requirements. I'll be happy to hear from you.

Important rules for e-mail writers

the original author of these rules to bear in mind as you whip out your e-mail notes is unknown. (P.S. Remember to capitalize the beginning of sentences. The rules of grammar don't turn up dead just because you're writing in the informal digital medium.)

1. Verbs HAS to agree with their subjects.

2. Prepositions are not words to end sentences with.

3. Avoid cliches like the plague. (They're old hat.)

4. Be more or less specific.

5. Don't use no double negatives.

6. Proofread carefully to see if you any words out.

(For more really really good rules, see Chapter 10.)

✔ My resume will tell you more about me, but nothing beats conversations. Use the Reply button if you'd like me to call in a few days to arrange a meeting.

✔ I look forward to talking with you soon about your promising opportunity and my ability to do the job you want done.

✔ If you like what you see on my resume, I'll be happy to get your e-mail about when we can meet and talk.

✔ It would be my pleasure to meet with you soon. You can reach me by e-mail or telephone.

✔ Thanks for your time. I look forward to hearing from you.

✔ Thank you very much for posting this position, and I earnestly anticipate speaking with you personally.

Helping to hear from you

Also mild mannered, these closers go a step further than those above and softly pressure the reader to contact you by providing a telephone number or e-mail address.

✔ Thank you for your time and future response. My cell phone number is —.

✔ My resume capsulizes my background, but a personal meeting would better reveal my qualifications. Can we talk? Please call me at the number above.

Pack paper for your interview

Take along to job interviews an attractively printed cover letter, like those in Chapters 14 and 15, as well as a paper copy of your formatted resume. Your offer to the interviewer: "I have a paper copy of my resume if that would be helpful." Then hand over both your letter and resume. It's a touch of class.

✔ Analysis of your advertised position suggests I am well qualified to provide the leadership and track history you specify. I look forward to hearing from you soon. My cell phone number is —; my e-mail address is —.

✔ Your consideration of my qualifications is much appreciated. You can reach me at my home phone or by e-mail, noted above.

✔ I look forward to a discussion of why I'm the best candidate for this opportunity. My e-mail is —; my telephone is —.

✔ I hope to hear from you soon, because I have an attractive offer already and need to reply, but your position sounds absolutely perfect for my qualifications. My cell phone: #—.

✔ I welcome a meeting to discuss my qualifications in greater detail. My management experience would add to your medical management team. I'm away on assignment but check my e-mail — xx@xx.com — regularly.

✔ I enjoyed talking with you and look forward to meeting with you in the near future. E-mail me at — and I can be in your office the next day.

✔ Do you need more info than my resume provides? Please call me at —.

✔ If you'd like to discuss how my qualifications meet your requirements, let's talk at your convenience. If that sounds good to you, my cell phone is —.

✔ My resume follows. Thanks for reading it. Please call me at the number above, —.

✔ I'll make myself available to interview at your convenience: xx@xxx.com, (700) 000-0000.

✔ I'd appreciate the opportunity to translate my past achievements into future benefits for your company. If you maintain resumes and cover notes in separate databases, my e-mail is xxxx@xxx and my cell phone is —.

Remaining in control

More assertive than the above two groups of closers, this group says, "I'll get back to you soon." Sales teams use this approach.

✔ I look forward to our conversation. I'll e-mail you in a few days for a time.

✔ Since e-mail can't replace face-to-face discussion, I'll call soon to set up an interview.

✔ Thank you in advance for reviewing my resume. I enthusiastically anticipate discussing my qualifications in an interview. I'll e-mail you on Thursday to validate your interest.

✔ I look forward to speaking with you personally to discuss your specific needs and my ability to meet them. I'll call your administrative assistant next week to see what time would be most convenient for you.

✔ I welcome a personal interview to discuss how my qualifications can augment your company's excellent reputation for purchasing acumen. I'll e-mail you on Tuesday to see if we can meet.

✔ I'm excited about employment opportunities within your agency and hope to explore contributions I can make. I'll e-mail you within the week to see when your calendar is open.

✔ I hope to play an active role in the future prosperity of your organization. I'll contact you next week to talk about this job or other positions where your needs and my talents meet.

✔ As you requested, here's my resume. I'll check back with you next week to flesh out any blank areas. Thanks for your interest.

✔ My resume follows. I'll follow up by telephone next week to answer any questions you may have.

✔ I'll be in touch within a few days to confirm your receipt of my resume and to answer any questions. Your time is valuable, and I appreciate your consideration.

✔ Please interview me. I'll e-mail you October 20. My resume follows in ASCII text, but is also attached in a MS Word document; both are computer-friendly, in case you scan resumes into a database.

✔ As a resume is limited in the information it conveys, why don't we meet in person? If you need additional facts before arranging an interview, call me at —. Otherwise, I'll e-mail you next week to confirm your interest.

✔ I'm eager to sit down with you to discuss the contribution I can make to ABCDF as it works to create a regional planning group. I'll follow up with a call next week. Or you can reach me at —.

✔ Please contact me by phone —, or by e-mail at —. After looking me over, if you want to chat, let's do it!

✔ My salary needs are in line with the position's description and what I bring in abilities. I'll e-mail you Tuesday to see when we can explore specifics.

✔ I would like to discuss with you why this position has my name on it, and I'll call you at the beginning of next week to see what your schedule allows. Or if you need to reach me sooner, my number is listed above.

Contacting (third-party) recruiters

Encourage recruiters to keep track of you in their databases so that you'll be remembered when a good job comes through their offices.

✔ [to recruiter] Please keep my resume in your database and contact me when a good match turns up. My cell phone and e-mail are noted above.

✔ [to recruiter] Please contact me for additional information. I'll be available for employment in July, and I will relocate for the right offer at a minimum base of $110,000.

Highlighting professional characteristics

Use these kinds of closers if you need to emphasize that you are a rookie, a transitioning member of the military services, or one who requires the use of a CV (curriculum vitae).

✔ [rookie] Thank you for reading over my resume. I ask to meet with you personally if you have an interest in my professional potential. I will e-mail you next week to see if we can interview.

✔ [project assignment] My resume capsulizes my abilities. If you think my skills set would bring value to your company, then we should talk. I look forward to a personal meeting to discuss the possibilities of a mutually beneficial project.

✔ [rookie] I will relocate to San Diego in June. I'd appreciate a telephone or online interview before then if you'd like to have a sharper picture of how I could meet the needs of your firm. Please reach me at the number above.

✔ [professional or academic] My curriculum vitae follows, detailing my experience and expertise. If you sense that I meet your requirements, please contact me by e-mail at — and I'll get back to you quickly.

✔ [rookie] My internship experience and education, coupled with an eagerness to learn and a drive to achieve, would make me a good hire decision for your company. Can we discuss available positions?

An Executive Summary of This Chapter

Traditional paper cover letters have morphed into short cover notes combined with a resume in one document when sent online in plain ASCII text. This is the model you should use for the vast majority of your online job searches. You can use a longer cover letter on that rare occasion when you send it in a Word document attachment, preferably at the invitation of the recipient.

Stylistic changes in e-cover messages have occurred due to limitations of technology and the informality of the e-mail medium. A new paradigm begins for the unified cover note model: Right after the subject, begin your e-mail cover note with your contact information. Put only your name on the resume that follows because the two are joined — remember, it's a single document — and computers like to read from the top down. You may restate for emphasis your e-mail address or telephone number in the closing paragraph, or you may simply refer to your contact information listed above (below the subject line and before the greeting).

If you do send a cover letter as an attachment, however, do include your complete contact information on the letter *and* the resume because they probably will be databased separately.

In our fast-moving, digitally determined job market, cover communications lives. To send a resume online without a cover note or letter is a missed opportunity and shows the candidate doesn't think the company is worth the time and effort to write a cover.

But when you do write a cover, use logic. Don't emulate this ditsy and empty but real-life example: "After a 24-year career in residential real estate, I have decided to explore my second love of computers and programming. My ability to work with the public makes me a valuable asset to your team."

Chapter 3

Helping Your Cover Letters Find Work

In This Chapter

▶ Finding places to go with your letters

▶ Locating crucial company information

▶ Learning about an industry

When your RedHot cover letter is ready to go, what's next? Where should you send it? Who should read it? This chapter answers key distribution questions — and throws in extra leads about gathering important information to keep your letter fresh for each recipient.

Until the world embraced the Web a few years ago, you usually turned to print job ads, personal networking, and library copies of print directories to find people and places to send your cover letter and resume. You can still do all that. But increasingly, job seekers are turning to Internet resources. You say you don't have a computer? Your public library probably has computers you can use and staff to show you how.

Check Out These DotCom Resources

The following overview of DotCom (digital) resources illustrate what's available to you. ***Except where noted, all resources in this sampling are free to the job seeker.***

Big national sites

The full-service sites boast databases of tens of thousands of job openings and active resumes. Generally, they offer all the specialty functions noted — executive employment, niches, information technology, and so on — plus newsletters, polls, and other attractions.

CareerPath, for example, with its job ads from 90 newspapers, allows you to search by city. JobOptions works with Business Women's Network. Monster.com maintains a talent auction division.

When you're looking for something special, you may find it at a specialty site or at a big national employment site.

America's Job Bank	www.ajb.dni.us
Monster.com	monster.com
Headhunter.net	headhunter.net
JobOptions	www.joboptions.com
HotJobs	hotjobs.com
NationJob Network	nationjob.com
CareerBuilder	careerbuilder.com
Career Mosaic	careermosaic.com
CareerPath	careerpath.com
Careers.wsj.com	careers.wsj.com
BrassRing.com	www.brassring.com

Newspaper sites

Only a few years ago, Net naysayers were dismissive in their estimate of one's ability to use online resources to find a job locally. To a man, they thought the Net was best used for relocation. One of the most intriguing developments on the Net is the emergence of local sites with job offerings. Newspapers are a prime example — most have online editions that help you target a job in the city where you want to live, including your own backyard. The following sites can connect you:

AJR News Link (most newspapers)	ajr.newslink.org
Newspaperlinks.com (most newspapers)	newspaperlinks.com

Search engines

What once were sites designed to help you find what you needed online — search engines — are now virtual mega-malls. Jobs and careers are nearly universal offerings.

Yahoo! Classifieds	yahoo.com
AltaVista	av.com

Lycos	`lycos.com`
Infoseek	`infoseek.com`

One-stop sites

If you believe that the only one who got anything done by Friday was Robinson Crusoe, you haven't looked for job listings on sites that aggregate them. These resources gather under one cyber-roof the job openings listed on 30 or more job boards.

Upseek.com	`upseek.com`
infoGIST (free trial, then pay)	`www.infogist.com`
RecruitUSA	`recruitusa.com`
WantedJobs 2K	`wj2k.com`

Executive sites

When you're looking for high-end positions, consider specialty ventures that often charge a couple of hundred dollars for a six-month subscription. But not all the management-only job sites charge to view their wares.

SixFigure Jobs	`6figurejobs.com`
NetShare (subscription fee)	`www.netshare.com`
Exec-U-Net (subscription fee)	`execunet.com`
Search Base (subscription fee)	`www.searchbase.com`
Search Bulletin (subscription fee)	`searchbulletin.com`

Niche sites

One of the best types of places to search and list your self-marketing materials are the specialty sites for career fields. Many are maintained by nonprofit professional associations. Others are commercial.

Society of Human Resource Management	`shrm.org`
Medzilla (biotech, pharmaceutical, medical)	`medzilla.com`
StarChefs (foodservice)	`starchefs.com`
Chronicle of Higher Education	`chronicle.com`
Public Relations Society of America	`prsa.org`

Project Management Institute	pmi.org
Assn. of Internet Professionals	association.org
Law Jobs	www.lawjobs.com
Advertising Age	adage.com
Financial Job Network (global)	fjn.com
Gamasutra (computer animation, video games)	gamasutra.com
MBA Central	careercentral.com/mba

Guides to professional organizations

Similar to the niche category, you can use associations to network and research as well as find job listings. (One technique: Find an Internet-published professional article you admire, contact the author, and ask who you should call for job openings in the author's field; this approach requires schmoozing talent and probably works best for new graduates.) These sites point you to people and organizations in your target field:

American Society of Association Executives	www.asaenet.org
Associations on the Net (Int. Public Library)	www.ipl.org/ref/AON
Yahoo Business&Econ/Organizations/Professional	yahoo.com

Information technology employment sites

Virtually all advertising media are courting high-demand, high-tech employees. So look for something extra, such as discussion groups where you, if a techster, can meet and greet your own kind who may help you solve technical problems — or tip you to your next good job.

Brainbuzz.com	brainbuzz.com
DICE High Tech Jobs Online	dice.com
Techies.com	techies.com
ComputerJobStore	www.computerjobstore.com

New college graduate sites

Web sites for employers with fresh mortar boards on their minds are a growth industry — they're everywhere.

JobDirect	jobdirect.com
JobTrak	jobtrak.com
College Central Network	www.collegecentral.com
College Grad Job Hunter	collegegrad.com
Best Jobs USA	bestjobsusa.com
Internships.com	www.internships.com

Diversity sites

If you're in the diversity category, you may get some special insights and advisories by taking your cover letters to visit classy specialty sites.

Black Collegian Online	black-collegian.com
LatPro	latpro.com
Asia-Net	asia-net.com
Gay work	gaywork.com

Government sites

All levels of government have jobs to fill. Here are places to source those jobs.

FedWorld Information Network	fedworld.gov
State & Local Government	piperinfo.com/state/states.html
About.com (search on government jobs)	about.com

Company Web sites

In the old days, before 1997 or so, if you wanted to apply at a specific company, you made direct application in some way or tried to find a friend of a friend to get you in the door. In the Internet age, you still do all the same things, only the companies give you a lot more help by making it very easy to find out what they're up to and if they have advertised openings. Just crank up their Web pages and get enlightened.

Company WebPages (4,000 companies)	interbiznet.com/hunt/companies
JobOptions (6,000 companies)	www.joboptions.com
Fortune (Fortune 500 companies)	fortune.com

WetFeet.com (industries; companies)	`wetfeet.com`
CorpTech (high-tech companies)	`corptech.com`
Meta List High-Tech Companies	`job-hunt.org/companies.shmtl`
Google (insert company name, click on I feel lucky)	`google.com`

Auction and staffing sites

The Web has spawned a burst of ventures that border on being human auctions. The services enable you to offer your skills to the highest bidder. And sometimes you bid on projects employers offer.

Aquent	`www.aquent.com`
Contract Employment Weekly	`ceweekly.com`
NationJob's WorkExchange	`nationjob.com`
Interim	`interim.com`
Guru.com	`guru.com`
FreeAgent	`freeagent.com`

Recruiters' sites

Outside recruiters are responsible for spotting candidates for many of the very best jobs. (See Chapter 16.) Find them and their specialties online.

Recruiters Online Network	`ipa.com`
Recruiter's Network	`recruitersnetwork.com`
Net-Temps	`net-temps.com`
TheWorksUSA	`theworksusa.com`
Oya's Recruiter Directory	`i-recruit.com/oya`
Electronic Recruiting Exchange	`erexchange.com`
Riley Guide Directories of Recruiting Firms	`www.rileyguide.com`

International sites

The idea of working anywhere in the world is a temptation to individuals across the planet. The Net clears information hurdles that once kept all but the most adventurous at home.

Escape Artist   escapeartist.com

JobNet Australia   jobnet.com.au

NetJobs (Canada)   www.netjobs.com

U.S. regional sites

Would your cover letter like to take a trip to a specific region of the United States? These examples are merely the tip of the continent.

East Coast

Western New York Jobs (Buffalo, Rochester)   wnyjobs.com

Boston Job Bank   bostonjobs.com

PhillyWorks   phillyworks.com

Midwest

Missouri Works   works.state.mo.us

Connect Ohio   www.connectohio.com/jobs

Wisconsin JobNet Job Search   www.dwd.state.wi.us/jobnet

South and Southwest

Charlotte's Web JobPage (N.C.)   www.charweb.org/job/jobpage.html

Working in Tennessee   www.state.tn.us/work.html

West Coast

Bay Area Jobs   bayareacareers.com

Employment Wash. Seattle   members.aol.com/gwattier/washjob.htm

Hawaii Careers   lava.net/~kbucar/html/hawaii_careers.htm

Local employment sites

Okay, so there's no place like home. There are sites to search for your preferred and familiar turf.

City Search   citysearch.com

Yahoo! Metros (search for jobs by city)   local.yahoo.com

Personal job agent sites

Would you like to be golfing or shopping while a job opening finds you? That's what personal job agent technology is all about. You fill out a profile of what you offer and what you want, and when a position matching your requirements comes along, you're tipped off by e-mail. You decide if you want to follow-up.

CareerXRoads 2000 co-author Mark Mehler says their research team found 322 job sites offering personal job agents — more than twice as many as the number (144) in the 1999 edition.

FutureStep (Korn Ferry)	futurestep.com
Alumni Network (headhunters)	alumni-network.com
JobOptions Job Alert	www.joboptions.com

Finding Out about Companies

The following resources are useful both for compiling job sourcing lists and for mining details useful in writing your cover letters.

Companies Online	www.companiesonline.com
PR Newswire	prnewswire.com
Hoover's Online	hoovers.com
Thomas Register Online	thomasregister.com
About.com (search on employer research)	www.about.com
Corporate Window	corporatewindow.com

Employee Message Boards – New!

Would you still send a cover letter and resume duo to a company whose employees think that it's the bottom of the food chain? Now, Web-working the trenches of corporate America is opening an unprecedented era in opportunities for pre-employment research.

Employee message boards are becoming common, but, like talk radio, they tend to attract more complaints than compliments. So use common sense in deciding if you're reading the real skinny on advancement opportunities, coworkers, pay raises, and the names of scrappy managers to avoid. Small companies have yet to grow their own "fine whines," so stay on the prowl for personal one-on-one networking to find a friend of a friend who is an ex- or current employee who's willing to spill the company beans.

Vault.com (hundreds of various companies)   `vault.com`

Yahoo!/Business-Finance/Co.'s/Intraco.Groups   `clubs.yahoo.com`

DotCom job riches: Finding the whole bounty

The sampling of where to send your cover letters in this chapter is certainly not comprehensive. Some observers claim 100,000 sites dealing with jobs litter the Web. I never counted. But to compile your own list, here are books dedicated to job site discussions that I highly recommend.

✔ *CareerXRoads 2000: The Directory to Job, Resume and Career Management Sites on the Web* by recruiting industry leaders Gerry Crispin and Mark Mehler (MMC Group — `careerxroads.com`) is simply the best Net directory published. 500 sites are fully reviewed and cross-referenced with hundreds of additional sites indexed for jobs and resumes. San Francisco State University human resources professor John Sullivan and other experts provide introductory editorial content. If you sign up online, the authors will send you free quarterly bulletins.

✔ *Job Searching Online For Dummies,* **2nd Edition,** by Pam Dixon (IDG Books Worldwide, Inc. — `dummies.com`). This wonderful 2000 update includes a 400-site directory of job-search Web sites, and Dixon tells you what she thinks about each site. Dixon keeps the directory fresh on her personal Web site (`pamdixon.com`). But this book is far more than a directory: Known for her exhaustive, precise research, the author, who has top-flight technological skills, has plenty to say about the best techniques to use in Internet job searching, which is now "all grown up."

✔ *The Guide to Internet Job Searching 2000-01 Edition* by Margaret Riley Dikel and Frances Roehm (NTC/Contemporary Publishing Co. — `ntc-cb.com`). A former college librarian, Dikel is a pioneer Internet search consultant who is respected the Web over. Roehm is a public librarian who has a pulse on what readers want to know about job searching online. Together they produce a very easy-to-read and easy-to-understand guide to the Net, a guide heavy with listings of digital resources. Dikel periodically updates the resources in her famous free Riley guide (`rileyguide.com`).

A tutorial and tips for researching companies

Hundreds of Web sites are flush with helpful information about where your cover letter could help you find a job. But making sense of all of them is a reach. Debbie Flanagan, a human resource professional in Ft. Lauderdale, Florida, gets five gold stars for her terrific free tutorial, *Researching Companies Online*.

Find it at `home.sprintmail.com/ ~debflanagan/ index.html`. This resource is well worth the mile-long address.

Part II

RedHot Cover Letters That Say You're Hot

The 5th Wave   By Rich Tennant

DOUG BELIEVED IN USING A STRONG CLOSING IN HIS COVER LETTERS

HIRE ME DAMMIT!

In this part . . .

Y ou know that you're talented. You know that you're capable of doing any job for which you're qualified. What's more, you're pretty sure you're capable of doing a bang-up job if you put your mind to it. But even if you write as well as, or better than, you speak, couldn't you use a little help positioning yourself for the very best jobs?

This part orients you to key cover letter concepts, exposes myths, and reveals secrets of proactive and reactive letters that draw job interview offers by the dozen.

Chapter 4

The RedHot Cover Letter Kick-Off

● ●

In This Chapter
▶ Why you need RedHot cover letters
▶ Overcoming writer's block
▶ Answers to cover letter questions

● ●

A resume should almost never go out alone in the world of employment. A resume needs a cover letter as a companion. Years ago, a cover letter was strictly a transmittal message. It said: *Here's my resume* and very little else.

Today's cover letter does far more than ride shotgun for your resume. Today's cover letter is itself a marketing tool, personalized and bursting with vitality. Sometimes the letter is on paper, sometimes it's on a computer. Either way, today's cover letter offers a great chance to generate an employer's interest in interviewing you.

Who Says You Can't Write?

Perhaps you haven't yet gotten the hang of writing contemporary cover letters because you think you can't write your way out of a paper bag, let alone write a letter that will catch an employer's eye. Is that what you think — don't try because you can't write? I bet you can. And this book will prove I'm right.

All your protests add up to is the need to expend extra energy into getting your thoughts down on paper — or on a computer screen. This book is loaded with the writing aids and tips you need to do just that.

You Can Learn to Write Cover Letters

Here's the thing: RedHot cover letter writing is a *learnable skill*. It is not Pulitzer Prize writing; it is getting-you-an-interview writing. If your cover letter attracts an employer's interest, the employer will read your resume to confirm a positive first impression. (Conversely, some employers go straight to the resume and, if they like what they see, turn back to examine the other gems of information that grace the cover letter.)

Virtually anyone can learn to write effective cover letters. You *can* conquer the cover-letter challenge if you really care about improving your career.

The difference between RedHot cover letters and run-of-the-mill cover letters is

- ✔ Strong personalization
- ✔ High energy
- ✔ Relevant information
- ✔ Moderately informal
- ✔ A breath of fresh air

A cover letter with each of these qualities is RedHot! The difference in the way you write is not night and day. What sets RedHot letters apart is a nuance of tone: greater zest, more vitality, more enticement — without extraterrestrial attempts at being clever.

Put your heart and soul into learning to write cover letters with passion! With apologies to Robert Frost: *No interest in the writer, no interest in the reader.*

In the competition of today's marketplace, you cannot afford to spend plenty of time perfecting your resume and then throw together a routine cover letter to slap on top. Putting your cover letter on autopilot downgrades your entire self-marketing package. Think about it: your marvelous resume and the boilerplate letter — what an odd couple to send marching out to do battle for you in the job world.

The Advantages of RedHot Cover Letters

Why should you bother to write a RedHot cover letter? Here are 11 good reasons.

Good first impression

A RedHot letter, as your first knock-on-the-door, grabs the attention of the resume reader: *Hey, you RezReader, slow down, stop, look at me!* The attention flows when you spotlight specific skills important to the reader. A RedHot letter causes the reader to look at your resume with heightened interest by answering the question in most employers' minds — *What can you do for us?*

Focus on employer

A RedHot letter focuses on the employer, in contrast to the resume that focuses on you. Psychologists are right — we all like to think about ourselves. That goes double for employers. Use words like *offer* and *contribute* over *growth potential* and *career opportunity*. A RedHot letter is a superb employment tool to address the benefits that you bring to the employer.

Matchmaking with benefits

Salespeople are told: *Customers buy benefits, not features.* Your letter personalizes your qualifications in terms of benefits and conveys them directly to a particular person. It tells the employer why you have what she wants. You stand out from the crowd by correlating your top skills, knowledge, and achievements with the employer's priorities. You can clearly state why this organization is a perfect place for you to make a contribution.

Up-to-speed image

A RedHot cover letter shows that you're in tune with the innovations affecting businesses today. In fast-breaking industries, employers assume that new graduates have current knowledge.

The family of job letters

Although this book title refers to cover letters, the title is something of a misnomer. This book covers the entire range of letters for job search needs, not only letters that respond to recruitment advertising and calls from executive recruiters. You'll find networking letters, broadcast letters, thank-you letters, and offer acceptance and rejection letters, as well as recommendation letters you write yourself. For the full range, see Chapters 6, 7, 14, and 15.

Job hunters more than 15 years out of school should make a point of showing that they do not believe the way they worked yesterday is the best way to work today and tomorrow. They should mention major changes the target industry is undergoing and explain what they have done to keep pace. The cover letter is an ideal place to convey that you are on the curve as new business worlds stir.

Shows savvy

A RedHot letter demonstrates your ability to understand and fulfill a company's specific needs. It shows you are smart enough — and committed enough — to scout the company's products, services, markets, and employment needs.

Presells you

A RedHot cover letter presells your qualifications, encouraging the reader to imagine you as qualified, personable, and savvy — the type of person to spend 30 minutes of a finite lifetime checking out. A strategic letter prepares the reader to like you. A good cover letter is like having a TV show announcer warm up the audience before the star appears.

You keep control

A RedHot cover letter puts control in your hands. It sets up a reason for you to call the employer, if the employer doesn't beat you to the phone. By promising to call, when you do telephone, you can truthfully get past the gatekeeper by saying that your call is expected.

Adaptability: A practical matter

Cover letters should be personal, of course. Whenever possible, write to a person, not a company. But, for practicality, you should first develop a core cover letter.

Once the core letter is polished, your cover letter has the versatility of a basic blue suit or black dress that goes from morning until evening with only a slight change of accessories. A core letter can be dressed up in any number of ways to address specific situations. You may develop several core cover letters — one for each career field. Write a new opening, plug in the target job specifics, and you have a whole new letter.

Career-changing bonus

It's not a magic bullet by any means, but your cover letter can be directed to help you change careers. When your most recent work experience is different from the career field you wish to enter, use your cover letter to accent your skills that best match the new field. Should you mention why you want to switch? Generally, I wouldn't; doing so just calls attention to your less-than-perfect match for the job. At times, though, it may be necessary. Suppose that you worked for four companies, each of which was sold. You might conclude your letter by saying

> *I am well qualified for a small company where wearing many hats is useful. I gained broad experience in different environments during 19XX-20XX at four companies: A, B, C, and D. Each company was acquired, resulting in changes of management. Despite departures of key personnel, excellent references are available.*

You: A three-dimensional person

With a RedHot cover letter, instead of being just a name and a set of qualifications, you come alive as a real person with benefits to offer, goals, ideas, and personality. A well-done cover letter suggests that you're knowledgeable, able, talented, and take pride in your work. By contrast, a poor or boring letter suggests that your work will be likewise.

Reveals critical thinking

A RedHot cover letter shows the employer how your mind works — how you state your position and then pull everything together in a lucid rationale. In a related evaluation, your cover letter proves that you can communicate in writing — useful for sales letters, memos, and reports.

The Disadvantages of RedHot Cover Letters

There aren't any.

Many Job Hunters Have Writer's Block

Perhaps the biggest reason you're struggling with writing cover letters is that you need to rethink your career goals. You really can't do your best writing about where you want to go until you know where that is.

Even when you're certain of your direction, you may still be stuck at square one. This phenomenon is called writer's block.

One cure writers use is *freewriting*. Writing becomes a problem for some people when they try to start at the beginning. When you freewrite, take about 15 minutes to randomly scratch out your thoughts on paper or bang away at your computer keyboard. Do not slow down to organize or edit. After you've pushed your pen for the full 15 minutes, read over your work. Mark ideas, words, and phrases that you can use in your letter. You may wish to freewrite several times until your thinking ink warms up.

Another technique to stop staring at a blank page is to answer the following questions. Find a friend to help you brainstorm, making notes as you go.

1. Whom do you picture reading your letter? What is that person wearing? In what environment is that person reading your letter — a well-ordered office or a room that looks like a teenager's retreat?

2. Which qualities do you want to emphasize in your letter?

3. Why will your letter be interesting and important to the reader?

4. What benefits do you bring to the reader's company?

5. What special skills or talents set you apart from the competition?

6. Why do you think your employability (person-specific) skills will help you fit into a new company?

7. How are your previous jobs similar to those you now seek? If the jobs are different, what skills are the same and transferable?

8. What do you like about the company to which you are applying?

Here's a tip for people who speak better than they write but must learn to write cover letters: Audiotape your letter with a voice recorder. Ask a friend to engage in a discussion about the job. Tell the friend why you are a hot prospect to fill the job. From that tape may come sound-bite excerpts that lift your letter out of humdrum status.

Keep in mind as you embark on the process of learning to write RedHot cover letters that your first draft is probably going to be shredder-bait, but your editing and refining can fix almost anything.

No Hard-and-Fast Rules

Just as absolutes do not exist in resume writing, neither do they exist in cover letter creation. You won't find a "best" way to do cover letters. As University of Pennsylvania career counselor Mary Morris Heiberger says

If there were a best way . . . all employers would have to be clones of each other, sharing identical tastes, priorities, and opinions.

Packaging and Presentation

Use a computer word processor and laser printer to turn out a fine-looking letter. Choose standard business size (8½" x 11") paper in white or eggshell.

Aim for a letter with no warts, no typos, and clean as a whistle.

Overcoming WhatIf Worries

WhatIfs (what-if questions) are legitimate worries when writing cover letters whose solutions may not be obvious.

WhatIf Worry	Answer
WhatIf I'm responding to your recruitment ad — to whom should my cover letter be addressed?	Send your RedHot cover letter with resume (see my book *Resumes For Dummies*, 3rd Edition) to the individual or department named in the advertisement. Follow instructions.
WhatIf the instructions say to send the letter and resume to the human resource department?	Not at all. New technology means that the resume will likely go into an electronic database and be stored for a long time; you may be considered for a number of open positions. In addition to following instructions, send a second RedHot cover letter to the name of the department hiring manager (your prospective boss). Say your resume is on file with HR (human resources). Get the hiring manager's name by anonymously calling and hope to break through voice mail.

WhatIf Worry	Answer
WhatIf I don't know enough about the position to write a RedHot letter?	Look up job descriptions for similar positions and read recruitment ads in print and online. Try to make online contact with people in the target career field through Internet newsgroups and mailing lists. This step is a longshot, but try to get through on the telephone to a person who does similar work for a competitor.
WhatIf I'm responding to an executive recruiter — do I send the same materials?	Send the same resume but change the letter (see Chapter 16). Mention that while you're very interested in this position, you would like to be considered for other jobs if this one doesn't pan out.
WhatIf I'm initiating a possible opening at a company that has not advertised one?	Research to determine who has the authority to hire you. Send your self-marketing materials to that person. Even more effective is to meet your target at a professional meeting or find a third party whose name you can use as an introduction (see Chapter 15).

Get Ready to Write

If you want your career to take off, make your cover letters terrific! Take more risks, offer more surprises, and find fresh ways to sell your benefits and skills. Pledge to never send out a run-of-the-mill letter again. From now on, you're in RedHot mode!

Chapter 5

Cover Letter Myths That Chill Hiring

. . . .

In This Chapter

▶ Myths that could make a letter drop dead

▶ Other fictions that sell your letter short

. . . .

Many people think that cover letters are an optional exercise in the job-finding game. They look at the cover letter as a throwaway piece that no one pays attention to. They take shortcuts and fall for myths guaranteed to show prospective employers that you don't care enough to send your very best. Don't cut corners with your cover letters. Believing the myths that follow can kill your cover letter before it has a chance to sell your skills.

Your resume may not be resurrected if you don't protect it with a well-written cover letter. The only benefit to be derived from these false beliefs is the one your competitors get by having you fall from job candidate status.

It's Okay to Send Your Resume without a Cover Letter

False! Unless you like to send your resume into other people's trash cans, make sure that a cover letter accompanies your resume. Your cover letter stamps a personality on your resume — a personality that the reader may find tough to reject out of hand.

Your Cover Letter Summarizes Your Resume

False! A summary of the resume and the resume with a summary seem a little repetitive, yes? Use a cover letter to add a warm handshake to your resume and to zero in on why the employer should be interested in you. Your cover letter should put your resume in context — it should draw attention to your strengths and present nonresume material that can make the difference between you and your next closest competitor when the interviewing decision is made.

A Cover Letter Merely Introduces Your Resume

False! Your cover letter is much more than a routing slip for your resume. Your letter is also ultimately a silent force, enticing the reader to scour your resume. Some employers believe cover letters are more important than resumes when choosing candidates to interview. If your cover letter doesn't flesh out the person presented in your resume, you may never get to meet the reader.

You Can Routinely Use a Generic Greeting — "Dear Employer"

False! Imagine that your job is to screen job applicants, and every letter you read begins with *Dear Job Application Reviewer* or, in effect, *Dear Nobody*. Research your target organization until you have the name and gender of the person who will review your resume. Double-check for correct spelling and proper job titles. When you can't uncover the correct name and must rely on a generic greeting, *Dear Employer* is as good as anything. Don't assume gender and use *Gentlemen* for your salutation.

What do you do when you're answering a blind ad, and you don't know who will review your resume? If the ad gives a U.S. Postal Service box address for reply, you're in luck.

Postal regulations require that the postmaster of a U.S. Post Office must reveal, upon demand, the name and telephone number of any person or entity renting a postal box to "solicit business" when the box is physically located at that station. The postal regulation releasing the names of business renters of postal boxes is USPS Communication 352.44, "Disclosure of Names and Addresses of Customers," Paragraph 4, "Post Office Box Address, Section 1, "Business Use." If you are denied the identity of a business renter, ask for a referral to the nearest U.S. Postal Service consumer affairs representative.

Apparently you have to deal with the postmaster's staff at the facility where the box is located.

Must the identity of individuals who rent U.S. Post Office boxes *for personal use* be revealed? No, except to law enforcement and other designated government agencies.

Must the identity of businesses or individuals who rent *private mailboxes* (such as Mailboxes Etc.) be revealed? No, except to law enforcement and other designated government agencies.

If you do get a name and telephone number from a postal clerk for the name of a business box holder, make an educated guess as to which department is hiring. Call the company's receptionist and ask if John Doe (make up a name) is the manager of that department; the receptionist may correct the name for you. Truthfully say that you are writing a letter, get the spelling down pat, and send off your RedHot cover letter properly addressed to *Dear Somebody-by-Name*.

Keep Your Cover Letter Really, Really Short — Like a Paragraph

False! The length of your cover letter depends not upon absolute rules of measurement, but upon the amount of content you have to convey. When the letter escorts a resume, I suggest limiting the letter to one page, with one to six paragraphs; when your letter substitutes for a resume, two to three pages is the max.

Devote one paragraph for each salient point. The short-paragraph technique maintains your letter's richness even when skimmed at transwarp speed. *Your RedHot cover letter should be just long enough to accommodate all your priority attributes and to motivate the reader to review your resume and meet with you.*

A Handwritten Cover Letter Is Best — It's Personal

False! Handwriting is certainly personal — but for job letters the risks are too high. What are the risks? Employers may assume you are way behind the times if you don't use a computer's word processor, or they may be unable to read your penmanship. If an employer wants a sample of your handwriting, the employer will request one. Your only handwriting should be your signature at the end, written in black or blue ink. (Colored inks like red or green are seen as unprofessional. Don't risk a job for a color statement.)

Resumes and Networking Are Infinitely More Important than Cover Letters in a Job Search

False! Finding a job is not a one-trick pony. You need the tools of marketing materials — cover letters and resumes — in your quest for job leads, which include recruitment advertising response, networking, and direct application among the most productive techniques. No one component is provably more important than the others.

Anyone Can Find a Job — If Your Cover Letter Isn't Working, the Letter Is at Fault

False! Your marketing materials — a cover letter or resume — can become an easy focus for your anxieties about a job search. Many of the moving parts of the employment process are frustratingly placed beyond your control: voice-mail keeps you from reaching a preferred employer, job openings for your target seem to go underground, interviews fail to spark job offers.

By contrast, the preparation of a cover letter and resume is entirely under your control. When things go wrong, blaming the marketing materials is convenient (although often the blame is well placed). Consequently, job seekers often think if they can only whip their marketing materials into perfect shape, the other parts of the search will turn out favorably. The truth is, all parts of your search must be up and running.

Your Cover Letter Gets You a Job

False! According to this logic, a cherry pit gets you a cherry. A cherry pit planted in fertile soil gets you a tree and then maybe a cherry. A RedHot cover letter riding shotgun for a resume gets you an interview and then maybe a job. To succeed in your job search, you need a strategy for finding job leads (*Job Hunting For Dummies* by Max Messmer, IDG Books Worldwide, Inc., can help) and a FirstRate resume (see my book, *Resumes For Dummies*, 3rd Edition, for what puts your resume in the FirstRate class), supported by a RedHot cover letter. In addition, you need marketable skills, appropriate personal qualities, interviewing strengths, and the right references. It's the total package that determines who wins the job.

The Cover Letter Is Your Chance to Talk about Your Personal Life and Feelings

False! Your resume talks about you; your cover letter talks about your intended employer — and how your employer can benefit from the splendid assets you offer. Describe special benefits that set you above other applicants. Rambling about personal feelings and situations in an employment letter is a blatant display of self-interest and, worse, is boring. An exception can be made when you're seeking to relocate (provided you offer to pay for the move). Many employers appreciate the desire to be near family as a reason to relocate. No need to go into your uncle's stint in the nursing home — having family in the area is enough.

Include Salary History and Expectations in Your Cover Letter

False! Save the salary discussion for the interview. You can be eliminated at this stage if your salary history is considered too high, too low, or too static. Don't get into it. If an ad requests such information, write that your salary is negotiable and that you'd be happy to discuss the issue during an interview. See Chapter 18 for more information about how to handle the salary issue.

Once You Send a Letter, the Employer Carries the Ball

False! No matter how terrific you are, most employers have no time for hunting you down unless they need you right this very second. If you don't get an acknowledgment (probably an automated reply) that your cover note or letter arrived, call or e-mail to confirm. (See Chapter 2.)

The never-say-die telephone strategy of years past — which requires you to doggedly call back every ten days or two weeks — no longer works well. Companies are understaffed; interviewers are overworked. Harried interviewers resent you for breaking into their days with excessive telephone calls. Remaining connected through well-written postal letters, e-mail, and faxes that offer information the employer can use is a much better idea.

Sending Your Letter by Courier Is an Attention-Getter

False! Unless time is of the essence, save your money. Anyone who cares how your letter arrives usually doesn't have the power to hire you. Mail usually filters through office staffers before reaching hiring managers. Even a courier envelope that costs you a meal is likely to be opened by nonhiring hands. E-mail and faxes may get the hiring manager's attention, because they often route straight to your target.

When Mailing, Use a Standard Business Envelope

False! Before the dawn of electronic magic, folding a letter for a 4" x 9.5" envelope was standard. Now that your documents face a good chance of being scanned and stored by job computers, inserting your letter and resume flat and unfolded into a 10" x 13" envelope is safer. Creases from folding may damage your document's text in scanning systems. By using a larger envelope, you have a huge edge over thousands of other job seekers who don't know that their marketing materials should arrive scanner-ready.

Paper Quality Always Has a Great Effect on Your Image

False! And True! Both humans and computers read cover letters and resumes. For a finger-friendly read, paper quality counts. And the more rag content, the better.

For a computer-friendly read, the quality of paper doesn't matter at all — the finest paper becomes just another pretty electronic face. Your cover letter and resume paper should match and should be white or off-white smooth paper, sized 8.5" x 11". Avoid glossy or coarse textures that can cause scanners to misread. Don't use colored paper — especially blue, green, or gray, which may scan in as shades of gray that obscure your letter's text.

Chapter 6

Action Letters That Respond to Needs

. . . .

In This Chapter

▶ Meeting the five-member family of responding letters

▶ Writing when you know a job opening exists

▶ Responding to recruitment ads

. . . .

*T*he job letter family is easier to understand if you think of its members in two main groups:

> ✔ **Reactive:** Action letters that **respond** to needs
>
> Letters in this group are written when you know a job opening exists. These are reactive letters.
>
> ✔ **Proactive:** Action letters that **initiate** leads
>
> Letters in this group are written to inquire about a possible job opening. These are *proactive letters*. You can read more about initiating letters in Chapter 7.
>
> Also in this category are thank-you letters and other letters you are not required to write but that you initiate as a way to follow up on a possible job opening.

You can hardly believe your immense good fortune — you've finally learned of a job that seems just right for you!

Perhaps you found the job in a help-wanted advertisement in a newspaper or professional journal or saw the job posted on the Internet. Perhaps you got wind of it in your networking moves or heard the job described on a job hotline. Perhaps a friend called to say a job is opening where he works. No matter how you found out about the job, you know an opening exists, and you break speed limits to reply. You want — as quickly as possible — to show your intention of becoming a candidate for the position and ask for a job interview.

As you pull up short in front of a computer, you're confronted by a sudden thought: What sort of letter shall I write that will nail this job for me?

This chapter answers that question by introducing you to five basic action letter categories — each of which can respond to specific needs of employers. They are

- ✔ **Resume cover letter**
- ✔ **T-letter**
- ✔ **Blind ad reply letter**
- ✔ **Employment service letter**
- ✔ **Targeted resume letter**

In the next few pages, you discover the concept, mission, advantages, and disadvantages of the responding letter.

Model letters that illustrate responding letters are found in Chapter 14. Any of these five types can be formidable when used to heat up your chances of being called for a meeting. This chapter offers some thoughts on which type is most likely to ignite interest in your qualifications.

The Resume Letter: A Familiar Type

The resume letter is the one that escorts your resume when you respond to a recruitment ad. This letter is the one most commonly thought of when you hear the term "cover letter."

The resume letter is more than shrinkwrap for your resume, however. Another weapon in your arsenal of flame-throwing, self-marketing materials, the resume letter adds personality to a formal resume. In effect, your resume letter says:

> *I am highly motivated and have built a solid reputation (whether at school or at work) for tireless enthusiasm, resourcefulness, accuracy, and careful work — all essential skills for a (your occupation). Go ahead and read my resume. I'm hot stuff!*

The resume letter's mission

- ✔ To get your resume read
- ✔ To turn you into a three-dimensional being

Uncovering job ads

When it comes to sourcing jobs, one of the chief methods is to respond to job ads. Here are pointers to expand your connections.

✔ Check out newspapers, trade and professional publications, association newsletters, job hotlines, public employment service job banks, electronic bulletin boards, newspaper help-wanted classifieds on the Internet (see Chapter 3), and Internet recruitment advertising.

✔ Skim through ads in fields outside your own — you may find yourself fitting into a new career field or fitting a new field to your career.

✔ You should apply not only to ads you match exactly, but to any openings for which you may be slightly over- or underqualified. Employers often advertise for the perfect match but adjust their requirements as applications are received. Forget this tactic if you are over- or underqualified by a country mile.

✔ Stay alert to companies doing major recruitment — they may advertise only some openings but actually have many others of interest to you.

✔ Even if you're pushed for time, target specific readers with personalized letters. Employers sniff-and-trash form letters like spent socks.

✔ Even if rejected once by a company, continue replying (with revised letters) to the company's ad as long as it runs — their human tracking systems often have a poor memory. Dynamics change when job computers enter the picture. If you know (because you've called to ask) that a computer is tracking applicants, be extremely careful about sending multiple resumes. If your letters do not seem to describe the same person with the same set of skills and other qualifications, you will raise serious questions about who you really are. Computers usually retrieve by name and telephone number. If you are determined to send wildly different resumes, change the telephone number and use initials instead of your first name.

✔ Don't shy away from blind ads. (The employer's name is not given, only a box number or coded reference.) Your objective is to maximize every possible interview source.

✔ The traditional advice is to apply separately for each position with the same company. One application is enough when you know the company uses a job computer to track applicants. Your resume is entered in a database, which is then searched as different positions open.

Advantages of a resume letter

✔ Directs the focus of your resume
✔ Highlights your skills

Disadvantages of a resume letter

- ✔ One glaring typo or error and, for this employer, your whole life could wind up as a wad of recycled paper.

- ✔ Because this format is expected (conventional formatted letter plus a resume), the presentation must be outstanding or the letter risks boring the reader.

The T-Letter: The New Champion

My personal favorite is the T-letter, a dynamite letter that matches point-by-point the employer's priorities with the qualifications you offer. This letter can accompany a resume, or it can be written as a targeted resume letter (described later in this chapter).

I call it the "You-want/I-have" letter because, graphically, this type makes seeing why your application deserves consideration so easy.

The T-letter can be constructed in one of two basic ways:

- ✔ The ledger layout (see Figure 6-1) is the most common. In the left column, you write the employer's requirements that you find in the advertisement; across from each item, you write your qualification that meets the requirement.

- ✔ The staggered block layout (see Figure 6-2) is another way to show the fit between the employer's priorities and your assets.

Watch for clues

Sleuth the wording of recruitment ads before writing your response letter. Pay attention to special emphasis placed on requirements, especially if they are repeated. Be certain to mention those requirements in your letter. Tip-offs to crucial requirements are preceded or followed by such demands as

(Requirement) is a plus

Desirable

Very desirable

Must be

Must be capable of

Must have

Is required

Must be strongly versed in

Must be knowledgeable in

Should be strong in

Proficiency in

The T-letter's mission

✔ To present a RedHot profile of you, perfectly matched to the employer's interests

✔ To pre-market your knowledge of the employer and the industry

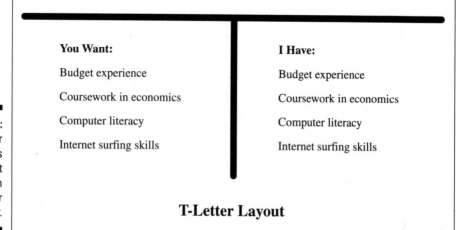

Figure 6-1:
The ledger layout is the most common format for the T-letter.

You Want:	I Have:
Budget experience	Budget experience
Coursework in economics	Coursework in economics
Computer literacy	Computer literacy
Internet surfing skills	Internet surfing skills

T-Letter Layout

Advantages of the T-letter

✔ Instantly appeals to busy readers by performing the matching between job requirements and applicant qualifications

✔ Shows understanding of employer's priorities and limited time — shows that you're resourceful

Disadvantages of the T-letter

✔ Unsuitable if you're not a close match. Without RedHot spin control on areas of weakness, may show too many deficiencies of knowledge or absent credentials, experience, or education.

✔ Without employer research, knowledge of field, and rigorous self-assessment (see Chapters 8 and 9), the cross-matching may be too sparse to compete with other applicants.

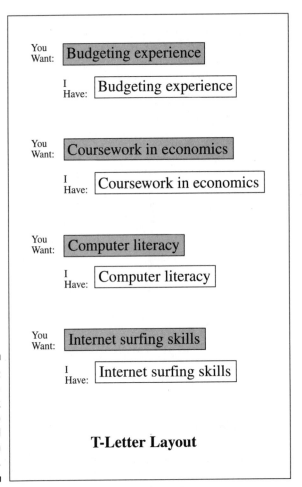

Figure 6-2:
The staggered block layout also works well with T-letters.

The Blind Ad Letter: A Leap of Faith

The ideal cover letter addresses a single reader by name. However, many recruitment ads virtually prevent any form of targeting — unless you're a good detective (see Chapter 5). The advertisers provide only an untraceable fax number, P.O. box, commercial mail facility box, publication box, or cloaked e-mail address. They bypass the advertiser's name, job title, and department, leaving you clueless.

Once you have tried your hardest to ferret out the name and identity of your recipient, you may still be left with only a ghost employer.

Why do advertisers run blind ads? Very occasionally an employer will run a bogus ad to survey the market or to out unhappy employees. A third-party recruiter may run a bogus ad to beef up a resume database. Because newspapers ads are too expensive to waste in playing games, bogus ads are more likely to be found on less expensive Web job-posting sites.

The many legitimate reasons employers place blind ads are to

- ✔ Attract a surplus of responses without the complications of incoming telephone calls

- ✔ Maintain secrecy while exploring the market before deciding on an internal promotion or replacement

- ✔ Keep job openings secret from competitors who'd love to know where the hiring company has holes in its armor

- ✔ Avoid being overwhelmed with an avalanche of job seekers when they lack the staff to process all responses

The blind ad letter's mission

- ✔ To attract the reader's attention and spark active consideration of your candidacy for the position

- ✔ To respond to requirements listed in the ad with a competitive lineup of qualifications, skills, and results (drawn from your data developed in Chapters 8 and 9) and your knowledge of the industry plus a motivation to learn new skills

Advantages of the blind ad letter

- ✔ As many job seekers doubt the legitimacy of blind ads, considering them a waste of time, blind ads are often ignored — reducing your competition.

- ✔ Use it to show creativity and resourcefulness (especially if you can track down the name of the advertiser), which may bring surprising responses from those you were hoping to reach.

Disadvantages of the blind ad letter

- ✔ Without enough industry research, you risk missing the mystery reader's bulls-eye interests.

- ✔ Ghost recruitment ads can decrease the chances that your inquiry will be acknowledged, wasting your time; without an identity, you can't follow up.

- ✔ Without employer identity, the ad could be your current employer or one you have already contacted via some other avenue — rare, but possible.

Job hotline reply letter

You called a hotline; now what? Most job hotlines offer the name of an individual to call or direct you to the employer's human resource department. In either case, your letter must address someone in particular, or your letter may be treated as junk mail.

Pay as much attention to job requirements given on the hotline as you would to a newspaper recruitment ad. The mission, advantages, and disadvantages are identical to those of other responding letters.

Usually you know the name of the company, but in a large organization, you may not be told the department or other particulars. When the hotline offers minimal information, dig around to find out more by calling the company's receptionist. If you're stonewalled by the receptionist or voice mail, follow the advice given for blind ad reply letters.

The Employment Service Letter

While shopping recruitment ads and online job postings, you may be asked to respond not to the employer but to the employer's third-party representative. You may be asked to contact

- ✔ Contract recruiters (specialists who fill short-term jobs, such as engineering contracts that last six months or longer) and temporary service consultants
- ✔ Executive recruiters and employment agencies
- ✔ Campus career center personnel

Be alert to wordings such as "client company," "our client," or similar expressions. This phrasing identifies the advertiser as an employment agency, executive recruiter, or other third-party employment service. Because these employment services represent an employer you hope to work for, address your letter to the employment service. If you know the name of the employer, you can state the employer's name in the RE: (Regarding) line or in the introduction to your letter.

Like most employers, employment services prefer letters that get to the point — preferably in less than one page. As with other RedHot cover letters, front-load your letter with your most marketable skills and experience (based on research for your career field).

The Targeted Resume Letter: All in One

The targeted resume letter is a combination of the cover letter and resume. It is also called a tailored letter. This letter is thought to be more personal, and thus more appealing, than the cover-letter-plus-resume duo.

This type of letter is more effective when sent directly to hiring managers rather than to the human resources department. In content, the targeted resume letter is similar to the broadcast letter described in Chapter 4.

To satisfy RedHot standards, incorporate employer research, skills, and information from your worksheets to showcase the jalapeño results employers are hungry for.

The targeted resume letter's mission

- ✔ To condense the resume and separate letter into two pages of friendly yet professional conversation
- ✔ To sketch a quick summary of your qualifications for the position — just enough for the reader to want more, but not enough to get you screened out of consideration

Advantages of the targeted resume letter

- ✔ Because these letters are obviously time-consuming to prepare, recipient may feel a greater obligation to read it rather than the letter-resume package
- ✔ Provides a less rigid, spartan context for information that may be dulled on a formal resume; with RedHot handling, can be a pleasure to read

Disadvantages of the targeted resume letter

- ✔ Time-consuming to write; without RedHot spice, the letter may not contain enough information to show you are qualified for the position; if your background is extensive, you may shortchange yourself.
- ✔ Targeted resume letters don't look like resumes and may be perceived by conservative employers as negatively unconventional, especially at managerial levels.

Close Your Letter with Freshness

Before moving on to action letters that initiate leads, one more thought about closing your responding letters:

Sincerely yours works fine. But how about a professional yet interesting closing, such as

> *Enthusiastic about joining your team,*
>
> *I look forward to meeting with you,*
>
> *Thanks for your consideration,*
>
> *Vigorously,*

What other lines can you think of to put morning dew on your responding letter?

For examples of responding letters, see Chapter 14.

Chapter 7

Action Letters That Initiate Leads

In This Chapter

▶ Writing when you hope a job opening exists

▶ Meeting the five-member family of initiating letters

▶ Pleasing by saying thank-you

The job letter family is easier to understand if you think of two main groups of members:

✔ **Reactive:** Action letters that **respond** to needs

Letters in this group are written when you know a job opening exists. These are *reactive letters*. You can read more about responding letters in Chapter 6.

✔ **Proactive:** Action letters that **initiate** leads

Letters in this group are written to inquire about a possible job opening. These are *proactive letters*.

Also in this category are thank-you letters and other letters you initiate as a way to follow up on a known or possible job opening.

You've toiled in the vineyards of responding letters, and now you wonder what else you can possibly do while you anxiously await call-backs and interviews.

You can seize the initiative and campaign for jobs that don't surface in recruitment advertising — jobs found in the *hidden job market*. This term refers to job openings or potential job openings that for one reason or another are not made public. In many cases, these are prime positions that become known through industry networking. Many of these jobs are filled from within the company (leaving another vacancy) or are filled by candidates known or recommended by someone known to the employer. These are the jobs to which your networking skills can lead.

You can track down those job leads and write letters to pursue them. Action letters that proactively initiate leads do heavy lifting in any RedHot job search.

This chapter introduces you to five basic action-initiating letter categories — each of which can open doors to employment (model initiating letters can be found in Chapter 15).

- ✔ **Networking letter** — used to open job options in the companies that you target and to ferret out more job leads from your contacts

- ✔ **Follow-up letter** — used to thank employers for interviews, to remind employers and contacts of your interaction with them, and to encourage hiring action

- ✔ **Broadcast letter** — used in mailing campaigns to potential employers and executive recruiters

- ✔ **Recommendation letter** — used as reinforcement of your qualifications (you draft the letter for a reference's signature)

- ✔ **Endgame letter** — used to accept or reject job offers

The Networking Letter: Reaching Out

Networking means making connections with people you may not yet know but who may be helpful in your job search. As author Max Messmer says in *Job Hunting For Dummies,* 2nd Edition (IDG Books Worldwide, Inc.), networking is based on the principle of being carried into a situation on another person's coattails: "It is easier to get information and help from people who either know you or know someone who knows you than from people who have never heard of you."

You can write networking letters to

- ✔ Employers
- ✔ Family
- ✔ Friends
- ✔ Coworkers (former and current)
- ✔ Fellow members of professional organizations
- ✔ Fellow members of service, religious, civic, fraternal, and political organizations
- ✔ Alumni, campus career center specialists, professors, and classmates
- ✔ Employees of other companies in your field
- ✔ Internet contacts

Some networking letters, using a mutual friend's coattails, make memorable connections with potential employers, asking them for a job or soliciting advice and ideas. Other networking letters ask everyone but potential employers for job leads or referrals.

The networking letter's mission

Use a networking letter to help you accomplish a number of useful goals.

When addressed to someone who can give you a job, your networking letter can be used

- ✔ To gain a job or referral by making a personal connection and establishing rapport. When you telephone, you can truthfully say that the employer is expecting your call (your letter specifies when you'll call)
- ✔ To gain priority over nonconnected applicants

When addressed to someone who can help you find a job, your networking letter can be used

- ✔ To get a referral or recommendation
- ✔ To get information on a target employer
- ✔ To get general advice on your course of action

Advantages and disadvantages

A well-written networking letter

- ✔ Establishes a broader base of job options
- ✔ Gives you priority over applicants who apply out of the blue
- ✔ Shows employers your personal connection with their companies and reduces their screening efforts

As with most things useful in your job search, networking letters have disadvantages as well.

- ✔ Writing networking letters requires time and resourcefulness.
- ✔ Even the greatest networking letter does not guarantee success in job leads.
- ✔ Without RedHot tact, you may be misinterpreted as presumptuous.

Networking letters to potential employers

When writing networking letters, mention

✔ How you came to write the letter (note reference or other lead)

✔ How your education and background have prepared you for the field

✔ Knowledge about issues the employer faces without appearing to tell the employer the employer's business; add lots of "as you know" qualifiers

Follow-Up Letters: Circling Back

Follow-up letters are sent after something has happened — agreement to grant a job interview, the job interview itself, or some other action that suggests you're being helped into the employment process.

The thank-you letter to employers

Even if employers are not swayed by your thank-you letter, sending one never hurts. Think of letter-writing as a muscle that needs exercise.

The thank-you letter's mission

Before the job interview, write a thank-you letter (e-mail is fine)

✔ To confirm the interview time and place

✔ To thank the interviewer for the appointment

✔ To add a selling point to increase the interviewer's anticipation of meeting you

After the job interview, write a thank-you letter

✔ To immediately remind the interviewer of you and make yet another good impression

✔ To add information or ideas not covered in the interview — perhaps ideas suggested during the interview itself

✔ To provide another reason for the interviewer to contact you about your candidacy

E-mail or snail-mail your thanks?

Should you send paper or e-mail thank-you letters after an interview? The debate continues. Paper is good because so few candidates write postal letters these days that doing so allows you to stand out from the crowd. If you're 25 or 30 years old, for instance, and a known whiz at things technological, a paper letter makes you look gracious and exceptional.

But e-mail is good because its ease of response invites the interviewer to conduct a dialogue with you, especially if you end the thank-you email with a question (such as "If I may ask, when do you expect to make a decision?"). E-mail also is the medium of choice for people over 40 who could use a bit of help in the youthful image department.

Advantages and disadvantages

When you write a thank-you letter

- ✔ You look well mannered, or at least aware enough to be an asset to the company.
- ✔ Unless you write a poor letter, a thank-you letter always leaves a positive impression.

There are no disadvantages.

Writing is one sure way to expose the quality of your thinking. Anytime you set word processor to paper, you risk making a poor impression if you don't think things through carefully. Stay aware of the importance of each word you choose. If your writing skills are not strong, ask a friend to review your letter before you send it.

The follow-up letter for a favor

You understand the need to write thank-you letters to potential employers. But remember all the others who help your job cause. Here's what I mean:

Suppose that last week you struck up a conversation with a woman at your gym, who turns out to be the administrative assistant at a firm you'd love to work for. She told you about an entry-level opening in its newest department, and she advised you to send in a resume and a cover letter.

You're not certain if she processes resumes and cover letters, but she's your only straight slide into the firm. Still sticky in your gym clothes, you're in front of your computer, coping with writer's block and a blank screen. You need a job letter — a follow-up letter — to remind her of your meeting, and you need to send it within the next 24 hours. Write it!

The follow-up letter is a close relative of the networking letter. Both cement a continuing relationship between networking contacts and employers with whom you have not yet interviewed.

The follow-up letter's mission

Use a follow-up letter

- ✔ To remind the contact of your connection
- ✔ To follow up when an employer (as a result of a contact or networking letter) invites you to send your resume
- ✔ To encourage contacts to forward your resume to employers
- ✔ To establish continued rapport in case an opening should arise in the future

Advantages and disadvantages

A follow-up letter

- ✔ Personally connects you to employer inroads
- ✔ Communicates an interested brand of aggressiveness and enthusiasm about an opening
- ✔ Provides the contact with a permanent reminder of a promise to help you

The downside of a follow-up letter, as with any writing effort, is that

- ✔ You may need to write a number of them before one produces a solid lead or interview.
- ✔ You may need to make several time-consuming attempts before you compose an effective letter.

The Broadcast Letter: Giant Mailings

You may have heard of the broadcast letter, otherwise known as the "direct-mail campaign resume letter." You may even have decided that this approach is your best bet for broadest job coverage.

The broadcast letter combines a resume with a cover letter. Advocates of broadcast letters say that the technique works when you invest in big numbers (like one or two thousand letters). The numbers shrink when you mail to executive recruiters (as noted in Chapter 16, sending to a select list of a few hundred executive recruiters is recommended as a good way to jump-start a job search).

Detractors say that the mass outreach of broadcast letters is a waste of time and money.

I've never seen a study scientifically proving whether broadcast letters work or not. If you try the technique, take care in selecting your mailing list and write one wowser of a letter.

The broadcast letter's mission

Use a broadcast letter

✔ To replace the resume

✔ To present your qualifications quickly to a hiring manager with the power to hire you (not human resource department personnel)

✔ To publicize your availability to employers in a hard-hitting, self-marketing format

Advantages and disadvantages

The broadcast letter has a number of advantages. It

✔ Combines resume and cover letter into one compact seller

✔ Includes pertinent information from your resume not usually found in other cover letters

✔ With RedHot sell, may save recruiters time and money in their searches

✔ Gets more attention than most junk mail

The disadvantages of the broadcast letter are that it

✔ Relies on getting the reader's attention in the first couple of seconds

✔ May appear lazy or vague without careful assessment of background

✔ Is time consuming, and you may receive few or no responses

The broadcast letter is a favorite technique of outplacement firms, and some cover letter readers may consider it overplayed.

If your broadcast letter does not address specific individuals, or if it addresses the wrong individuals, you may as well feed it to the neighborhood dinosaur.

The Recommendation Letter: Getting Endorsements

The employer you've been hopping around on pins and needles waiting to hear from just left a message on your e-mail asking for several letters of recommendation.

Don't panic — write your own recommendations! Remembering that just about everyone in the working world is as busy as (if not busier than) you, contact individuals in a position to recommend you (such as previous employers, professors, and leaders of organizations or clubs).

If your references are willing to sing your praises, offer to draft a letter for their fine-tuning.

For your references' convenience and your peace of mind, find out what word-processing program they use. Draft the letter(s) in that program and e-mail them as attachments or save them on floppy disks. If you put your letter on a disk, postal mail or hand-deliver it with a printed copy.

The Endgame Letter: Wrapping Up

You're well into your job search. Maybe your search has stalled out and you need to restart it. Or perhaps you've been offered a job. You still have letters to write.

- ✔ Resurrection letters
- ✔ Acceptance letters
- ✔ Rejection letters

The *resurrection letter's* mission is to remind an employer of your application (perhaps they stalled their recruitment) or to revive your application after having removed yourself from consideration. In short order, remind the reader of

- ✔ Your last communication with the employer
- ✔ A positive narrative of what has happened since that time
- ✔ Your top selling points for the position (include another copy of your resume)
- ✔ A statement of your continued interest in the position and the company's search

The *acceptance letter's* mission is not only to thank the hiring party, but also to define the terms of your employment as agreed upon in your interview/job offer negotiations. Such terms include

- ✔ Salary
- ✔ Job title
- ✔ Benefits
- ✔ Contract terms

The difference between fizzle and sizzle

In drafting your recommendation letter for another's signature, bear these thoughts in mind:

- ✔ Identify your reference — who the person is, what the person does, and where the person does it.

- ✔ Give a clear statement of who is being recommended (you) and for what position.

- ✔ Add a narrative of the reference's relationship to you — how long, in what capacity, how closely, and what projects were shared.

- ✔ Include a time when the reference can be contacted for more information.

- ✔ Provide a flash-list of your top skills, judgment, work habits, reliability, productivity, compatibility, field knowledge, attributes, and achievements, as well as how these qualities benefit the prospective position.

- ✔ If your references prefer to write their own letters, review with them the preceding points in case they have fewer, less RedHot details in mind. Take no chances. A wishy-washy recommendation can cool your candidacy.

While this letter may seem like overkill, your terms are in writing in case anything goes awry. Send one to each individual directly involved in your recruitment.

The *rejection* letter also is a wise time investment; if you don't answer other employers' job offers, you may create enemies.

✔ Courteously thank employers for their time, interviews, and consideration.

✔ Inform them that you have already accepted another offer (you may not wish to say from whom) and are no longer available.

✔ Include any hopes you may have to work with them in the future.

Whether making friends or covering your flanks, EndGame letters finalize the end of your job hunt.

For examples of initiating letters, see Chapter 15.

RedHot phrases for acceptance letters

"I am delighted to accept your offer to become your company's (job title)."

"I appreciate the confidence you demonstrated by selecting me to be (job title)."

"This letter is my acceptance of your offer to join (name of company) as (job title)."

"I look forward to becoming a part of your team as (job title), beginning (start date)."

"I eagerly anticipate the challenges in the position as (job title) that you have offered me."

"I would like to express my gratitude in accepting the position of (job title); I look forward to the challenges and responsibilities that the position offers."

Part III
Working Out What Sizzles

The 5th Wave   By Rich Tennant

"Do you think being able to play N64, Dreamcast, and Playstation could be considered transferable skills?"

In this part . . .

*E*ven in an era when employers are insisting that
skilled labor shortages will bite us in the New
Economy, isn't your goal to land the best of the best jobs
for your package of interests, skills, and lifestyle prefer-
ences? No more than you would enter a 5K walk without
giving a thought to conditioning your body should you try
to dash off your cover notes and letters without thoughtful preparation.

Even the best writers sometimes creep at the speed of
dark. This part helps you to find your best voice with
worksheets and up-to-date skill listings that'll shoo you
into position for the finest job you can get.

Chapter 8

JobSeeker's Skills Finder

*I*n the New Economy, it's not who you know but what you know.

The new high-tech global economy's attention is riveted on *skills* — useable knowledge. Inquiring employers want to know: What skills do you have that allow you to do the work you seek?

Why Are Skills "Suddenly" So Special?

Haven't skills always been a high priority in hiring plans? Yes, they have. But the degree of importance assigned to skills is exploding as you read these words. We're living through rocket-paced change, which brings with it not only opportunity but big problems for those who do not have the skills (and who can prove that they have them) to come into a workplace and do the work the employer wants done *now*!

Not only do huge numbers of young people go ill-equipped into an economic tide that, awash with world changes, is flowing against them, but older adults, too, are increasingly at risk as they age and age discrimination spreads.

Remaining Employable in the World Marketplace

Whether you are a professional, manager, technician, or blue-collar worker, be aware of several trends in the acquisition of skills:

- ✔ Skill requirements are increasing in response to rapid technological change. (*Tip:* Avoid jobs where you work with outdated technology and equipment — your skills base will wither and the bloom will be off your rose.)

- ✔ Advances in technology (mainly the Internet) are revolutionizing the manner in which skill training is delivered. (*Tip:* Thousands of Web sites sponsored by career firms, distance education schools, and professional organizations offer not only skill training but skill certification.)

- ✔ Companies that are large enough to have training departments will become learning organizations. You will be encouraged to think of your skills base as a "continuing journey."

Small businesses are creating most of the new jobs. But small companies have fewer resources to use in training new hires. That means you're pretty much on your own to acquire the skills you need for most of the jobs in the New Economy. (Exactly how you acquire the skills you require is a subject for another book.)

Large companies, although offering fewer jobs in the aggregate, are still the best places to work to acquire up-to-date skills you can market on future jobs.

Even when you have an enviable collection of skills, how do you market them in your cover letter?

- ✔ *Inference.* Your prior education and experience suggest your competencies: "With my degree in civil engineering, I am competent to design contemporary roadways."

- ✔ *Assertion.* You claim you have the skills: "I can design and sell a program of services to the Spanish-speaking market."

- ✔ *References.* Others claim on your behalf: "My former manager, Carlyle Sangi, says I put together a budget better than anyone she knows."

- ✔ *Certification.* Testing and peer evaluation document your abilities: "As a certified industrial ergonomist, I can evaluate your workplace and make required changes to conform to new OSHA rules."

Where There's a Skill, There's a Way

Skills are also called *competencies*. Analyzing them only looks easy. The task can prove challenging even when you know what you're doing. A practical way to organize skills for job-seeking purposes is to divide them into three basic types: transferable skills, employability skills, and technical skills.

- **Transferable skills:** Transferable skills are your most important skills — portable skills that you can use in job after job. They answer an employer's question: "*Can* you do the job?" Because they apply to a variety of jobs, they can be considered *nonspecific.* For example, employers value communications skills in jobs ranging from apple grower to zookeeper. You can transfer these skills from job to job, or even from one career field to another career field. Another term for transferable skills is *cross-functional skills,* which you use to perform activities that occur across jobs.

- **Employability skills:** Employability skills are personal skills that answer the employer's questions: "*Will* you do the job? Will you do the job in harmony with other employees?" Also called *adaptive* or *self-management skills,* these skills can be considered *person-specific.* For example, reliability, honesty, enthusiasm, and getting along with others illustrate characteristics included in employability skills. Employability skills suggest character and attitudes — who you are and how you work.

- **Technical skills:** Technical skills are job-related skills, suitable for a particular type of job. They also answer an employer's question, "Can you do the job?" Often you can't easily move technical skills from one employer to another, so these skills are considered *job-specific.* For example, the ability to use a certain brand of mold-injection machine classifies as a technical skill.

  Here's a common-sense tip: Mention your technical skills only when you are certain that a prospective employer can benefit from the technical skills you bring. Unless you are positive the employer can use your technical skills, stick to transferable skills in your cover letter and resume.

Discovering Your Skills

Because the skills concept is such a hot issue, I give you a couple of checklists to help you round up and brand those you own. Don't get creative and adopt a skill just because it looks good on paper or when you're not sure what the word means. If you don't know what a word or term means, look it up or don't use it. You can expect to be grilled on your skill claims during a job interview. Prepare to support each skill claim.

Skills: Your count or mine?

It's a matter of opinion how skills are classified. Some advisers, for instance, divide skills into only two categories: work content and functional.

Work-content skills are used to perform a specific type of job, such as financial planning or computer programming; they are learned through school or work experience.

Functional skills are transferable, learned across careers, jobs, and industries.

The classification scheme isn't important. What counts in a job search is being able to sell yourself by identifying your skills.

Read through the following two checklists of transferable skills and employability skills and mark those words and terms that apply to you. Include the terms as part of your skills language to take with you and use for resumes, cover letters, and job interviews. The checklists are not exhaustive but are a good start; you may think of other words and terms to use as well.

I don't include a technical skills checklist because those skills vary according to each individual's job area.

Transferable Skills Checklist

A

❏ Accelerating

❏ Accomplishing

❏ Accounting

❏ Accuracy

❏ Achieving

❏ Activating

❏ Active

❏ Active learning

❏ Active listening

❏ Adapting

❏ Addressing

❏ Adjusting

❏ Administering

❏ Advertising

❏ Advising

❏ Aiding

❏ Allocating

❏ Altering

❏ Amending

❏ Analyzing behavior

❏ Analyzing costs

❏ Announcing

❏ Anticipating

❏ Appearance

❏ Application

❏ Appointing

❏ Appraising

❏ Appreciation

❏ Arbitrating

❏ Argumentation

❏ Arranging

❏ Articulation

❏ Assembling

❏ Assessing cost

❏ Assessing damage

❏ Assigning

❏ Assisting

❏ Attaining

❏ Attending

❏ Auditing

❏ Augmenting

❏ Authoring

❏ Automating

B

❏ Balancing

❏ Bargaining

❏ Blending

❏ Bookkeeping

❏ Boosting

❏ Bridging

❏ Briefing

❏ Budgeting

❏ Building

C

❏ Calculating

❏ Calibrating

❏ Cataloging

❏ Categorizing

❏ Chairing

❏ Charting

❏ Checking

❏ Clarifying

❏ Classifying

❏ Clerical ability

❏ Coaching

❏ Coaxing

❏ Cognizance

❏ Coherence

❏ Collaborative

❏ Combining

❏ Comforting

❏ Commanding

❏ Communicating

❏ Comparing

❏ Competence

❏ Compiling

❏ Complimenting

❏ Composing

❏ Compromising

❏ Computing

❏ Condensing

❏ Conducting

❏ Confidentiality

❏ Conflict resolution

❏ Conforming

❏ Confronting

❏ Consolidating

❏ Constructing

❏ Consulting

❏ Contingency planning

❏ Contracting

❏ Controlling

❏ Converting

❏ Convincing

❏ Cooperation

❏ Coordinating

❏ Copying

❏ Correcting

❏ Correlating

❏ Corresponding

❏ Counseling

❏ Counteracting

❏ Counterbalancing

❏ Counting

❏ Creating

❏ Creative writing

❏ Crisis management

D

❏ Data collecting

❏ Data entry

❏ Debating

❏ Decision-making

❏ Deductive reasoning

- ❏ Defending
- ❏ Defining problems
- ❏ Delegating
- ❏ Delivering
- ❏ Demonstrating
- ❏ Depicting
- ❏ Describing
- ❏ Designating
- ❏ Designing
- ❏ Detecting
- ❏ Developing ideas
- ❏ Devising
- ❏ Diagnosing
- ❏ Diagramming
- ❏ Diplomacy
- ❏ Directing
- ❏ Discretion
- ❏ Discussing
- ❏ Dispatching
- ❏ Dispensing
- ❏ Displaying
- ❏ Distributing
- ❏ Diversifying
- ❏ Diverting
- ❏ Documenting
- ❏ Drafting
- ❏ Drawing
- ❏ Duplicating

E

- ❏ Editing
- ❏ Educating
- ❏ Effecting change
- ❏ Elevating
- ❏ Eliminating
- ❏ Empowering
- ❏ Enabling
- ❏ Enacting
- ❏ Encouraging
- ❏ Engineering a plan
- ❏ Enhancing
- ❏ Enlarging
- ❏ Enlisting
- ❏ Enlivening
- ❏ Enriching
- ❏ Envisioning
- ❏ Equalizing
- ❏ Escalating
- ❏ Establishing objectives
- ❏ Establishing priorities
- ❏ Estimating
- ❏ Evaluating
- ❏ Examining
- ❏ Exchanging information
- ❏ Executing a plan
- ❏ Exhibiting
- ❏ Expanding

- ❏ Expediting
- ❏ Extracting

F

- ❏ Fabricating
- ❏ Facilitating
- ❏ Figuring
- ❏ Filing
- ❏ Finding
- ❏ Finishing
- ❏ Fixing
- ❏ Fluency
- ❏ Following through
- ❏ Forecasting
- ❏ Foresight
- ❏ Forging
- ❏ Forming
- ❏ Formulating
- ❏ Fostering
- ❏ Founding
- ❏ Framing
- ❏ Fulfilling
- ❏ Fundraising
- ❏ Furthering

G

- ❏ Gauging
- ❏ Generalizing

❏ Generating

❏ Grammar

❏ Graphics

❏ Grouping

❏ Guessing

❏ Guiding

H

❏ Handling complaints

❏ Harmonizing

❏ Heading

❏ Healing

❏ Helpful

❏ Hypothesizing

I

❏ Identifying alternatives

❏ Identifying causes

❏ Identifying downstream consequences

❏ Identifying issues

❏ Identifying needs

❏ Identifying principles

❏ Identifying problems

❏ Illuminating

❏ Illustrating

❏ Impartial

❏ Implementing

❏ Improving

❏ Incitement

❏ Increasing

❏ Indexing

❏ Indoctrinating

❏ Inducive

❏ Inductive reasoning

❏ Influencing

❏ Information gathering

❏ Information management

❏ Information organization

❏ Information receiving

❏ Informing

❏ Infusing

❏ Insightful

❏ Inspecting

❏ Inspiring

❏ Installation

❏ Instilling

❏ Instituting

❏ Instruction

❏ Integration

❏ Interaction

❏ Interceding

❏ Interpersonal skills

❏ Interpretation

❏ Interrupting

❏ Intervening

❏ Interviewing

❏ Introducing

❏ Investigation

❏ Isolating

❏ Itemizing

J

❏ Joining

❏ Judgment

K

❏ Keeping deadlines

❏ Keyboarding

❏ Knowledge of subject

L

❏ Language

❏ Launching

❏ Laying

❏ Leadership

❏ Learning

❏ Lecturing

- ❑ Listening for content
- ❑ Listening for context
- ❑ Listening for directions
- ❑ Listening for emotional meaning
- ❑ Listing
- ❑ Locating
- ❑ Logical reasoning
- ❑ Long-term planning

M

- ❑ Maintaining confidentiality
- ❑ Maintenance
- ❑ Managing
- ❑ Maneuvering
- ❑ Manipulation
- ❑ Mapping
- ❑ Marketing
- ❑ Masking
- ❑ Matching
- ❑ Mathematics
- ❑ Measuring
- ❑ Mechanical ability
- ❑ Mediating
- ❑ Meeting
- ❑ Mending
- ❑ Mentoring
- ❑ Merchandising

- ❑ Minding machines
- ❑ Minimizing
- ❑ Modeling
- ❑ Moderating
- ❑ Modifying
- ❑ Modulating
- ❑ Molding
- ❑ Money management
- ❑ Monitoring
- ❑ Motivating

N

- ❑ Negotiating
- ❑ Nonpartisan
- ❑ Number skills
- ❑ Nursing
- ❑ Nurturing

O

- ❑ Objectivity
- ❑ Observing
- ❑ Operating vehicles
- ❑ Operations analysis
- ❑ Oral communication
- ❑ Oral comprehension
- ❑ Orchestrating
- ❑ Organizational effectiveness

- ❑ Organizing
- ❑ Outfitting
- ❑ Outlining
- ❑ Outreach
- ❑ Overhauling
- ❑ Overseeing

P

- ❑ Pacifying
- ❑ Paraphrasing
- ❑ Participating
- ❑ Patterning
- ❑ Perceiving
- ❑ Perfecting
- ❑ Performing
- ❑ Persuasion
- ❑ Photography
- ❑ Picturing
- ❑ Pinpointing
- ❑ Planning
- ❑ Plotting
- ❑ Policy-making
- ❑ Polishing
- ❑ Politicking
- ❑ Popularizing
- ❑ Portraying
- ❑ Precision
- ❑ Prediction

- ❏ Preparation
- ❏ Presentation
- ❏ Printing
- ❏ Prioritizing
- ❏ Probing
- ❏ Problem-solving
- ❏ Processing
- ❏ Producing
- ❏ Professional
- ❏ Prognostication
- ❏ Program design
- ❏ Program developing
- ❏ Program implementation
- ❏ Projection
- ❏ Promoting
- ❏ Proofreading
- ❏ Proposing
- ❏ Protecting
- ❏ Providing
- ❏ Public speaking
- ❏ Publicizing
- ❏ Publishing
- ❏ Purchasing

Q

- ❏ Quality control

R

- ❏ Raising
- ❏ Ranking
- ❏ Readiness
- ❏ Reading comprehension
- ❏ Reasoning
- ❏ Reclaiming
- ❏ Recognition
- ❏ Reconciling
- ❏ Recording
- ❏ Recovering
- ❏ Recruiting
- ❏ Rectifying
- ❏ Reducing
- ❏ Referring
- ❏ Reformative
- ❏ Regulating
- ❏ Rehabilitating
- ❏ Reinforcing
- ❏ Relationship building
- ❏ Remodeling
- ❏ Rendering
- ❏ Reorganizing
- ❏ Repairing
- ❏ Repeating
- ❏ Reporting
- ❏ Representing
- ❏ Researching

- ❏ Resolving
- ❏ Resource development
- ❏ Resource management
- ❏ Response coordination
- ❏ Restoring
- ❏ Restructuring
- ❏ Retrieving
- ❏ Reversing
- ❏ Reviewing
- ❏ Revitalizing
- ❏ Rhetoric
- ❏ Rousing
- ❏ Running

S

- ❏ Saving
- ❏ Scanning
- ❏ Scheduling
- ❏ Schooling
- ❏ Science
- ❏ Scientific reasoning
- ❏ Screening
- ❏ Scrutiny
- ❏ Searching
- ❏ Selecting
- ❏ Selling
- ❏ Sensitivity
- ❏ Sequencing

- ❏ Serving
- ❏ Setting up
- ❏ Settling
- ❏ Shaping
- ❏ Shielding
- ❏ Situation analysis
- ❏ Sketching
- ❏ Social perceptiveness
- ❏ Solidifying
- ❏ Solution appraisal
- ❏ Solving
- ❏ Sorting
- ❏ Speaking
- ❏ Spearheading
- ❏ Specialization
- ❏ Specifying
- ❏ Speculating
- ❏ Speech
- ❏ Stabilizing
- ❏ Stimulating
- ❏ Stirring
- ❏ Storing information
- ❏ Streamlining
- ❏ Strengthening
- ❏ Structuring
- ❏ Styling

- ❏ Substituting
- ❏ Summarizing
- ❏ Supervising
- ❏ Supplementing
- ❏ Supporting
- ❏ Surmising
- ❏ Surveying
- ❏ Sustaining
- ❏ Synthesis
- ❏ Systematizing
- ❏ Systems analysis
- ❏ Systems management
- ❏ Systems perception
- ❏ Systems understanding

T

- ❏ Tabulating
- ❏ Taking instruction
- ❏ Talking
- ❏ Teaching
- ❏ Teamwork
- ❏ Technical writing
- ❏ Tempering
- ❏ Terminology
- ❏ Testing
- ❏ Theorizing

- ❏ Time management
- ❏ Training
- ❏ Translating
- ❏ Traveling
- ❏ Treating
- ❏ Troubleshooting
- ❏ Tutoring
- ❏ Typing

U

- ❏ Unifying
- ❏ Updating
- ❏ Upgrading
- ❏ Using tools

V

- ❏ Values clarification
- ❏ Visual communication

W

- ❏ Word processing
- ❏ Working with earth
- ❏ Working with nature
- ❏ Working with others
- ❏ Written communication

Your top transferable skills

Select your top six transferable skills from those you marked in this chapter. Keep these top transferable skills in mind as you look for validation of each one while doing the worksheets in Chapter 9. (You'll also unearth additional transferable skills in working your Chapter 9 worksheets.)

1. _____
2. _____
3. _____
4. _____
5. _____
6. _____

Employability Skills Checklist

A

- ❏ Ability to learn
- ❏ Abstract thinking
- ❏ Accepting consequences
- ❏ Ability to learn
- ❏ Abstract thinking
- ❏ Accepting consequences
- ❏ Accepting criticism
- ❏ Accepting freedom
- ❏ Accepting supervision
- ❏ Accommodating
- ❏ Active
- ❏ Adventurous
- ❏ Affable

- ❏ Agile
- ❏ Alert
- ❏ Ambitious
- ❏ Amicable
- ❏ Animated
- ❏ Appealing
- ❏ Approachable
- ❏ Artistic abilities
- ❏ Aspiring
- ❏ Assertive
- ❏ Astute
- ❏ Athletic
- ❏ Attendance
- ❏ Attention to detail

- ❏ Autonomy
- ❏ Awareness

B

- ❏ Benevolent
- ❏ Benign
- ❏ Bold
- ❏ Brave
- ❏ Bright

C

- ❏ Careful
- ❏ Caring
- ❏ Casual
- ❏ Cautious

❏ Charismatic

❏ Charitable

❏ Charming

❏ Cheerful

❏ Chivalrous

❏ Clever

❏ Colorful

❏ Commitment

❏ Common sense

❏ Compassion

❏ Compliant

❏ Composure

❏ Comprehension

❏ Concentration

❏ Conceptualization

❏ Concern

❏ Confidence

❏ Congenial

❏ Conscientious

❏ Conservative

❏ Considerate

❏ Consistent

❏ Constant

❏ Contemplative

❏ Cordial

❏ Courageous

❏ Courteous

❏ Creativity

❏ Critical thinking

❏ Cunning

❏ Curiosity

D

❏ Daring

❏ Decisive

❏ Dedicated

❏ Deft

❏ Deliberate

❏ Dependable

❏ Desire

❏ Determined

❏ Devoted

❏ Devout

❏ Dexterity

❏ Dignity

❏ Diligent

❏ Discipline

❏ Dogged

❏ Drive

❏ Dutiful

❏ Dynamic

E

❏ Eager

❏ Earnest

❏ Easy-going

❏ Economical

❏ Efficient

❏ Eloquence

❏ Empathy

❏ Energetic

❏ Engaging

❏ Enjoys challenge

❏ Enterprising

❏ Entertaining

❏ Enthusiasm

❏ Entrepreneurial

❏ Ethical

❏ Exciting

❏ Explorative

❏ Expressive

❏ Extroverted

F

❏ Fair

❏ Faithful

❏ Fast

❏ Firm

❏ Flexibility

❏ Focused

❏ Forceful

❏ Fortitude

❏ Friendly

❏ Funny

G

- ❑ Generous
- ❑ Gentle
- ❑ Genuine
- ❑ Gifted
- ❑ Good-natured
- ❑ Graceful
- ❑ Gracious

H

- ❑ Hard-working
- ❑ Hardy
- ❑ Honest
- ❑ Honor
- ❑ Humble
- ❑ Humorous
- ❑ Hustle

I

- ❑ Imagination
- ❑ Immaculate
- ❑ Impetus
- ❑ Improvisation
- ❑ Incentive
- ❑ Independent
- ❑ Industrious
- ❑ Informal
- ❑ Ingenious
- ❑ Initiative

- ❑ Innovative
- ❑ Inquisitive
- ❑ Integrity
- ❑ Intelligence
- ❑ Interest
- ❑ Intuitive
- ❑ Inventing

K

- ❑ Keen
- ❑ Kind

L

- ❑ Likable
- ❑ Lively
- ❑ Loyal

M

- ❑ Maturity
- ❑ Memory
- ❑ Methodical
- ❑ Meticulous
- ❑ Mindful
- ❑ Modest
- ❑ Motivation

N

- ❑ Neat
- ❑ Nimble

O

- ❑ Obliging
- ❑ Open-minded
- ❑ Opportunistic
- ❑ Optimistic
- ❑ Orderly
- ❑ Original
- ❑ Outgoing

P

- ❑ Patience
- ❑ Perfectionist
- ❑ Persevering
- ❑ Persistence
- ❑ Personable
- ❑ Pioneering
- ❑ Pleasant
- ❑ Poised
- ❑ Polite
- ❑ Positive
- ❑ Powerful
- ❑ Practical
- ❑ Pragmatic
- ❑ Presence
- ❑ Pride
- ❑ Progressive
- ❑ Prompt
- ❑ Prudent
- ❑ Punctuality

Q

❏ Questioning

❏ Quick-thinking

R

❏ Rational

❏ Realistic

❏ Reasonable

❏ Receptive

❏ Reflective

❏ Relentless

❏ Reliable

❏ Reserved

❏ Resolute

❏ Respectful

❏ Responsible

❏ Responsiveness

❏ Restraint

❏ Retention

❏ Reverent

❏ Risk taking

❏ Robust

S

❏ Safety

❏ Savvy

❏ Scrupulous

❏ Self-esteem

❏ Self-motivating

❏ Self-reliant

❏ Self-respect

❏ Sense of humor

❏ Sensible

❏ Sharp

❏ Showmanship

❏ Shrewd

❏ Sincere

❏ Smart

❏ Sociable

❏ Spirited

❏ Stalwart

❏ Stamina

❏ Staunch

❏ Steadfast

❏ Steady

❏ Striving

❏ Strong

❏ Studious

❏ Sturdy

❏ Style

T

❏ Tactful

❏ Tasteful

❏ Tenacious

❏ Thinking

❏ Thorough

❏ Thoughtfulness

❏ Trustworthy

U

❏ Unbiased

❏ Understanding

❏ Unprejudiced

❏ Unpretentious

❏ Unselfish

V

❏ Venturing

❏ Versatile

❏ Vigilant

❏ Vigorous

❏ Visualizing

❏ Vivacious

W

❏ Warm

❏ Wary

❏ Watchful

❏ Willingness to follow rules

❏ Wisdom

❏ Work ethic

❏ Work habits

❏ Working alone

❏ Working under pressure

Your top employability skills

Select your top six employability skills from those you marked in this chapter. Keep these top employability skills in mind as you look for validation of each one while doing the worksheets in Chapter 9. (You'll also unearth additional employability skills in working with your Chapter 9 worksheets.)

1. _____
2. _____
3. _____
4. _____
5. _____
6. _____

Basic Skills Employers Want

You know the skills *you* have to offer, but how do you know which of those skills *to* offer? According to a study by the American Society for Training and Development and the U.S. Department of Labor, reading, writing, and arithmetic are no longer enough for a perfect job candidate. Based on the study, here's the hot gossip on employers' favorite skills.

The main skills employers want fall into four categories:

- **Effective communication:** Employers seek candidates who can listen to instructions and act on those instructions with minimal guidance. They want employees who speak and write effectively, organizing their thoughts logically and explaining everything clearly.

- **Problem-solving:** Problem-solving ability can aid you with making transactions, processing data, formulating a vision, and reaching a resolution. Employers need the assurance that you can conquer job challenges.

- **Organization:** Life in the working world requires prioritizing and organizing information. The tidier your mental file-folders, the clearer your focus.

- **Leadership:** Leadership consists of a strong sense of self, confidence, and comprehensive knowledge of company goals. These are qualities that motivate and inspire, providing a solid foundation for teamwork.

Give Serious Thought to Certification

A professional certification can be a kind of passport, identifying you as a citizen of a career field with all its rank and privilege. In other words, professional credentialing is one way to document your ownership of the skills you claim.

Not all credentials are worthy. A credential is worth the effort it takes to get it only if it has industry recognition and respect. Even so, given the circumstances, certification is almost sure to become a growth industry before the century ends.

Crash course on certification

Differences in certification exist, but for ease of communication, I include other terms of validation such as *registered, accredited, chartered, qualified,* and *diplomate,* as well as *certified.* Whether the professional designation carries statutory clout or is voluntary, common elements include professional experience, often between two and ten years, sometimes reduced by education. Education standards are included, which may call for minimum levels of both academic and professional education.

Certification examinations, which may be one or several, are uninviting to many professionals — generally, they require time-consuming study and may include both experience-based knowledge acquired working in the field, and curriculum-based knowledge gained by assigned learning texts.

Grammar grill: Watch the tense

The checklists I provide contain nouns and adjectives as well as verbs, which are usually expressed as gerunds (words ending in *-ing*). Watch the verbs: They hold the potential for ambush. Here's what I mean:

Saying that you are employed from "20XX to Present" suggests that you are still working. Use the present tense of verbs for current activities. Some people, who really are working, forget about this and use the past tense of verbs. That error invites the employer to think:

"She is trying to put one over on me. This applicant is really out of a job, but wants me to think that she is currently employed."

If you have the skills and are using them now in your job, use the present tense.

The same tense structure holds true for resumes. Refer to your current job in the present tense, and to past jobs in the past tense. Don't worry about tense disagreement on the same pages; now is now and then was then.

Employers' HotSkills buzzwords

1. Listening
2. Communicating clearly
3. Problem-solving
4. Showing leadership
5. Goal-setting/achieving

6. Self-motivating
7. Showing confidence
8. Organizing
9. Conceptualizing
10. Negotiating

Membership in the certification-granting organization may be required, as well as professional recommendations. Rarely does certification come cheap. Costs can run from a few hundred to a few thousand dollars.

What's certification worth?

Is certification worth your effort?

Certification has strong appeal in your early career — say, the first 12 to 15 years — as a technique to control your earnings environment. But in business, certifications lose their luster at the vice-presidential level and above. Why? Certifications zero in on specific skills, while top managers are more concerned with the big picture. For consulting, medicine, law, and technology careers, professional certifications never lose their punch, especially for those who hope to work internationally.

The credential may be a license awarded by a state board, such as the familiar certified public accountant (CPA), or a voluntary program sponsored by a professional organization, such as the designation of accredited in public relations (APR) awarded by the Public Relations Society of America.

Because a given professional certification may not carry stripes for your sleeve, much less stars for your shoulder, investigate first. Clues to look for include the following: Do recruitment ads call for the professional designation? Do trade journals mention it? What do practitioners in your field advise?

- ✔ As you change jobs more often, certification can be a kind of passport. It shows that you're a player in your field's global body of knowledge and that you have documented standards and achievements.

- ✔ Certification can be very helpful if you become sidetracked into too narrow a specialty or stagnate in a company with antiquated technologies or find yourself boxed in by a hostile boss. The boss can still claim that you lack interpersonal abilities, but a professional designation leaves little room to say you're short on technical skills.

- ✔ You may earn more money going the certified route. A study of management accountants showed those holding the certified management accountant (CMA) designation outearn those who do not by about $9,000 to $15,000 yearly.

Need more clues? Check your library for a standard reference: *Guide to National Professional Certification Programs* by Phillip Barnhart (HRD Press). It details more than 500 certification programs, indexed by occupation.

No Frills, Just Skills

Now that you can speak a few words in skills talk, turn to the worksheets in Chapter 9. You'll review your education, jobs, and other experiences to find examples of the skills you claim — and you'll look for other skills you may have overlooked. By now you know that all this fuss over skills is because **Skills Sell!**

Chapter 9

Worksheets: Sorting Out Your Qualifications

In This Chapter

▶ Identifying your strengths and the facts that support them

▶ Discovering the positive differences you can make

Before you can write a RedHot cover letter, you need raw materials to spotlight the RedHot features that interest potential buyers. The following worksheets identify your most marketable features; they also encourage you to translate those features into benefits for your target employer.

Worksheets are strength builders because filling them out helps you recall all the good things you have done. For instance, in reviewing your last job or college post, think about these issues:

✔ What did you do?

✔ What did you direct others to do?

✔ What did you manage, create, approve, or instigate?

✔ What was the outcome of your actions?

— More profits? (How much?)

— More revenue? (How much?)

— More accounts (How many? What are they worth?)

How Did You Make a Difference?

Define your skills and what you bring to a new job. Consider what would have happened to others affected by your performance in your last position had you not been there.

After you finish the main worksheets, use the four summary exercises to reinforce the concept that you make a difference.

Education and Training Worksheet

(Photocopy and fill out one worksheet for each experience.)

Name of institution/program _____

Address/telephone _____

_____

_____

Year(s) _____ Degree/diploma/certificate _____

Overall GPA _____ Major GPA _____ Class rank (if known) _____

Work-relevant course and grade received _____

_____

_____

_____

_____

Knowledge acquired _____

Skills acquired _____

Accomplishments/experience (with concrete examples) _____

_____

Relevant projects/papers/honors _____

Merit scholarships _____

Quotable remarks by others (names/contact data) _____

_____

How does education/training relate to the objective of the letter? _____

_____

_____

Paid Work Worksheet

(Photocopy and fill out one or more worksheets for each job you've had.)

Employer's name (postal address, e-mail address, Web site, telephone, fax)

_____

_____

_____

Type of business/career field _____

Job title _____

Dates _____

Direct supervisor's name, contact information (use this person's name if a good reference; otherwise note coworkers or sources of good references)

_____

Major accomplishments (Promotion? Awards? Business achievements — "increased sales by 30 percent" or "saved company 12 percent on office purchases." What credit can you claim for creating, implementing, revamping, designing, or saving? Jog your memory by recalling problems faced and action taken.)

    Problem faced _____

    Action taken _____

Skills acquired _____

_____

Job responsibilities _____

Quotable remarks by others (names, contact data) _____

_____

_____

_____

Relate paid work to the objective of the letter _____

_____

_____

Unpaid Work Worksheet

(Photocopy and fill out one or more worksheets for each organization.)

Volunteer organization site (postal address, e-mail address, Web site, telephone, fax) _____

_____

_____

_____

Type of organization _____

Volunteer job title _____

Dates _____

Direct supervisor's name, contact information _____

_____

Major accomplishments (What credit can you claim for creating, implementing, revamping, designing, or saving? Jog your memory by recalling problems faced and action taken.)

  Problem faced _____

  Action taken _____

Skills acquired _____

_____

Job responsibilities _____

_____

Quotable remarks by others (names, contact data) _____

_____

_____

_____

Relate unpaid work to the objective of the letter _____

_____

Hobbies/Activities-to-Skills Worksheet

(Photocopy and fill out one worksheet for each activity.)

Name of hobby, organization, or club (location) _____

_____

_____

_____

_____

Dates _____

Title/position (officer/member) _____

Elected (yes/no) _____

Accomplishments _____

_____

_____

_____

_____

_____

_____

_____

Work-related skills acquired _____

_____

_____

_____

_____

_____

_____

Selling From Interests

Top 4 Free-Time Fun Activities

Skills Required

Phrases That Sell You

Selling From Strengths

Ten Adjectives That Describe Your Strengths

_____   _____

_____   _____

_____   _____

_____   _____

_____   _____

Five Things Others Say You Do Well

Qualifications: What They Are, How You Got Them, and Why They're Valuable

What	How
Your occupation	How you acquired this qualification
Your skills	
What: *Network Engineer* ▶	How: *Completed CNA & CNE certification* ▶
What: *Word Processing Applications* ▶	How: *Night school classes* ▶
What: *Spanish Fluency* ▶	How: *Major in college* ▶
What: *Leadership Skills* ▶	How: *Elected President of college senior class* ▶
What: ▶	How: ▶
What: ▶	How: ▶
What: ▶	How: ▶

Why It Matters

So what? What benefits does this qualification bring your target employer?

Why: *Computer network will operate with less downtime*

Why: *Productive immediately*

Why: *Spanish-speaking customers will find it easier to deal with company*

Why: *Can provide guidance to new summer interns*

Why:

Why:

Why:

Part IV

Writing RedHot Cover Letters

The 5th Wave   By Rich Tennant

"Some of these cover letters include too much personal detail. This one has a centerfold."

In this part . . .

*Y*our cover letter should be warm and friendly, you
bundle of personality you, and filled with skill-selling
talk that is grammatical and spelled correctly.

This part helps you jump through the cover-letter-writing
hoops. You'll find a great deal of information about
common grammar errors. You'll get tips on writing a
dazzling opening line. And you'll work through a RedHot
Cover Letter checklist to make sure that the best you lives
in your letter.

Chapter 10

Language That Snap-Crackle-Pops

*V*isualize your reader and write specifically for that reader. Speaking directly to your reader may seem obvious, but this tenet is one of the most overlooked aspects of effective writing. Writing to a real person makes your letter more personable and interesting to read. It shows you have considered your reader and want that person to understand what you have to say.

If your blank sheet of paper is beginning to look like the place where you'll spend eternity, rip a page from a magazine featuring a picture of someone who could be reading your letter, tape the picture to your computer, and write to that specific person. Who cares if you select a picture of a conservative middle-aged man with gray hair when in reality the reader of your letter is a vivacious, young woman with bouncing red curls? No matter. The process — the visualization allowing you to target a particular human being — is what counts.

Refreshing Your Language

Once I asked a friend who writes and publishes career books if he genuinely likes to write. "Well, no," he responded, "I like to have written."

That sentiment sums everything up for many who do almost anything to avoid writing but who know that they can't escape this lifetime without learning to write certain things — a cover letter is one of those things.

Make this task easier for yourself not only by reviewing a few rules of grammar, but also by reminding yourself to answer the big "So why?" and "So what?" questions in every letter.

Why are you writing?

So why are you writing? Never assume the purpose of your letter is obvious to your reader. You are writing a cover letter — or another type of job letter — ultimately aimed at employment.

If you are writing a cover letter, you want to land an interview. Say so. Try to maintain control by saying that you will be in touch at a specified time to see if an interview is possible. When this approach seems impractical, like when you respond to a blind recruitment ad, close with a benefit you offer — "My former boss describes me as the best multimedia designer in the state. Can we talk?"

If you are writing another type of job letter, tell your reader exactly what you want. Leave no room for guessing.

What does it matter?

For each sentence you write, ask yourself, "So what? What does this information mean to my reader — a benefit gained, a loss avoided, a promise of good things to come — what?" Don't, for instance, merely list a bunch of skills and achievements — what good will those skills do for the person who reads your letter?

Must you always interpret for the reader the benefit of your skills and achievements?

  ✔ Yes, if a ghost of an outside chance exists that the benefits of your skills and achievements are not evident to the reader. The former chancellor of a university in Berlin may need to explain how her skills relate to the running of a university in Ireland.

  ✔ No, if the listing of your skills and achievements is so strong that an eighth grader will get the message. The former President of the United States would not need to explain how his skills relate to the running of a university in the U.S.

For more illustrations of when you must interpret your benefits, look over the model cover letters in Chapters 14 and 15.

Getting in the habit of asking yourself "So what?" boosts the power of your job letters by 100 percent.

Technical versus nontechnical language

Tailor your language to your reader. If you are an engineer writing to another engineer, use technical language. If you're an engineer writing to a director of human resources, your reader may not understand technical engineering language, so you need to explain any technical terms in simple, everyday language. If you use technical language when writing to a nontechnical person, you're likely to lose your reader.

Concise but thorough

Your reader may be pressed for time, so you should aim to write a concise but thorough cover letter. You may wonder how being both concise and thorough at the same time is possible. Think of this task as giving a lengthy explanation in as few words as possible. Tell your reader as much about yourself as you can, but don't make your reader wade through extra words and unnecessary details. Consider the following example:

I am a person who believes that the values of fervent dedication, cooperative teamwork, dynamic leadership, and adaptive creativity really make up the cornerstones and are the crucial components of any totally successful sales venture.

Revised using concise but thorough language, the same sentence now reads:

Dedication, teamwork, leadership, and creativity are essential to successful sales.

Use short, simple words, sentences, and paragraphs. Avoid cramming too many ideas into each paragraph. Logically break long paragraphs into several short ones.

Simple, direct language

The goal of any written work is communication. To make that communication easier, use simple, direct language that gets your message across clearly and concisely. Don't use your thesaurus to find words that may make you look smarter and the recipient of your letter dumber. Instead, use your thesaurus to find the word best suited for the meaning you want to achieve. For example,

Eschew superfluous obfuscation

makes more sense translated as

Avoid unnecessary complication

For more direct language, use specific terms; avoid generalities or vague descriptions. Use numbers, measures, and facts — detailed information — rather than unquantified descriptions. Consider the following example:

I saved the company a fortune when I instituted a new system for scheduling.

Now read the same example revised for specifics:

I saved the company more than one million dollars in production when I instituted a new system for production scheduling.

Table 10-1 provides a list of word baggage to avoid and RedHot words to replace them.

Table 10-1	RedHot Replacements
Instead of	*Write*
able	can
about	approximately (be precise)
above	this/that
absolutely	(eliminate)
according to	said
ad	advertisement
advanced planning	planning
advise	write/perform
aforementioned	this/that
ahold	reach/get hold of/obtain
alright	all right
along the lines of	like
alot	a lot
a lot of	many/much
arrived at the conclusion	concluded
as per	according to
as to whether	whether
at a later date	later

Instead of	Write
at the present writing	now
at the present time	now
attached hereto	attached/enclosed
attached herein	attached/enclosed
bachelor's degree	bachelor's
bad	poor/inappropriate
beneficial success	success
better than	more than
between each	between every/beside each
between you and I	between you and me
bit	(eliminate)
but however	but *or* however
but that	that
cannot but	(eliminate)
can't hardly	can hardly
city of San Francisco	San Francisco
close proximity	close *or* proximity
close scrutiny	scrutiny
close to the point of	close to
cohese	cohere
concerning the matter of	concerning/about
concerning	about
continue on	continue
disregardless	regardless
due to the fact that	because
each and every	each *or* every
end result	result
entirely completed	completed

(continued)

Table 10-1 *(continued)*

Instead of	Write
equally as	as *or* equally
estimated at about	estimated at
every other	every (second) day
ex-	former
fewer in number	fewer
file away	file
for the purpose of	for
for the reason that	because
for your information	(eliminate)
gather together	gather *or* together
good success	success
he is a man who . . .	he . . .
he or she	he
idea	belief/theory/plan
i.e./e.g.	that is/for example
if and when	if *or* when
important essentials	essentials
in accordance with a request	as you requested
inasmuch as	since/because
in connection with	about/concerning
in excess of	over/more than
in order to	to
in respect to the matter of	about/regarding
in spite of	despite
in the amount of	for
in the area of	about
in the field of medicine	in medicine
in this day and age	now/today

Instead of	Write
irregardless	regardless
join together	join *or* together
keep continuing	continue
kindly	please/very much
kind of	rather/somewhat
known to be	is/are
know-how	knowledge/understanding
large portion/number of	most of/many
last but not least	(eliminate)
like for	like
like to have	(eliminate)
lot/lots	(eliminate)
love	(eliminate)
magnitude	importance/significance
master's degree	master's
more essential	essential
more perfect	perfect
more specially	specially
more unique	unique
most carefully	(eliminate)
most certainly	(eliminate)
mutual cooperation	cooperation
mutual teamwork	teamwork
near future	soon
needless to say	(eliminate)
new innovation	innovation
new record	record
now pending	pending

(continued)

Table 10-1 *(continued)*

Instead of	*Write*
of between/of from	of
optimize	increase efficiency
outline in detail	outline *or* detail
overall	comprehensive/final
per	(eliminate)
per diem	daily
per annum	yearly
period of	for
plan ahead	plan
please be advised	(eliminate)
point in time	now
presently	now/soon
qualified expert	qualified *or* expert
rather unique	unique
reason is because	because
reason why	because
regarding	about
represent	composed/made up of
respecting	about
revert back	revert
scrutinize closely	scrutinize
seem	(be more specific)
seriously consider	consider
several	many/numerous
should/would/must *of*	should/would/must *have*
spell out in detail	spell out *or* detail
subject	(be more specific)
subject matter	subject

Instead of	Write
subsequent to	after
sufficient enough	sufficient *or* enough
take for example	for example
take into consideration	consider
target	goal/objective/quota
thank you in advance	(eliminate)
that	(eliminate if possible)
there is/are/was/were	(eliminate)
true facts	facts
try and	try to
unknown	unidentified/undisclosed
unthinkable	unlikely/impossible
very unique	unique
was a former	was/is a former
way in which	way
whatsoever at all	whatsoever
with the exception of	except/except for
yet	(eliminate if possible)
you know	(eliminate)

Active voice versus passive voice

Active voice uses verbs to indicate a motion or action. Using active voice makes your writing more dynamic and interesting. With active voice, you identify who does what — and how!

On the other hand, passive voice (as in this sentence) is characterized by passive verbs and is a description of a state of existence. Because passive voice is generally weak, avoiding it is beneficial. Some passive verbs include *be, is, was, were, are, seem, has,* and *been.*

Revising the preceding paragraph for active voice results in the following:

Passive voice, on the other hand, characterized by passive verbs, indicates a state of existence. Because passive voice generally weakens writing, try to avoid it.

Passive voice just sits there, without vigor and without action. Take responsibility for your achievements. Be active.

Past/present tense

For the most part, use present tense as you're writing (as noted in Chapter 8). After all, your letter is something you're creating now. When you refer to accomplishments or achievements, use past tense.

When your resume says you are currently employed (20XX–Present), remember to use the present tense if you refer to your current job in a cover letter. If you slip and use the past tense, the reader may assume you've left the job and are pretending to be currently employed.

Fundamentals of Grammar and Punctuation

Grammar slips sink jobs. Many employers see language skills as an important aspect of potential job performance, and nothing says language skills like attention to grammar and punctuation. To help you over some areas that many cover letter writers find tricky, here is a brief overview of frequently made mistakes and how to correct them.

Sentence fragments

Sentence fragments signal incomplete thoughts. They neglect essential components. For example,

Although I work in Detroit, making $200 an hour.

This fragment is missing the subsequent subject and verb needed to finish the "Although I work . . ."

To test your sentences, speak each one aloud, out of context. Imagine walking up to someone and saying that sentence. Would the sentence make sense, or is something missing? If so, add the missing information.

Although I work in Detroit, making $200 an hour, I would prefer to work in Atlanta to be near my family.

Run-on sentences

Run-on sentences are two complete sentences written as one. For example,

I finished writing my cover letter, it's great!

This run-on should read:

I finished writing my cover letter. It's great!

Each sentence contains a complete thought and should stand on its own.

Run-on sentences stand out as grammatical errors and signal either a lack of attention in English 101 or a lack of precision in your editing skills. If you don't care enough about your cover letter to make sure that it's grammatically perfect, a potential employer may wonder how much you'll care about precision in your job.

Dangling participles

Dangling participles are words ending in *-ing* that modify the wrong subject. For example,

Running across the water, we saw a huge water beetle.

This sentence literally means that we saw a water beetle while we were running across the water — a rather incredible situation. You should revise the sentence to read:

We saw a huge water beetle running across the water.

Dangling participles undoubtedly cause chuckles, but they indicate imprecision or lack of care, qualities no potential employer appreciates in a prospective employee.

Misplaced modifiers

Like dangling participles, misplaced modifiers modify the wrong subject, often resulting in hilarious miscommunications. For example,

Ben taught the dog, an inveterate womanizer, to bark at all blonde women.

The dog is an inveterate womanizer? Probably not. Revised, this sentence makes more sense:

Ben, an inveterate womanizer, taught the dog to bark at all blonde women.

Semicolons

Semicolons can be tricky, so you should probably avoid them if you don't feel comfortable using them. In essence, semicolons are weak periods; they indicate a separation between two complete sentences that are so closely related they "shouldn't" be separated by a period.

As you can see, this definition is not too specific. Because no definite rule exists for the use of semicolons, you may simply use periods between every sentence. You won't break any rules, and you'll avoid using semicolons incorrectly.

The only rigid rule for semicolons is as follows: When you introduce a list of complete sentences by using a colon, separate each sentence with a semicolon. For example:

I accomplished the following: I networked all the computers, company-wide; I designed a new system for scheduling; and I broke the world's record in typing speed.

Again, you can avoid this use of semicolons in your cover letter by placing each item on a separate line set off by bullets. No punctuation is necessary at the end of each line. For example,

I accomplished the following:

- *I networked all the computers, company-wide*

- *I designed a new system for scheduling*

- *I broke the world's record in typing speed*

Punctuation in parenthetical expressions

If a parenthetical expression occurs in the middle or at the end of a sentence, place the punctuation outside the parentheses. Some examples include the following:

Cover letters are essential (see Chapter 4).

Cover letters (and resumes) are essential.

Cover letters (and resumes), essential to the job search, are easy to write.

Question marks and exclamation points, when part of a parenthetical expression occurring in the middle of a sentence, are the exception to this rule. Some examples include the following:

The interview (or was it an inquisition?) was a disaster.

My cover letter (a masterpiece!) took four hours to write.

If a parenthetical expression stands alone as a sentence, place the punctuation inside the parentheses. For example,

(I will discuss these skills in a moment.)

Commas in a series

Whenever you have a series of terms separated by commas, use a comma after the next-to-last term for clarity. Some examples include the following:

Cover letters, resumes, and interviews make up part of the job-search process.

Dear Mr. Barnes, Ms. Collins, and Ms. Schultz:

This technique is called the *serial comma*. Serial commas are not used in newspapers because they slow down reading. Be consistent in your use of commas. Don't use a serial comma in one paragraph and no serial comma in another that calls for one.

Hyphenating words for clarity

When you use two words together as a description of another word, use a hyphen. Examples include

next-to-last job

long-range plan

To test whether you should use a hyphen, take out one of the descriptive terms and see if the description still makes sense. For example,

> *next-to-last job*

without one descriptive term, becomes

> *to last job*

Doesn't make sense, does it? Because the three words "next to last" cannot be used individually as a description and still make sense, you need hyphens between them.

The same rule applies for two nouns used together to express a single idea. Examples include

> *light-year*

> *life-cycle*

For greatest accuracy, check a dictionary.

As with most things in English, you find exceptions: Words ending in *-ly* do not need a hyphen when used as part of a description unless they are used with a present participle (a verb ending in *-ing*). For example,

> *professionally written resume*

> *descriptively accurate cover letter*

> *friendly-sounding cover letter*

Abbreviations

Only use abbreviations if you have previously written out what the abbreviation stands for. For example, do not write UCSD if you have not previously written University of California, San Diego (UCSD). Never assume that your reader knows or will be able to figure out what an abbreviation stands for.

Some exceptions: Abbreviations such as AIDS, LSD, and DNA are so well known that they do not have to be defined. Also, some technical jargons commonly use abbreviations. In that case, write to your reader. If your reader will understand the abbreviation, use it.

If you're writing to a nontechnical person who may not understand, write out an abbreviation the first time you use it, perhaps with a brief description. If the abbreviation is a technical term normally not spelled out, provide the abbreviation with a brief description. For example,

> *GSI, a programming language*

> *LYCOS, a search engine*

Consecutive numbers

When you use two numbers in a row, avoid confusion by writing out the shorter of the two numbers:

> *six 9-person teams*

Or revise your sentence to separate the numbers:

> *six teams of nine people*

Numbers at the beginning of a sentence

Whenever a sentence begins with a number, write out the number rather than use numerals. Better yet, revise the sentence so the number does not appear at the beginning.

Commas

In general, use commas anyplace you would pause if you read the sentence aloud. If you're a person who pauses often while speaking, this suggestion probably won't work for you. My advice is to ask several people to read your letter for punctuation and grammar and follow their suggestions. Or get a good punctuation guide and follow it.

Capitalization of trade names

Trade names, like Band-Aid, Kleenex, and Xerox, should be capitalized. Avoid using these trade names to refer to a class of things or to an action. For example,

I need a Band-Aid.

Use bandage unless you specifically want the brand-name product.

I need to Xerox some papers

is also technically incorrect. Write

I need to photocopy some papers.

Capitalizing for importance

Resist the urge to Capitalize words to make them Stand out as Important. Doing so looks Contrived and Juvenile. It's also wrong.

Capitalize titles of departments, companies, and agencies

Any official name of a company, department, agency, division, or organization should be capitalized. Examples include

U.S. Department of Labor

Department of Safety

Don't capitalize words such as department, company, or organization when used as a general word rather than as part of a specific title. For example,

I work for a division of Chrysler.

Table 10-2 provides a handy chart to help you through the grammatical thicket.

Table 10-2	RedHot Grammar Guide		
Error Term	*Definition of Term*	*Don't Do This*	*Do This*
Subject-verb disagreement	Subject and verb don't agree, resulting in a grammatically incorrect sentence.	Our team, as well as the company, *value* ambition.	Our team, as well as the company, *values* ambition.

Error Term	Definition of Term	Don't Do This	Do This
Active voice vs. passive voice	Active voice relates an action (good); passive voice relates a state of existence (bad).	*I was trained* in all aspects of public relations.	U.C.I. *trained me* in all aspects of public relations.
Sentence fragment	Phrase lacks a subject and/or verb, revealing an incomplete thought.	*Unlike some applicants.*	Unlike some applicants, *I bring* talent and diversity.
Run-on sentence	Contains more than one complete thought; may lack punctuation.	Every writer knows how important grammar is, *I* know you really value marketing, and sales skills, in your business correspondence.	Every writer knows the importance of grammar. *I also* understand you value marketing and sales skills in your business correspondence.
Subject-pronoun disagreement	Pronouns don't agree with subject, resulting in a confusing or easily misunderstood sentence.	When *someone* reads, *they* should pay attention to details.	When *someone* reads, *he (or she)* should pay attention to details. *Or,* When *people* read, they should pay attention to details.
Misplaced modifiers	Incorrect placement of a description of one subject in a sentence with two subjects; result is confusion.	Falling more than 500 feet, we watched the daredevil bungee jump off a cliff.	We watched the daredevil bungee jump, falling more than 500 feet off a cliff.

Organizing for RedHot Impact

Poor organization is one of the big reasons people's cover letters fail to make the RedHot category. Poor planning results in poor organization. Start with a rough outline that identifies the contents and how the contents will be organized in your cover letter.

Most publishers require an author to write a table of contents — the TOC (pronounced "tee-o-see"). The TOC shows how the book will be organized. This requirement keeps the author from wandering away from a logical development of the topic. The TOC can be changed as the book develops, but its preparation serves as a map when you begin writing. Review Chapter 8, describing the anatomy of a cover letter, and then draft your own TOC.

Formats for organization

Following are several formats to suggest how your letter can be organized. Any organizational format can be used with any occupation.

Problem/solution

The problem/solution format starts with "Here's the problem" and ends with "Here's how I solved it." Case histories and success stories blossom in this favorite format for cover letters and resumes.

Inverted pyramid

News stories use this format. You start with a lead paragraph summarizing the story, with the following paragraphs presenting facts in order of decreasing importance. In your cover letter, you state a comprehensive goal, career desire, or position at the beginning and then provide specific examples in the following paragraphs to support your aim.

Deductive order

Much like the inverted pyramid, the deductive order format starts with a generalization and ends with specific examples supporting the generalization. For example, you can start by making a general statement about a skill. Then support that statement with facts.

Inductive order

Begin your letter with a story or anecdote and then lead the reader to the conclusion that can be drawn from the story or anecdote. You explain how that story or anecdote supports your ability to succeed at the job you've targeted.

List

Separate your letter into distinct points and set off the points with headings, bullets, or numbers. Put the most important point first. This format is especially effective for enumerating skills or achievements. This format is usually combined within another format (such as the T-letter in Chapter 6) for extra punch.

Ask yourself, Why?

When you finish writing your letter, read it over just to check its organization. When you read it, each line should fit into the other. You shouldn't really notice that a new sentence has begun. You should feel "prepared" for everything that you're about to read.

To avoid jarring the reader with an abrupt change of subject, ask yourself, "Why did I place this sentence or paragraph after the one before it?" If the answer is not obvious in your letter, the flow of your text is probably choppy and unclear to the reader. Analyze what's not working and rewrite until the letter reads smoothly.

Three blazing tips

1. Highlight short sentences and lists with bullets, asterisks, or em dashes. For example,

   • Won Orchid award for building

   ✔ Won Orchid award for building

   – Won Orchid award for building

2. Start with a short quote that reflects the employer's policies or values.

3. Reword portions of the employer's mission statement or other documents and work these phrases into your letter as you describe your skills, work ethic, and values.

Chapter 11

Zooming in on Cover Letter Anatomy

In This Chapter

▶ Connecting the parts of a RedHot cover letter

▶ Writing a letter that says "Hire Me!"

▶ Taking a quiz — Do you know your cover letter's anatomy?

*I*n case you've forgotten or never learned the parts of a job letter, review these building blocks.

Contact Information

Your address, telephone number, e-mail address, and URL (Internet World Wide Web address) appear first on the letter. As you can see from the sample letters in Chapters 14 and 15, you can place your address in the middle or on either side of the page. Just make sure that your Web address is on a line of its own.

You have a choice about where to place your name. You can either place it (preferably in larger letters) above your address, or you can type it below your signature. The only stipulation: Don't put it in both places. It's a waste.

Computer-friendly cover letters place the telephone number, e-mail address, and Web address on separate lines below your residential address for better scanning. You can also separate two items on the same line.

Date Line and Inside Address

Place the date two lines below your contact information and place the inside address two lines below the date. Aligned with the left side of the page, enter the name of the person to whom you're writing (with Mr. or Ms. designation), followed on the next line by the company name, followed on the next lines by the address. If you know the position the receiver of your letter holds, include that information on the same line as the receiver's name or on the following line.

On the right side of the page, aligned with the inside address information, you can include a line labeled *RE:* to highlight the reason for correspondence.

Salutation

Your salutation says, "Hello!" in the form of *Dear Person-Who-Can-Hire-Me*. It's like the eye contact that establishes a connection and begins the dialogue. Do your best to identify the person who will read your letter and address that person directly. Not only does your reader appreciate being addressed by name, but also, this personal bit separates your letter from the ones written by people who didn't take the time to do a little research into the company. Chapter 2 gives you some tips on how to go about finding the name.

If you can't uncover the name of the hiring manager, write *Dear Employer* or *Good Morning*. It's cheerful and feels more personal than *Dear Sir or Madam* or *To Whom It May Concern*. Remember to complete the salutation with a colon (:) to indicate more information to come.

Because no one enjoys reading mail addressed to a generic person (remember all the junk mail you've trashed addressed *Dear Resident*?), try, try, try to discover the name of your reader. It's courteous, it takes initiative, and it indicates genuine interest in the company and, most importantly, in the job.

Introduction

Your introduction should grab your reader's attention immediately. As the "head" of your letter, it appeals to the head of your reader, sparking interest that will compel your reader to keep reading. It subtly says, "Read Me!" and states the purpose of the letter.

All sorts of rules have been given for ways to start your cover letter. Some say, "Don't start with I." Others advise shock value and creativity, a risky approach for some. The most important rule is to engage the reader's interest. What does the reader need in an employee that you can draw attention to from the get-go? For more information on RedHot opening lines, check out Chapter 12.

Body

The body of your letter provides essential information that the employer should know about you — skills, achievements, and quantified statements about your past accomplishments. These skills may double as the interest-generating element of your letter as well. Unless your cover letter also serves as your resume, the body of your cover letter should be one to six paragraphs in length for eye-friendly appeal.

The body should include a brief background summary of your relevant experience. I suggest including it somewhat like this: "As an accountant at Donne Brothers Company, I accomplished the following: _____" This is information that the reader can get from your resume, so don't spend too much time on it in your letter. But don't be tempted to leave it out. Without this key selling point, your reader may never get to your resume.

The information that you include in the body of your cover letter gives tangible evidence of your potential contribution to an employer. It provides your reader with facts to digest and satisfies hunger for a valuable employee. Make sure that these facts are tasty, enticing your reader to devour your resume and call you in for an interview.

Conclusion

The last leg of your letter aims to stimulate action on your behalf. It gets your reader's blood pumping and legs moving toward the telephone to call you before anyone else does.

Motivating your reader to action requires a sincere "thank you for your time and consideration" and a contact date. Always tell your reader when you will call (no more than one week in the future) to confirm receipt of your letter and resume and coordinate a time for an interview. Including this information ensures that you'll act; you promised. Your word is on the line. If you call, a potential employer certainly can't ignore you — someone at least will have to move to answer the telephone. And if the news is not good, at least you're not home waiting by the telephone for a call that never comes.

Closing, Signature, and Enclosure Line

The closing section says, "Good-bye." It's the handshake before parting, sincere and warm with promise of meetings to come. *Sincerely* and *Very truly yours* are the most popular, but other choices include *Best regards, Warm regards,* and *Sincerely yours*. Don't forget to put a comma after your closing line.

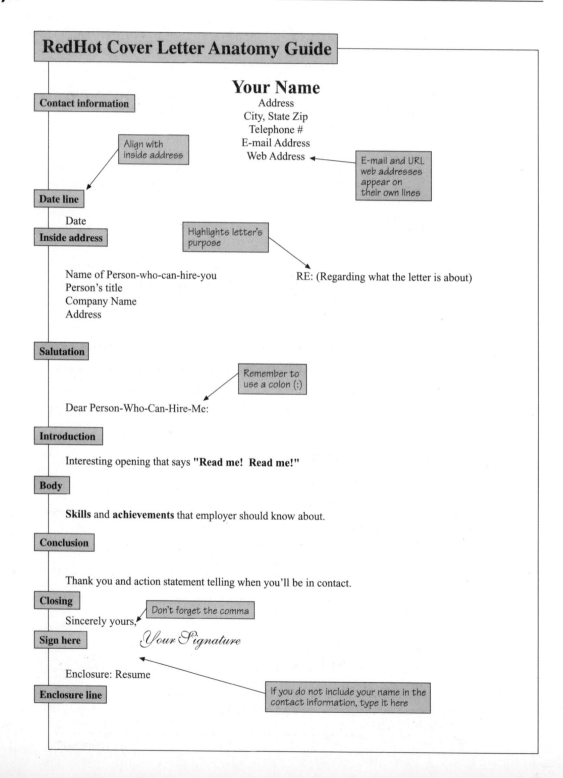

Don't forget to sign off. If your name *doesn't appear* in your contact information, type your name below your signature (four lines below the closing) so that there will be no confusion about spelling.

If your penmanship runs to chicken-scratch, try to make your signature legible. Any employer prefers to be able to read what someone handwrites rather than have to interpret it.

Once you've motivated your reader to action, the enclosure line provides a direction. Indicate everything else that you've sent with your cover letter, such as resumes or portfolios. This line directly follows your typed name or signature.

Now Test Yourself

Now let's see how much you know. Take the following 40-question true-false quiz, which tests some of the knowledge presented in this chapter as well as your general knowledge of cover letters (see Chapters 4, 5, and 10 for more information). Place an X under T (for true) or F (for false).

Your RedHot Cover Letter Anatomy Quiz (Part 1)

	True (T)	False (F)
Contact Information		
1. Includes your nickname(s)		
2. Includes your name (no abbreviations)		
3. Includes your direct mailing address(es)		
4. Lists all your e-mail and Web addresses on address line		
5. Includes your telephone number and other numbers (pager, message, office) but excludes ex-employer numbers		
6. No parentheses placed around telephone area codes		
Date Line		
7. Date is written in full or in brief (abbreviate or number months)		
8. Date is on its own line two lines below contact information		
Inside Address		
9. Includes recipient's name, spelled correctly, two lines under date		
10. Includes recipient's job title and designations, if any (Ph.D., M.D., C.P.A.)		

(continued)

Your RedHot Cover Letter Anatomy Quiz *(continued)*

	True (T)	False (F)

11. Includes recipient's company (spell out acronyms; NASA = National Aeronautics & Space Administration)

12. May hail multiple readers with "Messrs," "Misses," "Mesdames"

13. Includes recipient's address

Salutation

14. Uses "Dear — " "Greetings — " or "Good Morning — " two lines under inside address — greets with friendly tone

15. Includes designation (Mr., Ms., Dr.)

16. Ends with semicolon (;)

Introduction

17. Grabs the reader's attention at once, two lines under salutation

18. Lists who referred you and objective in first line

19. Mentions any mutual acquaintances or previous contact

20. States the position you apply for by job title

21. Names advertisement (plus publication and date) or contact that led you to apply

22. Lists your top sales points, experience, credentials, or accomplishments

Body

23. Lists personal information verbatim from resume

24. Lists information about you but targets employer's interests

25. Details how your qualifications and qualities contribute to employer

26. Discusses what you didn't like at your last job

27. Discusses how your skills relate to known job requirements

	True (T)	False (F)
28. Explains why you apply to this specific employer — what interests you		
29. Discusses your familiarity with the industry, including employer's competitors		
30. Discusses what you stand to gain (financially) by working with this company		
31. You can write as many as six paragraphs or as few as one in the body		
32. Discusses salary history and requirements in detail		
33. Discusses personal issues and money troubles to evoke the reader's sympathy		
Conclusion		
34. Thanks the reader for his or her time and interest		
35. Motivates the reader by asking employer to call you at a specific time or date		
36. Initiates action by mentioning that you look forward to discussing the position further with the reader		
37. Tells the reader what follow-up measures you will take		
Closing		
38. Two lines below last sentence, uses a complimentary closure statement like "Sincerely yours,"		
39. When enclosing a resume, "Enclosure: Resume" appears at the bottom-left corner of the cover letter		
40. Signature appears at bottom in blue or black ink		

Understanding Your Score

Most of the statements above are true. However, false statements may have sounded true, so I will comment only on false statements. If you got 35 right out of 40, you're RedHot material. If you only got 30 right, you should review this chapter as well as Chapters 4, 5, and 10 and the samples in Part V.

Here are explanations of the False statements:

1. Nicknames detract from a professional image.

4. E-mail and Web addresses each need their own lines (or be widely separated by white space on the same line) because computer scanners can't distinguish them from other number patterns, such as telephone/address numbers. (See Chapters 4 and 11.)

6. Telephone area codes appear in parentheses, for computer scanners to distinguish them from other numbers in the heading. (See Chapter 4.)

12. Messrs., Mesdames, and Misses went out of print with the manual typewriter. Use the name of each addressee (and designation) when possible. (See Part V.)

16. Easily confused with the colon, the semicolon (;) divides a two-part sentence. The colon follows salutations to flag more information to follow. (See Chapter 10.)

23. Personal information reinforces your chances for an interview only when it is somehow relevant to the position; never repeat your resume in the letter, because your letter's main focus is to snag the reader's interest in reading the resume, not to give away the resume itself. (See Chapters 4, 5, and 11.)

26. Omit all negative information. Complaining about your last job looks long-winded and unprofessional on paper and may lead to assumptions that you are difficult to work with. (See Chapter 5.)

30. Address the employer's financial interests, not yours. (See Chapter 4.)

32. Salary issues are complex. See Chapter 18 to understand them better. Try to save salary talk until the interview, but if you respond to employer's request for salary history or requirements, say as little as possible and speak in ranges: "Am in the $XX to $XX range (Confidential)."

33. People are not hired out of sympathy. Let positive attributes and qualifications speak for you. (See Chapter 4.)

35. Asking the reader to contact you is unrealistic. (See the sample, subtle substitutes in Part V.)

Chapter 12

Grabbing Attention with Your Opening Line

In This Chapter

▶ Opening statements that stand out from the crowd

▶ Examples of hot properties

▶ Plug-in-the-blank statements to help you get started

▶ Loser opening statements

Suppose you receive a letter that begins

Time flies when you're having fun.

That oldie probably won't entice your reading interest.

But suppose you receive a letter that begins

As Muppet Kermit the Frog says, "Time's fun when you're having flies."

That line is different. That line is funny. That opening lassoes your eyes, roping you into reading further. You keep scanning to find out what message such a whimsical letter could possibly be communicating.

I'm not suggesting you start job letters with frog quotes or other whimsical statements, but I am pointing out that you must work to grab attention. Build a fire under your cover letter by opening with words that intrigue, words that excite, words that zing!

Hey, There! Yes, I'm Talking to You

Learn to write openings that fire up the reader and move the reader along without wasting tons of time. Interviewers are overloaded — whole days are a blur for them, and they have no spare minutes to decipher what it is you can do for them.

Consider the harried interviewer pouring over an arcane or boring cover letter: "Why am I wading through this slush? I'm not. Let's sail this sucker right into the trash with the other gibberish."

If your cover letter starts off with tired blood, your reader will likely be too bored to keep on reading.

Two Tips to Open Your Letter

The best information to put into your opening line is a name: the name of the letter's recipient or of a mutual friend. Name dropping virtually guarantees that your letter will be read. To get attention, nothing beats the coattails of someone the letter's recipient likes or respects.

Even if the gatekeeping clerical staff doesn't know the names you drop from Adam's house cat, you'll increase your letter's chances of landing on the right desk.

The second-best information to put into the opening line is a clear statement of what you want, followed by the benefits you offer — qualifications you have that directly relate to the qualities the hiring company seeks. Skills are mother's milk to opening statements on cover letters.

Don't waste space in your opening lines by citing the source of a job opening notice — "I saw your ad in the *KoKoMo Express* last Sunday." Handle that in the "RE:" line in the upper, right-hand quadrant (see the sample cover letters in Chapter 14).

A Sampling of Sizzling Sells

Having trouble launching your first letter? I rounded up some of the best opening lines I could find — from real cover letters — and present them here to inspire you.

- ✔ "During your visit to UCSB last fall, I had the pleasure of hearing you address the issue of FuelCO oil rigs off the coast of Santa Barbara."

- ✔ "We acknowledged and discussed my diverse background when I assisted you through the Internet; I enclose my resume for your consideration."

- ✔ "Since you will soon be working on photo sessions for the Spring catalog, I have enclosed my resume and portfolio to show just how ideal my background in photography and design is for your marketing strategies."

> ✔ "Juliette Nagy mentioned your company has opened a division of sporting goods and suggested I contact you."
>
> ✔ "Your speech was inspiring, Miss Rogers. Soon I will have completed my master's in physical therapy, just in time for your entry-level openings in the PT ward."
>
> ✔ "Chaim Isenberg of the Grenwich and Co. accounting firm suggested I contact you regarding opportunities in your warehouse division in Champagne."

What makes these opening lines so great? Some mention names. Some connect to a common experience. Some reveal in-depth knowledge of the company involved. All show the letter writer as a person who cares enough to give time and attention to the presentation made in this self-marketing tool.

Exercises to Start Your Motor

Following is a series of plug-in-the-word statements to help you get started.

Name value phrases

As noted earlier, name value phrases help you connect your name with the interviewer's through the use of mutual contacts or associations. They give the interviewer one reason to pay attention to your application and a point of reference. If you're naming a person known to the interviewer, alerting that person to the fact that you're using his or her name is a good idea.

> ✔ **You know of no job opening, but the interviewer requests that you send a resume:**
>
> As you requested in our telephone conversation on (date), I enclose a copy of my resume for your review. A quick reading shows my well-developed skills in (a laundry list of your strongest skill sets).
>
> ✔ **You call about a job ad, and someone in the company tells you to send a resume:**
>
> As (name of individual) requested during our telephone conversation on (date), I am including my resume for your review.
>
> ✔ **A friend or important person suggests you send a resume:**
>
> On (date), I discussed your opening for (job title) with (so-and-so), who suggested I forward my resume to your office. We discussed the position's priorities; they seem to align perfectly with my education and experience. As my enclosed resume shows, my (a skill) and (an experience) will work great in your position.

✔ **You know the job title but can't reach a person by telephone:**

As your office requested, I am enclosing my resume in application for the (job opening title) opening. I understand your company values (a skill), (a type of experience), and (a work trait), and my experience illustrates such qualifications.

If you can't scrounge up a contact or any other "in," try the following general kinds of RedHots to spice up matches between your qualifications and the employer's requirements.

Power phrases

The following opening lines power through with a direct approach and a strong sell that emphasizes belief in yourself and your strengths.

✔ "I am particularly well-qualified for your position and would enjoy the opportunity to meet with you to explore how I can enhance your organization."

✔ "I was excited to read of your opening for (job opening title) in the (name of publication) on (date). Although we do not share any personal acquaintances, you will see from my enclosed resume that we do share many professional interests and goals, such as (mutual goals). Wanting a more personal introduction, I take the liberty of writing to you directly."

✔ "(So-and-so) thought my resume measures such achievement that he assured me he would pass my resume on to you; in the event it hasn't yet reached you, here's a copy."

✔ "For your convenience, I will keep this letter especially brief. The job you're trying to fill has my name on it, thanks to my qualifications in (skills) and (experience)."

✔ "Your position for (job title) strongly appeals to me because . . ."

✔ "If a meeting confirms my understanding of your open position (job title), I am confident that with my skills in (name skills), I can make an immediate and valuable contribution to (name of employer)."

You want what I am

Similar to direct-mail advertising, this pair of starters sells from the first sentence by directly linking your qualifications with those the firm is in need of.

✔ "I understand that your firm is in search of individuals with (skills) and (qualifications); don't you love finding the perfect match? In reviewing my resume, you will find that I possess all the attributes of that perfect match, from (skills) to (experience or attributes). I am delighted to learn of your job opening because I have been searching for a company exactly like yours to make real use of my experience."

✔ "Will your (department) reach its (company goal), or will it always (current company problem)? You'll never know without the best person for the job to follow through for you."

Cut to the chase

These opening statements show an awareness of the employer's need for time and efficiency.

✔ "My background demonstrates the skills you require in (name of position)."

✔ "As my resume shows, I have substantial experience in (field/position/skill)."

✔ "As we discussed earlier, my extensive professional experience can benefit any employer. However, (company name) is of special interest to me because . . ."

✔ "After developing skills in (appropriate to employer, list top skills, accomplishments from cooperative education or student job experience, or make connection between course work and research), as a graduating senior, I have begun to search for a position in (company/industry). I will graduate (date)."

Or

"After developing skills in (appropriate to employer, list top skills, accomplishments from cooperative education or student job experience, or make connection between course work and research), I recently graduated from (name of educational institution) and am searching for a position in (company/industry)."

✔ "I look forward to meeting with you to further discuss my background and to show you some of the (skills) that I have developed."

Network news phrases

You may not know of any job openings, but others in your field do. Don't be afraid to approach fellow members of professional organizations, friends of friends, or other people you know or are known to for help in your job search. Most people are happy to help if they can, and employers appreciate having a strong applicant pool from which to choose. Following are examples of some approaches you might use in asking for help.

✔ "If any opportunities come to your attention in (field or job title), I would appreciate your informing me. You can expect a call from me on (date)."

✔ "I appreciate any advice and/or referrals that you could pass on to me."

Broadcast letter phrases

The broadcast letter is sent to a variety of places in what is essentially a fishing expedition. This approach is not the best because it is not targeted. But it is a frequently employed tool and one that adds to your arsenal of techniques for finding your best job.

✔ "Among my qualifications, I am a (name your top attribute) aspiring to join a dynamic firm, such as yours, that could benefit from an individual who consistently contributes 150%."

✔ "Last year I earned (dollar amount) for (previous employer). I am confident my experience in (areas) could benefit (company applied to) as effectively."

Openings in dispute

Some advisers in cover letter-writing suggest the type of opening that could be considered condescending:

✔ "To maintain solid growth, a company must have marketing and sales professionals who can jump on a market before the competition does. My background proves I can do that."

✔ "When a customer calls for a quote, your firm's future is in the hands of the sales staff. I have big hands."

I personally can't support this type of opening because it presumes to tell the interviewer the interviewer's business. Think of a job seeker stating the obvious about industry needs and developments to a 30-year industry veteran who makes hiring decisions. If you're determined to take this approach, throw in a lot of "as you know" softening language.

Leadoff Strikeouts: Loser Opening Lines

Just as every baseball team needs a RedHot leadoff hitter at the top of the batting order, every cover letter needs a hard-hitting opener at the top of the page. These real-life cover letter leadoff lines never made it to first base.

Comments that follow in italics are from the employer's view.

✔ I was recently let go due to a reduction in force.

Nothing like starting on an upbeat note.

✔ Having recently completed an assignment in the Commonwealth of Independent States (the former Soviet Union), I am interested in pursuing and advancing my career opportunities into this arena.

Arena? What arena? Here. . . . There. . . . Where?

✔ In most organizations, job performance, whether excellent or inept, doesn't count, as long as you conform and play politics. I believe that performance does count! I have recently been notified by Dunnie Pharmaceuticals that my R&D position will be eliminated in the near future.

Does this translate to: I wasn't much of a team player? Is that why the writer's position is being eliminated?

✔ I am currently in search of a job; I have no particular preference in any area, for as you can see from my included resume, my experience includes a broad range.

One who will take anything masters nothing. As movie pioneer Sam Goldwyn said, "Include me out."

✔ I am writing in response to the position for a production coordinator advertised in the paper. I am very interested in advancing in my field and making a transition into the aspects of the communications profession described in your ad.

Do you want to advance in your field (which is what?), or do you want to make a transition, or do you want to do the work I need done?

✔ If you or someone you know could use a graphic designer, please pass my resume on to interested parties, or call me as soon as possible.

If you're asking me to be your agent, remember, agents get 15% off the top.

✔ My partner and I are dissolving our business after 15 years of working together. I am interested in a position at Fred & Associates and have enclosed a resume for your review.

A business divorce is rarely just one person's fault: Are you a pain in the patootie? And what is it you want to do for me?

As noted earlier, you don't get a second chance to make a first impression. Make sure that the first impression you make with your cover letter gives the interviewer reason to invite you in, not write you out.

Cover Letter Crimes

The writers of the highly imaginative letters below did not solve the case of the missing job interview. Their efforts are interesting, funny, charming, and amusing. But employers didn't bite. Generally, employers prefer more predictable letters, where your qualifications do the talking. Exceptions: Cover letters for creative fields, such as advertising, public relations, or marketing.

The crime of these letters is that their writers put so much effort into them — with no result. They're like some television commercials: You think they're whacky and cool, but can't seem to recall the name of their product.

Goals on Steroids

A desperate writer branded himself as unfit with the following homey lines: "Throughout my career I have accomplished many goals, yet there is one challenge I have not met. I have played one on one with Michael Jordan and beat him 40 to 5. I skated against Nancy Kerrigan in a competition and won first place. I discovered the cure for cancer and sold it to the government for a modest price. The only thing I have yet to do is work for you."

Repent, Cover Letter Sinner!

From the handwritten sheet of lined notebook paper to the five lines of felt-tip pen scrawl, this applicant shows a deep-seated need to go agnostic:
DEAR CORN CHIP GOD,
I PRAY TO THEE, THAT I MAY SOMEDAY WORSHIP YOU AT THE HIGHEST LEVEL BY WORKING FOR UNITED CORN CHIP COMPANY. YOUR FAITHFUL SERVANT

Loan Officer Giveaway

This applicant drew herself with arrows pointing to her professional attributes as a loan officer. She gave herself away without making one red cent:
"Strong knees -- holds up under pressure" "shoulders tested to carry a great deal of responsibility" "Quick on her feet -- will go the extra step" "Shiny shoes -- keeps herself neat & clean."

Candidate for Permanent Shore Leave

This applicant revealed both total desperation and low aspirations in one rookie swoop:
"I would lick the decks clean for a month, in order to get hired on with your company. I have been working for small companies since I've been a junior ship engine mechanic; I am ready for a real job."

Begging for a Broken Heart ♥♥♥♥

Red-flagged with homemade graphics of valentine hearts and the company product, corn flakes, this letter arrived on the desk of an un-named human resources director on February 14th:
"I've been a secret admirer of yours for quite some time. You were in my every thought during my college years. Every time I pour milk, all I can see is you. I have never asked another for such commitment, because I've been waiting for a cereal I could stay with forever. I know thousands of sutors are applying for your affection, but their attempts are nothing in my quest to win your approval. Long-distance relationships are hard, and I'd love to see you face-to-face, to demonstrate my sincerity.
Happy Valentine's Day."

Psst! Child Labor is Illegal These Days

Stapled to a fair (not RedHot) letter was a sheet of kindergarten penmanship paper, proving his life goal to be a pilot:

If *I* Could B e A*ny*one. Ma*r*k P. I would be a pilot b ecause I like the **ins**ter ment pannel. And I like *to* go in*si*ded the *cl*ouds and look down at the states a nd look at the cars. It would be ne at be*ca*use th *e* cars would loo k like ants and people would look li*ke* li ttle tiny s*pe*cts o f dirt. I'd li*ke* **to** work the radio, *I*'d li ke to talk to *the* control *tower* a*lso* I'd like to see h *ome* movies and land th e airp*l*ane o*n* the runway. A nd I'd like to *be* the *pi*lot for *I*nter*n*ation*al* F*li*g*ht* Airl i*n*es. (Wri *t* ten **w** *h*en I was 6)

Fire Discovered, The Wheel is Invented

Top 10 lists in cover letter form, now common, offer outrageous reasons for why applicants should be interviewed:
- From an applicant for a shipping company, "Thinks boxes are sexy and make nice end tables "
- From an applicant to a bottled water company, "We like our water guy."
- From an applicant to an interstate retailer, "Lives conveniently between Paris hub and Moscow headquarters."
- From an applicant to a cruise ship, "I run the tightest ship in the family business."

Chapter 13

A No-Fail Checklist for Top Results

• •

In This Chapter

▶ Mark your RedHot cover letter checklist

▶ Grade your cover letter before it's sent

• •

Make sure that your letter is not only read, but also becomes your invitation to an interviewing jamboree. Remember, your letter tells an employer what you can do for the company and offers plenty of reasons to meet you.

Your letter speaks about the benefits you bring to the job: your expertise, your mastery of technology, your personal qualities, your willingness to arrive early and stay late, your thoughts on saving the company money, and, perhaps, your pleasant or persuasive manner with people.

To be sure that you're on track, grade each cover letter with the following scoring sheet.

RedHot Cover Letter Checklist

A point value appears below each box. Most items are valued at 10 points; three items are so important to your success that they're worth 20 points on the RedHot range of high-powered persuasion.

The highest total you can reach is 300 points, including 20 points applying only to e-mail letters (and not everyone will prepare an e-mail letter).

If you're distributing your letter by e-mail, you need a full 300 points to be considered a hot-wired contender. Otherwise, if your letter points total 280, you've written a RedHot sensation!

Focus

20 pts.[1] My letter is employer-centered. As much as possible, it matches point-by-point what the employer wants; in effect, my letter says, "You want, I got." (The T-letter, described in Chapter 6, is a good format in which to accomplish this goal.)

10 pts. I address the person who will be reading my cover letter by name; I do *not* begin "Dear Prospective Employer" or worse, "Dear Sir" or "Dear Madam." (If you have absolutely *no* clue to identity, you get a free throw — give yourself 10 points.)

10 pts. My letter introduces me with a bang by mentioning mutual contacts or previous telephone conversations or meetings, or by using some other attention-grabbing statement that sells my hottest, most relevant qualifications.

10 pts. I hook the reader by naming the position I want — or my goal — in the first paragraph.

10 pts. My letter specifically tells an employer how I am equipped with the abilities to do the job the employer wants done; the letter does not focus on what I want.

10 pts. The overall theme of my letter specifically supports my objective.

10 pts. My letter highlights my most relevant qualifications; to the extent pertinent to the target job, my letter mentions my career achievements or education focal points.

Achievements and Skills

10 pts. My letter speaks of skills, not just responsibilities.

10 pts. My letter speaks of skills, not just responsibilities.*

☐ My letter speaks of skills, not just responsibilities.*
10 pts.

☐ For the most important skills, I cite at least one achievement; I measure achievements with real numbers, percentages, or dollar amounts to establish credibility.
10 pts.

Length

☐ For cover letters attached to resumes, my letter is concise and limited to one page, consisting of three to six short paragraphs; for targeted letters replacing resumes, my letter is limited to two, certainly no more than three, pages.
10 pts.

☐ I have avoided repeating the same words and phrases in my letter that appear on my resume.
10 pts.

Layout

☐ I use the same 8.5 x 11-inch white or eggshell paper for my cover letter as I do for my resume. (Scanners accept other sized paper, such as Monarch, but the operator must stop and reset the scanner. This extra step often causes cover letters to be thrown away.) My letter, resume, and envelope are the same type of paper.
10 pts.

☐ The layout is open: minimum 1-inch margins — 1.25-inch or 1.5-inch margins are better; my letter looks visually appealing.
10 pts.[2]

☐ My cover letter uses familiar, scannable typefaces (like Times Roman or Univers); it is word processed and laser-printed (not typewritten or handwritten, which makes me look old-fashioned).
10 pts.[2]

☐ My e-mail cover letter is sent in the body of the message, not as an attachment. (Many employers, virus conscious, are leery of opening attachments.)
10 pts.

☐ No handwriting is present on printed letterhead to correct an address or telephone number.
10 pts.

---

*This point is so important, it bears repeating. Check once, check twice, and then check again.

Proofreading

☐ My letter has no typos.
20 pts.[3]

☐ My letter has a return address and full contact information. If a resume is included, enough postage is on the parcel that the employer does not have to pay postage due, or I do not have to remail the entire package.
10 pts.

Contents

☐ I use powerful, selling words to give my letter that extra bite.
10 pts.

☐ My statements illustrate specific product, company, and industry knowledge — they impress by suggesting that I did my homework.
10 pts.

☐ My letter contains keywords (nouns) that can be sought and retrieved by job computers.
10 pts.

☐ I translate acronyms, technical jargon, or military lingo into plain English, as necessary.
10 pts.

☐ I have not shot myself in the foot by mentioning negative or special issues — if I do mention such an issue, I have presented it in a savvy way.
10 pts.

☐ I have noted my education and training as it relates to my job target.
10 pts.

☐ I have closed my letter by suggesting an interview and by saying I will call at a given time.
10 pts.

☐ My letter uses enough (but not too much) industry-specific jargon, establishing my familiarity with the career field.
10 pts.

Comments

[1]   20 points for accenting employer's needs, showing how you are a point-by-point match for the job.

[2]   20 points for conforming to computer technology (10 points for clean, familiar typefaces and 10 points for not burying your letter in an e-mail attachment). Letters that do not conform are left by the wayside because a job computer can't read them. Cover letters are considered a useful part of the applicant's file even in companies where cover letters are scanned into computers and not read by human eyes until a job match is made.

[3]   20 points for clean copy. Typos may make cover letter readers uneasy — if you're careless enough to misspell your application letter, what else will you be careless about?

Part V

RedHot Cover Letters: What They Look Like

In this part . . .

*E*xamples of highly effective cover letters — with educational tips noted in "call-outs" — give you plenty to work with in writing your own RedHotter.

This part shows you models from which to learn. Each of these sample cover letters is a candidate to be cut down and reformulated as a cover note (as described in Chapter 2). Bear in mind that the e-mail samples shown in this part are too long to use as-is in a cover note; instead, use this type of full-length message on the rare occasion when you send a cover letter as a word-processed document in an attachment (along with a separate resume attachment) to your e-mail.

Chapter 14

RedHot Responding Letters

. . . .

In This Chapter

▶ Resume letters

▶ T-letters

▶ Blind ad reply letters

▶ Employment service letter

▶ Targeted resume letters

. . . .

*Y*ou're on the move:

> ✔ You see an appealing recruitment ad in the paper.
>
> ✔ You cruise the Net and are rewarded with three job ads hinting at signing bonuses and stock options.
>
> ✔ Your six-months-ago pitch to a recruiter finally has his attention.

To keep momentum flowing, you rush to get your cover letter out the door. You need RedHot action! And here it is. . . .

These cover letters show patterns you can use to respond to a variety of job opportunities and situations in which you may find yourself. You have lots of options. But the main point is to convince the reader that the job shouldn't be filled before you have an interview.

Read through these samples. The names and identifying features have been changed for privacy. You'll also see some letters that help with tricky issues like rejecting a job offer or composing a recommendation.

I added notes to help you see what makes these cover letters RedHot. Use these models to trigger ideas for your own responding letters.

 As you know, technology is a moving target. So read these letters **for content**. *You can use the ideas on paper or you can format them in a digital version to use online.* Additionally, I include three e-mail letters in this chapter to suggest formatting options.

**Targeted E-mail
Retail Field Consultant**

From: Brian S. Letson
       890 A St., #12
       Wichita, KS 88896
       (750) 966-4242
       brian.letson@gte.net
Subject: My assets for field consultant position
To: Carol Priest <cpriest@fastshop.com>

Dear Carol Priest, HR Generalist, Fastshop Corp.

While researching the Fastshop Web site, I learned of your
open position of field consultant. Please interview me for
this position.

Among many assets I can bring are my documented abilities
to resolve complex personnel problems and increase
productivity and revenues while cutting expenses and waste.
My competencies include developing an annual budget
and keeping accurate records of all contracts, purchase
orders, and budgetary expenses.

My master's degree in marketing atop a bachelor's in
business management, plus my three years in customer
service, marketing, and sales are a bull's eye for your
position requirements. My plain text resume follows
immediately. (If you prefer reading a formatted Word
document version, please open the attachment.)

Respecting your Web site instruction, which says "No
Calls," I urge you to reach me on my cell phone, day or
evening, at 750-966-4242.

Most employers won't open attachments from strangers because they fear viruses or don't want to keep switching back and forth between programs when pouring through e-mails. The job seeker shows Net savvy by incorporating the plain text (ASCII) form of his resume within the body of his e-mail. Because ASCII resumes are not attractive to read and often lose their shape with odd-looking spacing and wraps, the job seeker also shows resourcefulness by including a smart-looking, formatted resume in a Microsoft Word document as an attachment. The two-fer is a good approach when e-mailing. No, do not make this a three-fer by postal mailing a paper version for good measure; that's over the top.

The job seeker follows directions by honoring the employer's dictum of No Calls, but includes a cell phone number, which conveniently can be reached day or evening.

Letter has no signature. One could be added when electronic signatures become commonplace.

E-Mail Job Board
Plant Supervisor

This cover letter and accompanying resume was e-mailed to the employer by a national job board whose online response form was filled out by the applicant. The employer, an energy company, identified itself in the job listing, but the applicant was directed to apply through the job board. Here's what the employer sees.

Date Submitted Nov. 9, 20XX
Time Submitted 15:52:23 pm
Employer ABC Utility Corp.
First Name Rudy
Last Name Schwarz
Address 8976 Lindberg Blvd.
City Atlanta
State GA
Zip 12345
Home Phone (777) 932-5432
Work Phone (777) 678-1400 cell
email rudyschwarz@hotmail.com

This lenghty letter would be attached as a Word document. To shorten for use as a cover note in ASCII, see Chapter 2.

Dear ABC Utility Corporation Employer:

The Navy spent a lot of money superbly preparing me for the position of senior supervisor engineer you advertised on MajorName Job Board. In one month, I'll complete a 12-year tour in the U.S. Navy and will be interviewing immediately after that.

My expertise is in plant operations, repair, and training. ABC Utility Corp. will benefit from my heavy-duty background in large pressurized water reactor and steam plant operation, and safety and environmental compliance. In addition to nuclear engineering, I have kept abreast of the engineering principles of fossil fuel and combined cycle alternatives.

I meet the requirements for a bachelor's degree from Thomas Edison State College in Trenton, NJ, and expect my degree to be awarded next month. I am reviewing mechanical engineering topics preparatory to the April, 20XX Engineer-in-Training and October, 20XX Professional Engineer examinations.

I have traveled to Europe, the Middle East, the Far East, and South America and would appreciate any travel opportunity. Thank you for your time and consideration as I continue to use my outstanding training and experience, this time in the civilian sector, specifically at your premier energy company. I look forward to hearing from you.

Sincerely, Rudy Schwarz

E-Mail Internal Candidate Letter Supply Chain Supervisor

The following application for Job #4567 has been submitted:

Applicant:	Sandra Gage Rivera
Applicant's SSN:	111111111
Applicant's Email ID:	Gagesan
Applicant's Pony Address:	Wisc. Bldg., Milwaukee
Applicant's Supervisor:	Jackie Linstrom
Supervisor's Email ID:	Linstja
Supervisor's Phone X:	1212

The Supply Chain managerial posting made my day; let me make yours by filling the opening and doing a great job. My strong background in supply chain management and 14 years of management experience make me an ideal candidate for the position of Supply Chain Manager III within the parts procurement division, as defined on the company's position-posting Web site.

My extensive cross-functional team leadership experience, background in financial analysis and budget planning, and excellent oral and written communication and negotiation skills, plus my MBA, deliver the competencies required for this position. I know my stuff! On an interpersonal level, I've maintained a good rapport with customers, vendors, and co-workers.

My resume follows with details. I'm very interested in taking on the responsibilities this position entails and look forward to an interview. How soon can we talk?

A salutation does not appear on this e-cover letter because it was sent internally by a current employee requesting advancement to a posted position. She merely filled out a form. But, depending on the bureaucracy and its culture, researching to find out who awards the position, then using a salutation addressed to all the decision-makers by name (Dear Jack Olson, Margot Rhine, Ted Baxter) might have been more effective; the risk is that you'll miss one or two decision-makers and that oversight could backfire.

As an internal applicant, don't assume you'll be interviewed or that you have the inside track. You have to promote your candidacy as strongly as an external candidate.

**Resume Letter
Social Worker**

KEVIN A. MIRAMONTES, SOCIAL WORKER
EAST COAST COLLEGE, 123-G ELEANOR HALL, BANGOR, MAINE 45678   (111) 213-1415
E-MAIL: MONTES@ECC.EDU

April 23, 20XX   RE: HOME PARENTING SUPPORT JOB # HPS 432

MS. KATARINA M. SWARTZ, HUMAN RESOURCES MANAGER
AREA HOSPITALS INC.
NORFAK NAVY BASE
1234 AVENIDA SALUD
NORFOLK, VIRGINIA 56789

DEAR MS. SWARTZ:

From my own childhood, I can remember the day I realized my parents (my father, a 20-year Navy man, my mother, a tough survivor of three children and 5 relocations) didn't have all the answers. Since then, I have pursued a life ambition to provide the kind of caring support and feedback military families like my own need. I can remember the graying family housing and the ever-present sadness surrounding Norfolk Navy Base. I am glad I can change that sadness -- the base needs good people who know how to sensitively, actively help its families.

Your opening for **home parenting support and crisis intervention services** caught my attention because it not only fits my background and academic concentration perfectly, but Norfolk is where mom and dad retired and I will be returning there after I graduate with a master's in social work on May 21st. At the East Coast College, I have concentrated on precisely the areas your position requires experience in, including:

- **Child/spousal abuse prevention, reporting laws, knowledge of military family dynamics, crisis intervention, multi-lingual counseling (Spanish & English) and advocacy**.
- While completing my master's degree, I have been involved with a internship program off-campus, studying child-abuse and **prevention in dual-parent English and Spanish-speaking families**.
- In the last year of my baccalaureate study, I assisted the famous sociologist, Dr. Mariah D. Hersch, in researching **the dynamics of violence in military families** for a book that was published last year.

As you will see in my resume, I have both academic and clinical experience in home parenting support and in military family dynamics. My personal background has also well prepared me to empower individuals and prevent abuse, providing support that military families so desperately need. As dedication requires, I will work any hours necessary to make a difference in the lives of parents and children at Norfolk Navy Base. I will contact you next week to discuss the opening with you.

Sincerely yours,

Kevin A. Miramontes

Enclosure: Resume

A lengthy but irresistible letter.

**Resume Letter
Purchasing Agent**

SHAWN FULTON

495 Pembrooke   Chicago, Illinois 67777   (708) 555-1212

June 1, 20XX

Mr. Aaron Langdon   **RE: Purchasing Agent**
Human Resources Manager   **Ad: San Diego Union**
Bentley Corporation   **May 26, 20XX**
PO Box 123
San Diego, California 92101

> Fulton's last job was "project manager," not "purchasing agent." Purchasing responsibilities clearly identified.

Dear Mr. Langdon:

My broad management experience in the fields of purchasing, logistics, distribution, and materials are an excellent match for the needs described in your advertisement.

Outlined below are some recent accomplishments exemplifying my additional capabilities in planning and budgeting as a project manager with purchasing responsibilities. This list serves as an illustration of the potential contributions that I can make to the Bentley Corporation:

> Ad called for salary history and references. Fulton asks for "mutual interest" before revealing salary requirements; references should not be overused.

   *   Saved $1.35 million and reduced overhead by 40% via a
       consolidated corporate air express services program for
       more than 1300 sites.

   *   Developed and implemented automated processing of
       over 25,000 purchase requisitions.

   *   Negotiated a design-build function for $13.8 million, 850-site,
       branch bank standards program, encompassing new
       merchandising fixtures and site refurbishings.

Once a mutual interest has been established, I will be pleased to discuss salary and references. For a beautiful spot such as San Diego, relocation costs are negotiable. I will contact you in the next week to discuss a convenient time to further explore how my skills and professional background will put my winter coat in storage and me on the road to San Diego.

Sincerely,

Shawn Fulton

Enclosure: Resume

> Usually it's best not to give away benefits like relocation costs up front. But when the labor market for a position is strong, relocation costs are likely to keep Fulton from becoming a candidate. Fulton anticipated an objection and neutralizes it in advance.

**Resume Letter
Hotel Management**

Patrick Howard Paul
345 Flower Street
Millsville, Arizona 75674
(555) 431-7890
E-mail: phpaul@prodigy.com

October 1, 20XX

**RE: Your advertisement.
for a Night Manager
at the Millsville
Best Hotels**

Mr. David R. King
Vice President Operations

Best Hotels
4515 Sand Street.
Scottsdale, AZ 75672

Dear Mr. King:

After working as a morning lark for a while, I'm ready to revert to my true nightingale status. I want that night manager's job!

As my resume indicates, I have worked as a front desk clerk at Motels In-The-Sand for two years. Having filled in for the night manager's days off for the last six months, I know how important it is to combine **solid accounting skills** with **good judgment**. I also know the pace can vary from slow to hectic with multiple crises needing attention in a single evening. I function well in chaos.

Now that I have tested the waters of this position, I want to jump in and perform the job full time, and where better to do that than at Best Hotels. I have read your annual report and know that your motto of "Service Day and Night" is a key to your success. I want to deliver that service as the Night Manager in Millsville.

My expertise in technology and management are at your disposal. I am confident that when we meet and further discuss your company's goals and my qualifications, you will agree that we are a match. I will call Thursday to schedule an appointment.

Sincerely,

Patrick H. Paul

Enclosure: Resume

> Find annual reports online
> at Annual Report Service
> (annualreportservice.com).
> Search online business news
> reporting services for other
> information to use in your letter.

**Resume Letter
Dietitian**

Namay N. Lee
**12345 Whiskey River Road
Lexington, Kentucky 65329
(606) 555-1695**

TWJ, Code D-U
P.O. Box 230013
Lexington, Kentucky 65329-0001
Posting

RE: Dietitian Position:
**University of Kentucky,
Career Center Job**

May 3, 20XX

Good Morning:

> Good Morning is one way to avoid saying Dear Sir on a blind box ad.

Can you remember what you ate yesterday? My guess is somewhere along the line you ate lactose, milkfat, soy lecithin, corn syrup, partially hydrogenated soybean oil, cocoa powder, soy protein -- the dietitian's impression of a candy bar -- but what about vitamins A, B, C, D, E, and even K? I'll show you how to get tasty, proper nutrition -- without the candy bars! I'd like first, though, to tell you how I learned how.

To receive my Registered Dietitian Certificate (1/5/9X), I accepted an internship at Kentucky State Hospital, here in Lexington. Two years and 2,088 caring, working hours later, I have my certificate, and one extensive, vitamin, calcium and protein-packed background in:

* **nutritional counseling of:**
   **pregnant women
   infants & children**

* **planning menus**

* **teaching nutrition classes**

As part of a satellite outreach program funded by the hospital, I also provided **community maternal-health care** in the rural areas outskirting Lexington, developing skill in counseling mothers-to-be toward healthier, happier lives and children.

As you will see in the attached resume, your opening in ABC's new Women, Infants & Children program sparked my interest as a rare and timely match between my experience and ABC's recruitment interests. Please feel free to contact me anytime.

Healthfully yours,

Namay Lee

P.S.: Vitamins A, B, C, D, E and K appear in my dietary plan for mothers-to-be, which I would love to discuss with you in person.

Enclosure: Resume

**Resume Letter
Dental Hygienist**

Barbara Ann Timothy
4683 Pannee Road
Addison, TX 75240
(214) 555-3695

April 2, 20XX

**Re: Dental Hygienist
with Periodontist Experience**

Donald Payne, DDS
2176 Belt Road
Richardson, TX 75263

Dear Dr. Payne:

Sparked by your need for a dental hygienist with periodontic experience, as posted in the Texas Dental Monthly on March 30, I can relieve your stress of finding the ideal person to fill the job. Beyond my demonstrated **technical abilities**, my qualifications most beneficial to your practice include:

- Associates Degree in Dental Hygiene, Taper Medical Center, Fort Worth, TX
- 7 years' experience in periodontist practice
- Patient education: benefits of good oral hygiene, periodontal conditions, proper cleaning and care
- Hygienist education: patient care, cleaning, x-ray, and periodontist procedures
- Preparation of clinical and laboratory diagnostic tests for dentist
- Ability to recognize dental decay and gum disease
- Spanish fluency

Based upon these career highlights and those detailed in my enclosed resume, you will notice that I fit the bill as *the* prime candidate for your opening. I would be delighted to speak with you further about the match between my qualifications and the needs of your practice. I will contact you next week to set up an appointment.

Sincerely,

Barbara Timothy

A letter impressive in its simplicity.

Enc: Resume

Resume Letter
Customer Service Representative

KATELYN DICKERSON
48 Hillborough Drive
Washington, DC 02006
(555) 555-1212
kson@ixpress.com

June 23, 20XX

Mr.Gerald Hail,
Customer Service Supervisor
Big Bee Brands
1515 Fashion Square
Washington, DC 04321

RE: CUSTOMER SERVICE REPRESENTATIVE

Dickerson's research shows this company has a serious personnel problem. She targets the reader by explaining how she will solve the problem.

Dear Mr. Hail:

Are you tired of your search for the one employee who can consistently get the job done? Are you weary of trying to find an associate who is self-motivated and self-directed so you need not stand over that person cracking a whip? I can help!

Respond to requirements listed in job posting.

I am long on effort and enthusiasm...
      but short on procrastination and 30-minute "coffee breaks."
            I achieve my goals at the end of the day, not the end of the week.

I am long on cooperation and a positive, friendly, productive atmosphere...
      but short on "finger-pointing" and cheap gossip.
            I am strong on interpersonal and communication skills.

I am long on customer satisfaction and exemplary service...
      but short on putting telephone customers on hold and phone calls.
            In my current position, I have a proven track record of 98% "excellent" in customer satisfaction surveys.

Mr. Hail, I'd love to have the opportunity to put my energy, drive and determination to work for Big Bee Brands. May I further discuss your requirements during a personal meeting with you or one of your representatives? I understand the position advertised in the most recent copy of the Fashion Journal will be available August 1st. I am ready, willing and, as the enclosed resume shows, *more than able!*

Sincerely yours,

Katelyn Dickerson

Leads reader to resume by hinting at impressive content.

Enclosure: Resume

Drake Fraser

1234 Pearl Street , Colleyville, TX 92120   **(123) 456-7891**

August 7, 20XX

Ms. Marion Carver,
Staffing Specialist
General Toys   **RE: Marketing Research Position**
12 Gallery Road
Irving, TX 75264

Dear Ms. Carver:

An opportunity to work for a company that creates toys! And better yet, toys that combine creativity, education and, especially, fun. Life doesn't get much better. For that reason, and because of my marketing experience for the past 15 years, I would be thrilled at the chance to work for General Toys.

As Rosa Reyes, your administrative assistant, requested during our telephone conversation today, I outline the requirements you are seeking as they align with my skills.

Generating reports and market analysis...
> **I have been in charge of all market analysis with my current company. Reports are based on basic demographic data and SIC codes.**

Making presentations and discussing marketing strategies...
> **I currently organize and present 60% of my company's analysis and planning workshops. In addition, I present our most recent data at board meetings, and generate presentations, graphs, pie charts, flip charts, videos and select guest speakers.**

Supervisory and management experience...
> **I have been supervising a staff of up to three associates for the past eight years. My ratings as manager are consistently high.**

Even if I don't ever get to play with the merchandise at General Toys, I would enjoy the opportunity to market them. When you believe in your product, work is play! I will call you again next week.

Sincerely,

DRAKE FRASER

Enclosure: Resume

> Enthusiasm sells!
> Hard-hitting points are NOT same ones that are on Fraser's resume.

Responding Letter Loan

Catherine Hill McAndrew
123 West Shore Lane
Small Town, NJ 12345
(201) 555-1212
chmca@hotmail.com

July 15, 20XX

RE: Mortgage Loan Officer

Ms. Marion Smith
Human Resource Manager
Big Money Mortgage
9 Central Park Street
New York, NY 14785

Dear Ms. Smith:

Tom Banks at your new district office in Newark, New Jersey tells me you're in the market for a Loan Officer, an exciting opportunity that I simply can't pass up.

My resume defines my skills in **marketing** and **operations**. In opening a new office in a state with unique lending guidelines and regulations, I feel both aspects of my past experience can benefit your company. For example:

- **I can build and maintain a client-base from ground zero.**
- **I have an extensive contact-base in the Tri-State area with high profile clientele in New Jersey and New York.**
- **I have experience as an operations manager with several major mortgage companies on the East Coast.**

Qualities that may not be readily apparent from my resume include being a person who embraces the ideas of respect and candor. I bring **integrity**, **intelligence** and **energy** along with my diverse background and abilities to the position.

My exceptional interpersonal and communication skills will be key to the development of this office. As a seasoned veteran in the field, I recognize the need to clearly communicate to fellow employees and clientele the many intricacies of the mortgage industry.

Thank you for taking the time out of your demanding schedule to review my resume. I will call you on Tuesday morning to arrange an appointment to meet with you personally to discuss more specifically what I can offer to Big Money Management.

Sincerely yours,

Catherine McAndrew

Enclosure: Resume

> McAndrew will make her telephone call half an hour before normal work hours -- and keep calling until she reaches Smith.

**Responding Letter
Web Page Designer**

Dylan Hasselhoff, Web Page Designer

Juliet Plaza, 12 Ave della Arte
Verona, 3344556 Italy
Telephone: 67-78-89-91
Web: www.tod.com
E-mail: dhassl@aol.com

January 28, 20XX

Ms. Donna Aldeo, Art Director
Studio di Roma
Allegrito Boulevard, 654 Braggadocio Balustrade, Ste. K-38

Dear Ms. Aldeo:

Veronica Laertes recommended I contact you regarding a design position with Studio di Roma. As a result of studying and teaching courses in Web Page Design, your organization's extensive public visibility has made a great impression on me. I was especially energized when Veronica showed me your innovative designs for young, previously unknown companies, such as the now famous Pastaio Uno chain restaurant. I want a role in **Studio di Roma -- with me as a team member it can be even stronger, tougher, and bigger.**

Use of boldface accentuates "selling motto" of letter.

My experience at the University of Paris Art Department includes:
• Three years' teaching computer illustration as part-time faculty
• Designing the University's Web Page
• Recipient of the Most Creative Web Design Techniques Award given by University of Paris Art Department -- selected from pool of 134 applicants

Did you know 40M Web Pages exist today and it's an exploding arena? Such gazelles as Mama Maria Semolina Products, EuroTravel, and the recently publicized Bather's Choice began their first marketing successes on the World Wide Web.

My design expertise has prepared me to do big jobs for the smaller companies you service. I eagerly look forward to discussing how my diverse contributions and your successful designers can work toward stronger marketing with tougher technology to make Studio di Roma bigger profits and higher visibility. **I have some stronger, tougher, bigger ideas to show you!**

Repeats selling motto to remind reader and exits with a bang!

Sincerely yours,

Dylan Hasselhoff

Please check my Web Page to review my portfolio.

**Responding Letter
Chemist**

Vincent Remady
11223 Farm Oaks Lane, Westminster, OR 55536
(555) 847-5555
vremad@uofw.edu

April 12, 20XX

Ms. Jane Winter
Unified Fibers & Plastics
Human Resources Director
6623 Concord Avenue
Westminster, OR 55536

**Re: Entry-Level Chemist: Job Hot Line,
University of Washington**

Dear Ms. Winter:

I would appreciate the opportunity to apply my **advanced education in chemistry**, to be completed in June, to the development of catalysts/materials in hydrocarbon processing and environmental applications for Unified.

My faculty advisor—Dr. Martin John—believes you will benefit from my previously acquired catalysis knowledge base. My educational research has spawned thorough familiarity with all aspects of catalysis structure and development. My qualifications include:

• **Thesis Focus:** selection, synthesis and test of heterogeneous catalyst on a borazine/olefin system and utilizing this heterogeneous catalyst to insert carbon monoxide into a boron-hydrogen bond

• 5 years' research experience with three published articles

• Strong background in instrumental analysis and computer skills

• American Chemical Society's award for research *initiated* by a graduate student (selected from a pool of 256 graduate student applicants)

My **ability to work independently with thoroughness, motivation and judgment** in combination with my education will provide valuable results for Unified. Expect a call from me within the week to arrange an appointment to further discuss your needs.

Sincerely yours,

Vincent Remady

Martin John, Remady's faculty advisor, knows Winter; so Remady drops John's name.

Enclosure: Resume

**Responding Letter
RF Engineer**

James M. Oldenstad
23476 Sparrow Lane
Framingham, MA 36952
(508) 555-3636
jolden@dachey.daridu.org

> Employers generally don't want both online and hard copies of your materials (too much data to manage) but if you feel impelled to follow up with a hard copy, this letter shows how to handle the double submission.

June 14, 20XX

Mr. Harvey Knott
Director, Employee Staffing
Veri Communications Inc.
36 Super Highway Road
Worcester, MA 36953

**Re: Senior RF Engineer Job Posting,
Veri WebSite**
Online Response 9-14-02
Hard Copy Duplicate

Dear Mr. Knott:

Communications has come a long way from the tin can and string era, after 10 years as an engineer it is terrific to still be excited about hottest new developments. While visiting your WebSite last night, to learn more about Veri Communications, I realized how advanced you are in the wireless arena.

The job listings show VCI's exponential growth! I want to contribute to that growth. When it comes to radio frequency technologies, I have:

• led a team of design engineers, technicians and technical support staff in the design and development of digital multiplexers, analog telemetry and high resolution video fiber optic communication products and equipment

• CATV projects management and engineering design competence

• experience with latest (NAMES OF SOFTWARE) design tools

• over 12 years' diverse and progressive engineering management experience, with 4 of those years operating in Total Quality Management environments

If you want a skilled and enthusiastic communicator, I'm your man. I'll call on Wednesday for an appointment that fits your timetable.

Sincerely,

James M. Oldenstad

Enclosed: Resume

Responding Letter
Speech-Language Pathologist

Marisa Tomlinger
11 Park Street Alfred, New York 14802
(212) 555-1212   ger@worldnet.att.com

September 13, 20XX

Ms. Judith Ann Parson, Director
New York Rehabilitation Center
P.O. Box 45677
New York, New York 10128   **RE: Speech-Language Pathologist position**

Knowing is not enough,
we must apply.
Willing is not enough,
we must do.
-Goethe

The quote is a nice touch.

Dear Ms. Parson:

Having been a Speech-Language Pathologist for nearly **10 years**, and having spent most of that time **working with children who have severe speech and learning differences**, I have learned to live by this concept. With this in mind, I hope you will seriously consider me for the position advertised in the Sunday *New York Times*.

I have an extensive experience base in the New York area that will especially contribute to the growth of New York Rehabilitiation Center. My concentrations include **childrens' speech therapy, speech analysis for all ages, adult speech therapy and phonetics instruction**. My written and oral proficiency in Spanish and Italian will enable me to extend my services to a broad community.

I look forward to the opportunity of meeting you to discuss my background in further detail, since this letter only touches on the highlights of my career. I will contact you next week to do so. Thank you for your consideration.

Sincerely,

Marisa Tomlinger

Enclosure: Resume

**Responding Letter
RF Engineer**

Jeffrey T. Donaldson
209 Hilltop Lane
Ridgewood, NJ 07825
(201) 555-7623
jtdonaldson@aol.com

June 12, 20XX

Mr. Ronald Redfinger
Senior Vice President, Human Resources
BITES Inc.
635 Colum Road
Morristown, NJ 07962

**Re: Posting for RF Engineer
Job Bulletin Board, Conference of
Human Resource Professionals**

Dear Mr. Redfinger:

How does an opportunity to lead BITES' compensation staff sound to me? Like a sound opportunity!

Helping fulfill CEO Mary Twists's goal of achieving higher productivity and operating margins is just the assignment I've been looking for.

As an asset to BITES Inc., my qualifications extend far beyond my focus in management compensation, to include research, public speaking and written communication skills used to enhance productivity, quality and value among employees and clients. My contributions to BITES will include:

- Benchmarking and updating of pay for performance strategies and measures, in conjunction with other members of the Productivity & Quality Center based throughout the BITES organization

- Development of reward and recognition programs that reinforce economic value creation, as well as strategic gains in customer satisfaction, internal processes, and innovation -- the drivers of future financial performance

- Continuous year-to-year improvement in the ways that the overall pay system is communicated, resulting in clear signals -- to employees, customers and shareholders -- of just what performance is expected and rewarded

As an expert resource to your business groups and divisions, I will **visualize and implement continuing excellence** to insure BITES remains on top of its corporate competitors. I will call on Thursday for an appointment to discuss your staffing needs.

Sincerely,

Jeffrey T. Donaldson

Enclosed: Resume

**Responding Letter
Production Technical Support**

Brian Russell
5701 Kentwood Place, Grand Rapids, MI 49504
(616) 555-1212

May 24, 20XX

Mr. Richard Taylor, Employment Director
Precision Operation Company
P.O. Box 3333
Detroit, MI 49508   **RE: Production Technical Support**

Dear Mr. Taylor:

A wise man once said, "Never turn down the opportunity to solve a problem ... it is the process by which we solve that problem that we learn the most." That "wise man" was my father. I guess that explains why I look at technical support and troubleshooting as an opportunity. Someday, with all the problems I have solved in my nine years in technical support, I hope to be a very wise man indeed!

In listening to your job hot line advertisement, I couldn't help but notice that an excellent match exists between your needs and my experience, which includes:

*   More than **5 years' experience in planning, scheduling, tracking and supervising a comprehensive, corrective and preventative maintenance program** involving a wide range of power generation, distribution and control equipment.

*   More than **7 years' experience in troubleshooting and repairing** 110, 220, 440 and 4160 VAC and 250 VDC electrical systems and equipment ranging from large motors and generators to portable electrical tools such as drills and saws.

*   Proficiency with **Windows 2000, Linux, OfficeStar** and other useful software.

I'll call on Tuesday to see when we can meet. I look forward to the opportunity to assist in solving your company's most challenging problems!

Sincerely,

Brian Russell

Enclosure: Resume   Interesting opening, but not pompous.

**Responding Letter
Registered Nurse**

Nelson R. Harbor
12 Ave Sausser, Parque du Bon, Panache, France, 3456798
Telephone: (01)-11-11-31
E-mail: Harb@comp.com

1/10/XX

Mr. Liam Nielsenn,
Recruitment/Retention Specialist   **Re: Case Manager Position**
Champagne Medical Centre
123 Ave du Monde, Champagne, France 3344567

Dear Mr. Nielsenn:

For the past eight years, I have worked in various positions at the Panache Sanitorium, including **Charge RN (two years), ICU (two years) and home health (six years)**. As you will notice in my enclosed resume, many of my positions have involved numerous responsibilities above and beyond the standard job description.

Your recruitment advertisement requests that applicants possess management experience in:

> *open heart cases, amputee medicine, head trauma, stroke trauma, pediatric rehabilitation, spinal cord injury, and infection control.*

I have managed teams of more than 10 nurses in:

> **open heart cases, amputee, nerve, burn, head, stroke and neck trauma cases, pediatric rehabilitation, spinal cord injury and surgery cases, and infection control.**

Such a background aptly prepared me for your case manager position.

My experience helped me adapt to all kinds of typical hospital situations, including failing life support equipment, understaffing, staff authorization, utilization revision and discharge issues, and team management. I have been **licensed in France for eight years, and I completed my CRRN Credential**. As my resume shows, my experience is well suited to the responsibilities of a case manager at a larger institution. I look forward to discussing the position further with you, and will contact you next week.

Without complaining about his job at Panache Sanitorium, Harbor subtly clarifies his interest in changing jobs.

Sincerely,

Nelson R. Harbor

In quoting the help-wanted ad, and then presenting his experience in the same layout (indented with the quote in italics, his experience in boldface), Harbor makes an undeniable visual and mental parallel between the employer's needs and his abilities.

Enclosure: Resume

**Responding Letter
Associate Executive Director**

Charles DeWitt
105 Chaucer Street
Golden, CO 80301
(303) 555-1212

June 27, 20XX

Ms. Sarah McMillan,
Executive Director
American Purchasing Management Inc.
3607 Jayton Road
Washington, DC 20203

**Re: Association Management
Job Posting E-Span
June 26, 20XX**

Dear Ms. McMillan:

After speaking with membership director Mary Milton about your job requirements, I am thrilled to discover an exceptionally compatible match between your needs and my skills. **In addition to association management experience**, described on my resume, I have worked in the purchasing management field. A synopsis of my purchasing background:

Your needs:

* Four-year degree

* Interfacing and materials
  management

* Negotiating skills

* Supervisory experience

My qualifications:

* Bachelor's degree in Business/Economics
  Master's degree in Business Management,
  and five years' experience with Purchasing
  and Materials Management

* Comprehensive management of materials
  for facilities and engineering services

* Success in negotiating cost-plus pricing
  strategies for goods and services

* Analytical, negotiation, communication and
  leadership skills.

I seem to have exactly the background you need to support your leadership. I will call to check on the progress of your search for an Associate Executive Director next week.

Sincerely yours,

Charles DeWitt

Enclosure: Resume

**Responding Letter
Accounting/Assistant Controller**

LAWRENCE J. KUHN
19 CHARLES LANE, SCHAMBURG, IL 60191
(555) 555-1212

Mr. Josh Thomas, President
Thomas and Associates
1300 N. Collingham Drive
Chicago, IL 61092

August 24, 20XX

RE: Your Accounting/Assistant Controller Position
(Referred by Mr. Doug Orr, VP)

> Refers to a
> mutual contact.

Dear Mr. Thomas:

As a management professional with demonstrated success in maintaining budgets and business reporting, I am seeking a new career challenge as an assistant controller. Doug Orr was confident we could mutually benefit from my expertise.

In speaking with Doug, a former colleague at Olds and Young, about the job requirements of your position, I discovered a compatible match between your needs and my experiences. They include:

Your Needs:	*My Offerings:*
* Four-year degree	* BS in accounting
* CPA Credential	* CPA + continued training
* Reporting experience	* Compiled data for weekly, monthly, quarterly and annual reports, inventory valuations, created balance sheet and cash flow analysis
* Computer Proficiency	* PC Lotus, WordPerfect, Excel, General Ledger Applications
* Accounting systems implementation	* 100% increase production through creation of streamlined systems and reporting

Offer me the chance to increase your productivity and we will both benefit from our ability to implement positive change. I will call early next week to discuss how we can explore this possibility further. Thank you.

> Ends with a friendly,
> constructive tone.

Sincerely,

Lawrence J. Kuhn

**Responding Letter
Senior Systems Engineer**

CHRISTOPHER PURCEL
333 Green Park, New Brunswick Borough 99317, London, U.K.   (11)-22-33-44

July 5, 20XX

Hannah Hoffman, Engineering Resources, Tech House
654 Woodredge Lane
Hillsborough, 44567, London, United Kingdom

It's no use saying, "We are doing our best." You have got to succeed in doing what is necessary.
--Winston Churchill

I fervently agree, Ms. Hoffman, with Churchill's no nonsense approach. In fact, in today's high tech world, his words have even more relevance! Part of "doing what is necessary," as you well know, includes hiring the right people to get the job done. I am the candidate who can get the job done. Below is a list of qualifications required as specified in your July 2, 20XX ad in the Financial Times, for **Sr. System Engineers**. As you can see, I do what is necessary, and then some.

> Using Hoffman's name in first line replaces customary salutation so quote has full impact.

BS DEGREE IN ENGINEERING...

    BS Degree in Electrical Engineering, Queens University

EXPERIENCE WITH SATCOM SYSTEMS...

    18 years' experience as systems engineer. Lead Systems Engineer on VSAT design analysis, and trade studies. Simulated, analyzed, tested network and terminal concepts. 68% improvements on all systems tested.

PROFICIENCY IN PROVIDING PRESENTATIONS AND ADVANCING BUSINESS...

    13 years' assisting customers in defining system requirements; presented technical material at customer meetings; wrote technical requirement documents. Developed ability to translate technical subjects to non-technical individuals, resulted in 80% of prospects purchasing system.

For more details on the information listed, please see the enclosed resume. I will call your office next week to discuss my qualifications more in depth.

Sincerely,

Christopher Purcel

Enclosure: Resume

**Responding Letters
Electronics Engineer**

ELISABETH MARTIN
1355 State Street
New Haven, CT 02222
(555) 555-1212
emartin@jfuribe.com

May 31, 20XX

Mr. Bill Truesdale, Staffing Representative
Aerospace Technologies
17 Manhattan Avenue
New York City, NY 10022

CONFIDENTIAL

Martin marks her resume Confidential hoping her boss won't find out she's looking around.

RE: Electronics Engineer

Mentions industry competitor to show field familiarity

Dear Mr. Truesdale:

Although I am currently employed by your primary competitor, I recognize that Aerospace Technologies indisputably represents "the best" in the aerospace industry. Therefore, I have been calling your job hot line for the past six months in search of just the right position to match my diverse professional background. Yesterday, I found it!

YOU SEEK...	*AND I BRING...*
a Bachelor's Degree	**Bachelor's of Science Degree** in Electronics/Engineering
5 years' engineering and management experience	5 years' experience as **Electronics Engineer, and Supervisor**
technology development experience	**Technology development and implementation**, including; radar, research equipment and fuel systems

Of course, this abbreviated list represents only the experience that most directly corresponded with your hot line, so I am also enclosing a resume. I am available to you at your earliest convenience and look forward to discussing my background with you. I will call next week in hopes that we can do this. Thank you.

Sincerely yours,

Elisabeth Martin

Enclosure: Resume

Martin has a master's degree in engineering and also 7 years of experience. She answers as the job hot line listing requires. She assumes the listing means at least a bachelor's degree and at least 5 years' experience; otherwise she may be rejected for being "overqualified."

Responding Letter Attorney

Rosa Vargas
P.O. Box 2632
El Paso, TX 79913
(505) 283-5555
rosavargas@yahoo.com

June 23, 20XX

P.O. Box 9980   Re: Senior Counsel:
Dayton, OH 67321   Your Advertisement
                                                        El Paso Law Monthly, June 20XX

To Whom It May Concern:

> Low-key professional letter responds to a blind box ad.

I currently serve as senior U.S. counsel to the largest law firm in Mexico, Rodriguez y Gonzalez Baz. My qualifications which parallel to the requirements outlined for a position as in-house Senior Counsel include:

- 15 years' international law experience
- Juris Doctorate from University of California, Berkeley Law School
- Certified by the American Bar Association, California Bar, Texas Bar
- Fluency in Spanish
- Strong legal research and writing skills

In my capacity as senior counsel, my responsibilities include:

- Representation of major US-based multinational corporations with business connections in Mexico and other Latin American countries
- Organizing internal legal staff of 5
- Directing communication between inside and outside counsel to insure effective business dealings
- Determining companies' compliance with US and Latin American laws, customs, and business practices

The requirement of multi-national involvement, particularly the Latin American division, matches my qualifications for this position. My exemplary international law and bilingual skills will provide definite benefits for your company. I enclose my curriculum vitae and references for your review. Although I am currently employed by a competitor, my demonstrated knowledge and dedication to productive international business relationships and passion for international law mark me as the ideal candidate to fill your opening. I will contact you Wednesday for an appointment.

> Vargas encloses references because the ad asked for them.

Sincerely,

Rosa Vargas

Enc: CV

**Responding Letter
Environmental Engineer**

Beth Walton
123 Brick Road
Baton Rouge, LA
75038
(456) 978-1011

February 2, 20XX

Mr. John Dodge, Partner
Dodge & Dodge Recruiters
Akron, OH 36252

Dear Mr. Dodge:

My professional experience and educational background make me a strong candidate for the **Environmental Engineer** position for which you are conducting a search.

Highlights of reasons why I will be a great asset to your client:

- **Ten years' experience as an industrial environmentalist**

- **Master of science degree in environmental engineering, cum laude, Ohio State University**

As you'll see in my enclosed resume, my additional stint in the aerospace industry gave me the opportunity to apply federal and state health and safety regulations in a range of manufacturing environments, with certification in:

- **Industrial/Environmental Hygiene**

- **Environmental Inspection & Design**

Your client needs people with as many talents as possible, who understand the environmental industry from more than one perspective. My professional experience in the aerospace industry plus my in-depth studies at Ohio State University will enable me to make crucial contributions. Feel free to contact me anytime -- I'll call you within a few days to discuss what I can do and how I plan to do it.

Sincerely,

Enclosure: Resume

Beth Walton

Responding Letter Cybrarian

Harriet Powers
5850 Day Street
Oklahoma City, OK 32843

March 17, 20XX

Mr. Albert Betti, CEO
Bakewell Financial Products Inc.
2635 New Street
Oklahoma City, OK 32843

RE: Your JobOptions posting: corporate cybrarian-- "Librarian of Cyberspace"

**Call me at (777) 538-9900
E-Mail me at:
harrpow@excite.com**

Dear Mr. Betti:

Can I online-review patent holdings and trademarks? You bet I can! I start with Derwood World Patent Index and TrademarkLookUp. Or Assists, ALIO, and U.S. Patents TotalText. Recently I checked for Bonda's patents without success, but a trademark search showed that Bonda Technologies Inc., has registered "WithMe" on October 21, 199X.

Can I dig out the latest online investment analysts reports? You bet I can! I start with InvestWorld, the major database of investment analysts' reports. Five reports were found that discussed Bakewell Financial Products. You enjoy a good reputation.

Can I uncover corporate structures? You bet I can! When you want to know who owns a company, what does the company own, what are its subsidiaries, I mouse over to the online database for Company Affiliations to answer these questions. I found, for instance, that Bakewell has one subsidiary listed: Bakewell Financial Products Ltd., in London.

I have formal librarian training and have worked part-time as an information broker for three years. Keeping a handle on the fast flying information a thriving company needs today is a challenge. I'm good at it! Is tomorrow too soon to talk?

Sincerely yours,

Harriet Powers

Powers proves: she can do the job with three smart examples followed by a "can do" affirmation for each. She has formal librarian training, but not a degree in librarianship. Because cybrarians -- for public, school or corporate libraries -- are still rare, she can afford to hold the resume for the interview. This letter was hand delivered to the company receptionist.

**Responding Letter
Computer Programmer**

Paula Smith
36 Home Avenue
Etobicore, Ontario M5P358
(416) 555-1676
E-mail: psmith@prodigy.com

January 13, 20XX

Mr. Craig McCormick   RE: Director Applications Development
VP MIS
Health Care Centers Inc.
26 Bellflower Street
Toronto, Ontario M5P355

> Smith is writing to a Vice President of
> Management Information Systems and using a
> mutual business acquaintance as the introduction.

Dear Mr. McCormick:

Bob Firth of HBE Computers told me of your desire to find a Director of Applications
Development -- he believes as I do that my qualifications are a perfect fit.

I am a Senior Manager of Application Development with experience managing the informational
needs of a Canadian company with over $200 million in annual revenues. As a key member of
the management team, I have directed the implementation of computer technology, which has
reduced expenses by 20%. This application has been used in both Canada and the U.S. The
following is the tip of the iceberg when it comes to my accomplishments:

>   *   Directed a $4.5 million corporate-wide UNIX development project;
>   the system is installed in 350+ sites around the globe.
>
>   *   Established network criteria for marketing and operations divisions,
>   then directed implementation. The network has run error-free
>   for over 12 months.

My reputation is that of a solid strategic thinker who digests complex information and builds
coherent, actionable structure from that information, and then proceeds to get the job done. I am
eager to meet with you to discuss your corporate objectives as well as the contributions I can
make as Director of Application Development.   I will contact you in a few days to set up an
appointment that fits into your schedule. Bob Firth may call you about me this week.

Sincerely,

Paula Smith

> Smith will make sure that Firth
> makes the call!

> Smith wants to
> go from a
> Senior Manager
> to a Director so
> she leads with
> something she
> directed.

**Responding Letter
Catering Manager**

JAMES T. LUMSDALE
Jlum@mindspring.com

888 West Clinton Drive, Phoenix, AZ 85020   (602) 555-1212

March 20, 20XX

Mr. Stan Acres, Human Resources Manager
American Catering Corporation
126 Sun Street
Phoenix, AZ 85032   **RE: Catering Manager Position**

Dear Mr. Acres:

    While attending a friend's wedding last Saturday, one of your caterers, John Bolton, told me you were in the market for a catering manager. I was so enticed I had to pursue this once-in-a-lifetime chance to join a catering company as classy as yours!

    I have been in the catering business for most of my life, so I couldn't help but notice the exceptional services American Catering offers! The food was superb -- not an easy task at an out-door wedding -- the staff was knowledgeable and took great pride in their work! I haven't witnessed a working environment like the one you have created in years maybe never.

    I know American Catering can benefit from my conscientious service and performance in a high-volume setting. Here is a brief list of my achievements...

    I have...
- **Nine years in banquet/special event catering, restaurant food services and operations.** ←
- **Extensive presentation, menu coordination, and multiple course experience.**
- **Won the Sun City Best Presentation Award for 2001.** ←
- **Hired and trained many new employees, especially in the past 2 years.**
- **Graduated from Comell School of Restaurant Management.**

    I have lived in the Phoenix area and established clientele and business associations for the last 10 years. As you know, word of mouth is the best advertisement. Between your reputation and my contacts, I will be a profitable addition to American Catering.

    I can't stress enough the outstanding work American Catering provided for my friends. I would be honored to join such an impressive group! I was immediately comfortable with everyone -- and would fit right in. You will be hearing from me early next week so I can fill in the details of my background.

Sincerely,

James T. Lumsdale

Lumsdale fortifies the accomplishments with award.

Boldface and bullets call attention to top selling achievement.

Thomas Jamison
3636 Arbor Road
Willmington NC 67589
(632) 121-2289

October 7, 20XX

Ms. Marjorie Walters
Engineering Technologies, Inc.
Manager Human Resources   RE: Engineering Position
44991 Harbor East   Entry Level
Willmington, NC 67589

Dear Ms. Walters:

The Career Fair to be held at NC State this November is an exciting opportunity for Engineering Technologies, Inc., to interview students interested in the entry level positions being advertised through the campus Placement Center. My job experience and high GPA (3.75) make me a prime candidate.

While finishing my degree evenings at NC State, I have acquired valuable career experience through full-time employment the last three years at Technological Applications Inc. (TAI), a small electronics contract manufacturer specializing in Surface Mount Technology.

Starting on the manufacturing line and working at various positions before being promoted to Supervisor, Test Operations, has given me hands-on understanding of the challenges of turning designs into working prototypes and full production units. TAI does not afford me the opportunity to work in the design arena; therefore, I am looking to move on once I receive my degree.

I believe my work experience combined with a practical classroom education at a respected university has given me valuable knowledge of today's industry, both academically and professionally. The references I can supply from TAI will also validate my dependability and creativity.

I would appreciate the opportunity to meet with your representative next month to discuss possible career opportunities with Engineering Technologies, Inc. I will call in a few days with the objective of setting up a meeting.

Sincerely,

Thomas Jamison

> Jamison deals with why he will not stay with his current employer. The positive message is reinforced by bringing up the references.

Chapter 15

RedHot Initiating Letters

· ·

In This Chapter

▶ Networking, direct e-mail

▶ Search firm, Web site auction

▶ Temp, contract, resume, summer job

▶ Follow-up, thank-you, recommendation

▶ Rejection, acceptance

· ·

*1*f you're the sort of person who'd rather drive than ride along as a passenger, grab the wheel with initiating letters.

Even in a tight labor market where jobs are bouncing off the walls, if you're among the unemployed — or if you want to make hay while the sun shines — these letters are excellent tools to ask others to help you source jobs and employers to hire you.

There's more: Another letter in this chapter relates to a newer twist in the job market — the auction format, where you put yourself out for bid — and follow-ups to interviews and networking encounters. You'll find letters that say thank you and others that guide you to express appropriate rejection or acceptance of a job offer.

Do you need a reference letter? In some cases, the writer welcomes a draft of key points from you. A recommendation sample is in this chapter, too.

The letters in Chapter 14 are examples of responding letters, in which you react to the actions of others. The letters in this chapter are models of how you can seize the initiative. Go proactive!

E-mail to Headhunter

From: Alberto Mendez <amendez@newnet.com>
Subject: Resume submission; plus 2 Word attachments
Date: Sun, June 18, 20XX 1:35: PDT
To: Jeremy Chasen <jeremychasen@nobyparson.com>

Dear Mr. Chasen:

I present my resume for consideration in the soap, perfume, cosmetics industry, for which my research says you recruit. Functionally, my background is in training. Trainees say that my platform skills are excellent, that I grab their interest and don't let go.

During the past 3.5 years since my graduation from Skidmore College — well known as an institution blending liberal arts studies with visual and performing arts, a plus for effective training presentations — I have worked at Great Looks Inc. preparing regional trainers of retail sales personnel. During this time, I have gained credibility for designing and organizing new courses using state-of-the-art technology as well as providing inspiring and motivating instruction. I'm ready for bigger challenges.

Salary history:
    Beginning salary $39,000 plus 5% bonus
    Ending salary $44,120 no bonus (company lost
                           money)

Please consider me for positions that start at $48,000 to $55,000 base. The opportunity to learn, grow, and work with cutting edge products and equipment are important to me. My first choice of locale is the West Coast; however, I will consider any urban area for an offer I can't refuse. My resume follows.

Sincerely,
Alberto Mendez
H: (858) 711-7111
W: (619) 230-2300 x 72
Pg:(619) 121-1212
amendez@newnet.com

Job seeker tells third-party professional recruiter immediately that he falls into his specialty area of recruiting; otherwise, the headhunter would have no interest and delete the letter. He cuts to the chase on what he wants, including salary history and expectations. Recruiters appreciate steps you take to make things easier and faster for them.

P.S. For your convenience, if you can better use an attractive hard copy for client presentation, I have attached Word files of this letter and my formatted resume at the end of the plain text version. I appreciate your interest.

Talent Auction Profile

About This Talent

Available	8/15/XX
Duration	No Preference
Desired Hrs	No Preference
Based in	Charleston, SC

Topflight Public Relations Pro

TARGET PROJECT:
Wide-angle spectrum
of communications, public relations.
From situation analysis and strategic
planning to implementation and
evaluation. Media relations; event
planning; product launches;
issues/crisis mgt.
SALARY:
 $75/$125 hr.
HOURS:
 No Preference
PROJECT LENGTH:
 No Preference
SITE:
 Off-site

TARGET COMPANY:
Savvy, any-size, any-industry
company or organization with
collaborative environment. Establish
goals,then turn me loose to bring back
top results.

TARGET LOCATIONS:
FL - USA
GA - USA
SC - USA
NC - USA
DC - USA
VA - USA

Comments about Talent Auctions

Talent auctions on Web sites are
everywhere. Here's how they work:
Either companies post projects for
which you, the job seeker, bid, or vice
versa — you post a "project wanted"
profile and sit back to wait for an e-
mail offer from an employer. Low or
high bidder wins.

Part of a talent auction profile equates
to a cover letter; the other part is a
generic resume.

The "cover letter" portion of your
talent profile usually appears on one
side of the screen (see the generalized
example at left), and your generic
resume appears on the other.

To compose a talent profile, you don't
submit a cover letter and resume, but
fill in the blanks of a digital form.
Your talent profile may be limited to a
specified number of characters, say
4,000, or about 800 words.

The trick is to make every word
persuade and sell your talents. The
best way to perfect your talent auction
profile is to study how others are
showcasing theirs. (See Chapter 3 for
a couple of places to look.)

Does the bidding-block idea work?
Statistical data has not yet surfaced
showing that the talent auction model
is or is not effective in connecting
people with jobs.

**Networking Letter:
Competitor's Employees**

Ari Trinh
Plano Research Department
101 Main Street, Plano, TX 75004
(213) 555-8888 days (213) 666-9999 eves
Aritrinh.altavista.net

Ms. Maya McDonald
Cooper Systems Inc.
202 Lacan Circle
Columbia, OH 44122

April 8, 20XX

RE: **Research Analyst position**

Dear Ms. McDonald,

Our mutual friend, **Cory Payne** recommended I write to you for assistance in my current job
search. I seek a position as an **operations systems analyst** or **statistical research analyst**. My
qualifications include:

      -SIX YEARS' EXPERIENCE AS A STATISTICAL RESEARCH ANALYST

      -MORE THAN 12 YEARS OF COLLEGE-LEVEL MATHEMATICS, STATISTICS

      -EXTENSIVE KNOWLEDGE OF STATISTICAL RESEARCH

      -PHD IN MATHEMATICS EDUCATION

      -MASTER OF SCIENCE IN OPERATIONS RESEARCH

      -BACHELOR OF SCIENCE IN MATHEMATICS AND STATISTICS

While my current position has been extremely rewarding, my financial needs require that I
change jobs for one that is more lucrative. I would appreciate any assistance you can give me in
providing job leads, contacts, or advice. You have worked in this field longer than I, and I would
like to learn from your greater experience. Be assured that I will return this favor in any way that
I can.

Thank you,

Ari Trinh

Enclosure: 6 resumes

> Trinh hopes his friend's name will
> generate search assistance or at
> least confidentiality for his search.

Networking Letter: Alumni

200 South First Street
Manhattan, KS 65042
(913) 776-6655
fields@cts.com

February 5, 20XX

Ms. Gaye Rivers
United Aerospace Co.
101 Summer Avenue
Springfield, AZ 90168

**RE: Aerospace Engineering position
sought by fellow alum of
Kansas State University**

Dear Ms. Rivers,

*When confronted with challenging problems,
knowing who to call upon for the answers is a valuable tool.*
Anonymous

As one alum to another, I'd like to feel that it's okay to call upon you for some answers to my challenging first job search as an aerospace engineer.

My experience and qualifications include:
- Bachelor's in aerospace engineering expected May 20XX
- Internship with American Signal Inc. for two summers (20XX and 20XX)
- Expect to graduate summa cum laude
- One-year senior design course
- Proficiency with CAD and panel method software
- Leadership and community service experience in Delta Delta Delta sorority
- Willing to relocate

If you know of positions open or people I should contact to best utilize my qualifications, please let me know. In addition, I would love to hear how you got started and progressed as a successful aerospace engineer. As a woman entering a predominantly male field, I can use whatever advice you can offer.

I appreciate any time you can take to relate your advice or assistance. I'll call you in two weeks for any ideas you may have.

Sincerely,

Marsha Fields

Marsha Fields

Enclosed: 3 Resumes

Fields pulls out all the stops in asking an alumna of her gender and discipline to help her find a job. She got Rivers' name from her career center office, which worked through the alumni office.

**Networking Letter
Friends and Family**

Rolf Andersen

100 Ocean Drive, San Rafael, Florida 33300
(305) 444-4444
anders@aol.com

Mr. Jack Robins
400 St. Louis Avenue
Ventura, NJ 07954

June 12, 20XX

RE: Sales and Marketing position

Dear Jack,

Remember that political bet you lost to me last Christmas? Well, I've figured out how you can pay me back. Instead of dinner as we agreed, how about a job? Yeah, I know you can't give me a job, but I certainly could use some good leads, advice, or contacts.

Last month, my employer, International Gadgets, started downsizing, and I was surprised when the company laid off my entire support staff -- my personal secretary, my office manager, and my accountant! Suddenly, the "International Relations Department" became "Rolf Anderson." I'm ready to move on.

I have a pretty hot resume -- but it takes more than a piece of paper to get a job. In case you think of someone to refer me to, let me refresh you on my background:

* Managed international accounts for Dixon & Preece, Madison Avenue

* Sold for Florida Interstate Travel -- foreign and U.S. customer base

* M.A. Degree, 3.85 GPA, International Affairs, with a concentration in International Business and Economics, University of San Rafael, Florida

I've been looking for something in international business consulting, international marketing (as liaison with international subsidiaries/distributors), or international investment brokerage (specializing in Latin America) -- but I'm trainable, and I'd love to broaden my horizons; I welcome any advice.

So you have a choice: either pay the 30 bucks you owe me, or help me out in a much bigger way.

Thanks for everything Jack,

ROLF ANDERSON

A good-natured spoof asking for help from a pal.

P.S. I'm enclosing several copies of my resume in case you think of the perfect recipient.

Networking Letter: Internet

Date: Mon, 18 Mar 20XX 13:12:40
From: PixStix <rtk@roseshire.ac.uk>
RE: JobPlace <JOBPLACE@NEWS.JOBWEB.ORG>
Newsgroups: jobweb.jobplace
Subject: Placement year...

I am a second year student at Roseshire University in England reading Geography. The third year of my degree course is termed a "placement" year as I must find a job for at least 52 weeks in the period from July 20XX to September 20XX before continuing into the fourth and final year of my degree.

I am looking for any companies or institutions worldwide (but especially in Australia, New Zealand or around the Pacific Rim) that have a temporary post such as this with a geographical/environmental interest. I am willing to pay any travel expenses to reach the job. If you could help me in any way I would be most grateful.

Thank you for your time,

Ryan King

rtk@roseshire.ac.uk

King posted worldwide on every job-related discussion group he could find. Unfortunately for King, the JobPlace mailing list (a feature of JobWeb, the World Wide Web site of the National Association of Colleges and Employers) is not designed to help people find jobs. Instead, it is a discussion group for professionals in career counseling. King wasted everyone's time. LESSON TO LEARN: Post a job appeal only where your message reaches a target audience whose members have the power to say "yes." See Chapter 3.

Direct E-mail/ Broadcast Letter

Ethan S. Nealen
11 Jamestown Road
Smithfield, RI 02917
(234) 567-8910
Ethansn@hotmail.com

June 17, 20XX

Ms. Gertrude Moser
Korris International
171 Random Lane
New Martinsville, WV 26155

Selling points in bold here.

Dear Ms. Moser:

While serving as a manufacturing **Director of Sales and Marketing**, I spearheaded the push for new products "out the door" -- doubling new product production within three years. As **Marketing Manager** for another manufacturer, I introduced exciting distributor incentive plans, changed product packaging and added fresh distribution channels -- **result: sales up 17% and profits 31%.**

My last company was sold, making me available for sales and marketing management with a key manufacturing organization such as Korris International.

As yet another example of the contribution I can make to Korris, I reduced the size of our packaging by 50% while improving box graphics. Direct results include:

- Increased manufacturing turns
- Lower shipping weights/costs
- Lower box prices to endusers, increasing market share
- Improved distributor margins
- Higher sales and production volumes

"Enduser" is industry jargon for end user.

My verifiable record gives me confidence that I can quickly contribute to your company's profitability by developing programs to capture real customer solutions -- not just another round of price discounting!

I would greatly appreciate the opportunity to discuss how my skills and experience can make a powerful and significant impact on your company's success. I will call your office in a few days to arrange an appointment.

Sincerely yours,

Ethan S. Nealen

This letter can be sent out (in plain text—ASCII) as e-mail to a selective list, or postal mailed.

In an up labor market, Nealen is wise to include his e-mail address on both his resume and cover letter. The employer can easily respond using the "reply" button and may even start an online dialogue. But in a down labor market when jobs are hard to get, the argument can be made that an e-mail address also makes it very easy for an employer to reply, "Don't call, we're not hiring."

**Direct E-mail/
Temp Letter**

Sheveron S. Adams
**12354 Beach Boulevard
Huntington Beach, California 98777**

March 11, 20XX

Mr. Brock Keifer
Manpower, Inc.
8989 Avenida Encinas
Huntington Beach, California 99860

Dear Mr. Keifer:

Can your clients use a top pick DRAFTER choice?

I have gained valuable drafting experience, and I'm looking for jobs where I can use my expertise to jump in and do great work from Day One. I am ambitious, self-disciplined, and work well under pressure without constant supervision. Previous employers (names on request) have called me "meticulous," "conscientious," and "dependable."

I believe my determination to achieve will prove to be an asset to your temporary services firm.

Thank you for your consideration. I look forward to talking with you soon.

> *Adams will call within the week to verify his marketing package (cover letter and resume) was received, and to ask about the frequency of drafting assignments.*

Sincerely,

Sheveron S. Adams

(809) 234-9898
E-mail: ShevA@Prodigy.com

Enclosure: Resume

> *Note no mention is made of enclosing a resume in the body of the letter; that task is handled at the bottom of the letter.*

> *Any letter can be distributed by e-mail (with a change of format; see Chapter 2) or postal mail. It is labeled Direct E-mail/Temp Letter to remind you.*

Direct E-mail/ Contact Job Letter

Juan Carlos Suarez
Villa de Rose, 20-4B
67895 Las Flores
Barcelona, 38671, Spain
Telephone: 11-22-33-44
Juancarlossuarez@aol.com

January 7, 20XX

Ms. Jillian Carson
Human Resources Manager
American Propulsion Inc.
PO Box 222222
New Castle, DE 19270
USA

> This powerful opening statement for a contract job assignment is carefully worded. It doesn't say Suarez has done this exact work, but refers to the type of "challenging project."

Dear Ms. Carson:

Your new Blazer contract -- the talk of the industry! -- sounds very interesting @md just the type of challenging project that I've spent the last six years doing.

That's why I seek a **project assignment** for a **senior industrial engineering position** with American Propulsion Inc. My contractual obligations in Europe with Global Aerospace are coming to a close soon. Briefly, my background includes:

- Manufacturing process planning
- Quality engineering
- Procurement experience
- Project development
- Configuration engineering
- Multinational consortium coordinator
- NATO secret clearance
- European aerospace industry specialist
- Computer savvy

My attached resume describes my superior qualifications for top-of-the-line aerospace engineering projects. I will be in the United States **on the East Coast from January 20 to February 19.** I'll contact you when I arrive to explore your staffing requirements. I look forward to meeting you.

Sincerely yours,

Juan Carlos Suarez

> The warp speed growth of the Internet means any letter can be distributed by e-mail or postal mail; you should consider cost and impact on a case by case basis. Traditional companies, such as banks, may be more responsive to paper, while high-tech cor.panies will prefer e-mail.

> Suarez won't be ready to start a new assignment until May, but notice he doesn't mention that fact. The January 20 to February 19 trip is for scouting purposes only. If he does a good job of selling his qualifications, the employer may wait for him.

Resume Letter Summer Job

Marek Tellison
65 Torkle Drive
Highland Park, IL 66666
(619) 777-8888 (Until May 2)
(708) 232-8653 (After May 2)
marek@rockfan.com
April 12, 20XX

Ms. Dionne Devereaux, Manager
Dolluloid Accounting Group
7175 Wacker Drive, 8th Floor
Chicago, IL 50026

RE: SUMMER INTERNSHIP 20XX

> Flash of personality balances numbers-oriented accounting—suggesting a serious but fun guy to have around.

Dear Ms. Devereaux:

"If you wish to reach the highest, begin at the lowest."
--Publius Syrus

I know my quoting Publius Syrus is a sign of youthful idealism—that's me! And I have the energy for hard work that goes with it.

Thank you for today's discussion of the summer internship opportunities present at Dolluloid. I am glad that **Peter Hare** referred me to you. The situations we discussed sound both challenging and exciting.

As mentioned, I will soon finish my junior year at San Diego State University as an accounting major, and I will be home in Chicago until early September.

As you pointed out, San Diego State University has provided me with an excellent background and foundation in both accounting and personal development. I have completed the following courses:

Financial Accounting courses:
   -- Managerial Accounting
   -- Intermediate Accounting I and II
   -- Accounting Information Systems
   -- Income Tax
   -- Micro and Macro Economics
   -- Financial Markets.

I am proficient with PC and Macintosh software including Word, Windows, Excel, Lotus 1-2-3, WordPerfect, Quicken, MacWrite, and AppleWorks.

(1 of 2)

Ms. Dionne Devereaux/Marek Tellison

As the President of the Alpha Pi Fraternity, I have continued to sharpen both my interpersonal skills and my leadership abilities. I am gaining valuable experience in leading, motivating, and organizing the combined efforts of more than 60 men. I have learned the importance of doing independent work in a timely and pressured environment as part of a greater team.

This understanding can be exemplified by our chapter's recent success in being chosen for the Grand Piano Award, presented to one of the three best chapters in the United States and Canada for 20XX-20XX.

I have also gained additional experience in interacting with school officials, advisors, and prominent community leaders.

I believe these skills will assist me in supporting your staff to strengthen client relationships, and enable me to perform as a contributing team member.

I was able to advance my business background with an internship at Moe, Hauk & Smith (San Diego) during the fall of 20XX. With my soon to be awarded accounting degree, as well as my membership in the Student Accounting Association, I feel very secure about my accounting abilities as an entry-level employee of your company.

I look forward to further discussing a summer internship position with you. I am very excited about any opportunity that I might have to capitalize on my accounting background and assist your company's needs this summer. Thank you very much for your time and consideration.

Sincerely,

Marek Tellison

Enclosure: Transcript

Follow-Up to Meeting

4444 Milky Way Drive
Sun Beach, CA 90090
(900) 606-4004
rayl@worldnet.att.com

June 21, 20XX

Ms. Alex Sunni   RE: Associate Editor Position
Editor
Astronomical News Magazine
33 Nova Lane
Carlsbad, CA 92124

> Leight begins with a
> shared experience,
> much stronger than
> "Here's my resume."

Dear Ms. Sunni:

I truly enjoyed meeting you last Saturday at the Carlsbad Sundowner's Club. It's always
refreshing to spend time with fellow senior star-gazers, and I want to thank you for sharing your
amazing knowledge of black holes with me.

As you requested, I have enclosed my resume for your review. Your job opening for an associate
editor sounds fascinating, and with my 20-plus years of experience in writing, research, and
editorial work, I can bring a wealth of professional experience to this position. In addition, my
education in astronomy and my years of gazing through telescopes invest me with a personal
interest in the growth of your magazine.

I look forward to speaking with you soon so that we can discuss specifics of how I can contribute
to your magazine.

Best Regards,

Ray F. Leight

Ray F. Leight

Enclosure: resume

Follow-Up to Telephone Call

999 Rocky Plaza
Mountain City, TX 76444
(765) 432-9876
stone@worldnet.att.com

July 14, 20XX

Mr. Juan Cedres, CEO   RE: GIS position
Map Attack
888 Boulder Street, Suite 8
Pebble Beach, TX 77665

Dear Mr. Cedres:

Thank you for taking the time to speak with me yesterday about the possibility of creating a position for a Geographic Information Systems Specialist. As you requested, I have enclosed a resume for your consideration.

As we agreed during our telephone conversation, Map Attack's expansion will depend upon innovative software. My knowledge of **AML**, a GIS programming language, and my up-to-date education in **geography** and **computer science** enable me to create mapping software for commercial distribution as well as for company-wide distribution of easy-to-read plans and reports.

I welcome the chance for a personal meeting with you to discuss in more detail how I can help ease Map Attack's growing pains.

Sincerely,

Dustin Stone

Dustin Stone

Enclosure: resume

Thank You for Job Interview

Grant Wang
4590 Tinwood Circle
Roswell, NM 88202
(777) 316-9808
gwang@net.com

October 30, 20XX

Mr. Jeffrey Hano
Staffing Specialist
Human Resources Center
Fountain Corporation
PO Box 46234
Medford, OR 44444

> Adding new information sets your thank-you letter apart from the Thanks-Aunt-Martha-for-the-socks variety.

Dear Mr. Hano:

Thank you for interviewing me yesterday for a mechanical engineering position. You said you'll soon be routing my resume to several departmental managers. I'll look forward to hearing from interested managers -- I believe I can show them how I meet their needs for a high-performance mechanical engineer.

We were so occupied talking about my skills with hydraulic equipment and precision machining that I am not certain I fully described my experience with **hydro-electric plant technology** yesterday, but I note in today's newspaper that Fountain expects to land a major contract to build a plant in a developing nation. I enclose a summary of my hydro-electric plant experience with this letter and would be happy to detail my experience with you or with the appropriate departmental manager.

Many thanks. I hope we'll have much more to talk about soon.

Sincerely yours,

Grant Wang

Enclosure: Hydro-electric resume addendum

> Sending a resume addendum is, generally speaking, not a good idea—separate papers slip through the cracks. But here, timing counts. A new contract means heavy new staffing efforts—lots of work. Hano will remember interviewing Wang just a couple of days ago and perhaps see a way to lighten his recruiting load.

Thank You for Job Interview

Edie M. Schustermann
12345 North Sunder Court
Home: (678) 910-1112
Message: (131) 415-1617
E-mail:ann.ddd@edu

March 18, 20XX

Ms. Bethany Marsh, Marketing Director
World Wind Travel Gear, Inc.
444 Roving River Way
Fort Worth, Texas 56789

Dear Ms. Marsh:

I can hardly wait to work for you! I appreciate the time you spent interviewing me today for a **MARKETING TRAINEE POSITION**. I was excited to learn the position requires several annual trips to the Australian office. Although we only had time to discuss my education and work experience in detail, I wanted to remind you about my exposure to the Australian market.

During my undergraduate studies in international relations, I spent three informal summer months in Sydney drinking in *shrimp-on-the-barbie* culture. It was a great experience in bridging my US background with the way things are done Down Under. I made good friends with several advertising account executives at the Ayers Rock News, and I developed contacts with personnel at two major Bemberg travel agencies.

Please don't forget my Australian connection when you decide how to fill the ranks of World Wind Travel Gear's young adult marketing staff.

> While we were talking, I realized how well my Australian-flavored background fits into your organization -- from the directions of your advertising campaigns to your target market. This job has my name on it!

Sincerely yours,

Edie M. Schustermann

> Her GPA won't win awards so Shustermann compensates by emphasizing another selling point—the summer she spent scooting around Sydney. Always look for a way to compensate for a weakness.

Thank You for Job Interview

Maxwell Hong
123-D North Circle Drive, Toronto, Canada 44567
Telephone: 22-33-44-55
Internet WWW.BUILDNET.FREELANCE\MAXHONG
E-mail: mhong@aol.com

September 7, 20XX

Mr. Brent C. Nababy, Vice President
21st Century Developments
5555 Hassau Broadway
Toronto, Canada 44568

Dear Mr. Nababy:

Thank you for the opportunity to interview for a sub-contractor coordinator position. I was impressed with the warmth and efficiency of your offices, and your genuine interest in acquainting me with your staff and company goals.

During our discussion, I told you about my background in sub-contractor coordinating experience. Although our conversation focused on hiring policies, top contacts, and scheduling strategies, I wanted to underscore our mutual priorities. The latest issue of *Building Issues* brings to my attention a priority we share: "Beating the competition's quality by miles."

I have always strived to reach high quality results by using the most appropriate materials, and by studying the quality of materials used by other companies. Among my favorite suppliers, you may recognize the following names: Namath Re-bar, Drywall By-the-Mile, and Lionel Fixtures.

Such high standards have been so central in my work that I feel compelled to join such a demanding company as yours. Thanks again for the interview. I look forward to contacting you next week to check on the progress of your search.

Sincerely,

Max Hong

Opens with personable style and quick reminder of interview.

Reviews salient points made during interview.

Mentions contacts not included on resume.

Signs off with intent to follow up.

Includes interests not fully covered in interview, uses company motto.

Thank You for Referral

222 Phantom Way
Ghost Town, CA 92126
(444) 123-1231
Dorcaswraith@msn.com

October 31, 20XX

Ms. Susan Specter
Spirit Products, Inc.
333 Incorporeal Circle
Apparition, CA 92137

RE: Referral to Paula Geist

Dear Ms. Specter:

Your help with my job search has been out of this world! Thank you for all of your advice. Most specifically, thank you for referring me to Paula Geist at Geist, Deeman, and Hant.

I have left several voice-mail messages for Ms. Geist this week. Yesterday, her assistant informed me that Ms. Geist returned from a business trip three days ago, so I expect to hear from her soon.

I have enclosed a copy of my resume for your perusal. A million thanks in advance if you think of anyone else I should call. I hope you know how much I appreciate all of your kind assistance.

With sincerest gratitude,

Dorcas Wraith

Dorcas Wraith

Enclosure: Resume

If Geist doesn't call Wraith, Specter may follow up, asking that Geist do so. Note subtle suggestion that Specter continue to refer Wraith to other potential employers.

Acceptance Letter

Brooke Lancaster
34567 Unity Square
Troy, MI 48098

February 15, 20XX

Drew McCallister
Sales and Marketing
Walters and Sons Construction Firm
5577 Fairview Drive
Grand Rapids, MI 49503

> Lancaster writes more than an acceptance letter: He incorporates his understanding of conditions offered. While not legally binding, if a dispute occurs, Lancaster at least has some paperwork to confirm his understanding of the offer.

Dear Mr. McCallister:

I am pleased to accept your offer for the position of Assistant Supervisor of Sales and Marketing for Walters and Sons Construction at a starting salary of $3,500 per month, plus reimbursement for relocation costs up to a maximum of $12,000. As we discussed, I will receive the standard benefits package, which includes health coverage and retirement contributions.

I am looking forward to extending my ideas and expertise into the sales and marketing division of your company. My extensive background in sales and marketing will allow me to get started immediately with minimal training. Within three weeks, as we predicted, I should know the company well enough to relieve you and Maria Espinoza of the bulk of the marketing and sales responsibilities so you can focus more intently on the regional expansion of Walters and Sons Construction.

As you are aware, I am currently securing my living situation to relocate to Grand Rapids. I expect to conclude this endeavor by mid-March, in which case I will be able to begin working by March 28, 20XX. If this arrangement is inconvenient or you would like to present another option, please let me know. I will contact you by March 2 to cement final arrangements.

I am excited to join your team and thank you for the opportunity to participate in the growth and dynamism of Walters and Sons Construction.

Thankfully yours,

Brooke Lancaster

(718) 692-7777

Rejection Letter

Trevor Taylor
3456 Griffin Place #7
Rogers, AR 72757

January 7, 20XX

Grant Focault
Human Resource Department
GreenTree Corporation
Rupert, ID 83350

Note the grace with which Taylor turns down a job. Focault may be promoted to an even bigger newspaper and offer Taylor an even better job someday.

Dear Mr. Focault:

I would like to extend my thanks to you for offering me the position as **Features Editor** for the *Idaho Daily Times*. I feel fortunate to have had the opportunity to discuss this position with you.

I was quite impressed by you and your team at the paper. However, since we last talked, I have accepted another editorial position for a publisher in my area. Because of the location and my inability to relocate, I feel this position better suits my present needs.

Again, the opportunity to learn about your newspaper and its operations has been an enlightening experience. I am confident that your success will extend into future endeavors, and I am sorry that I cannot join your team at this time.

Best Regards,

Trevor Taylor

Recommendation Letter

March 15, 20XX   **Re: Higher Education Faculty**

To Whom It May Concern:

Susan Reardon has been a valued associate and friend for over fifteen years. During that time I employed her as an editorial/research supervisor for two long periods. Currently she is working with me as a writer/consultant for a book I plan to publish in the next year.

I first met Susan when she was a senior in high school. Even then I considered her editorial skills to be superior in the field; she proved an invaluable resource for research and editorial knowledge. Since then, she has developed an enormous range of interests and talents, from calculus to art history, that can bring true diversity to her teaching objectives and perspective.

Susan has tremendous skills in writing and communication which can only help in reaching her students' interest. Her editorial work is consistently reliable, independent, and polished, attesting to her professionalism and dedication. In the past year she has undertaken a variety of projects which show talent, range, and creativity. These projects include an effort to combine her analytic and communicative skills by developing a series of children's mathematics books.

Susan possesses a genuine commitment to mathematics education encompassing the needs of elementary-age students, to whom her manuscript is targeted, as well as encompassing the needs of college students whom she has taught. In addition, she is passionate about bringing mathematics to those who are under-represented by the traditional profile of mathematicians. Her own educational experiences fostered a concern for the shortage of women and minorities in mathematics. Her passion for mathematics and commitment to teaching, combined with her superior communication skills and professionalism, make her well-suited to work toward the goals of the community college system as she is eager to do.

Susan is contagiously enthusiastic about her field and well-prepared to introduce new students to mathematical concepts with innovative and flexible teaching approaches. Susan will be an asset to any mathematics department. Please feel free to call me if you have any questions.

Sincerely,

Michele-Ann Lawrence

Michele-Ann Lawrence
(121) 672-1111

This letter is placed in Reardon's credentials file at her university career center.

Part VI
The Part of Tens

The 5th Wave   By Rich Tennant

ALTHOUGH EX-PAPERBOY MITCH WROTE A GOOD COVER LETTER, HE HAD TO WORK ON HOW HE PRESENTED THEM

In this part . . .

No self-respecting *For Dummies* book is complete without The Part of Tens. This part sums up ten tips (more or less, who's counting?) for just about everything to help your job search succeed — working with recruiters, answering job ads, avoiding the salary question, handling negative references, and creating letters that even a computer can love. Read through this information to get you that last mile to the all-important job interview.

Chapter 16

Ten Tips for Working with Recruiters

*E*xecutive recruiting is a business with more than its share of fast-talking salespeople — salespeople who can sell you right into the best job of your life.

A specialist in executive recruiting is called an *executive recruiter, executive search consultant, technical recruiter* (if recruiting for technical jobs), and by that colorful term *headhunter.* Recruiters plying their profession on the Internet are sometimes called *e-recruiters* or *e-cruiters.*

By any name, the recruiter is a third-party professional in the pay of employers. (In-house recruiters, who are human resources department employees of the hiring company, are not considered third-party recruiters.) The recruiter is on a mission to find top-of-the-line employees and is not — hear this! — *not* working for you, the job seeker. No matter what a recruiter assures you, the recruiter's loyalty is to the source of business, the employer.

In slow job markets, recruiters prefer that you not bug them, especially by telephone — send in your resume and wait. In fast job markets, you can use e-mail to follow up a bit more often, especially if you can identify other good candidates (who are not competitive with you, of course). The old law of supply and demand is at work — as one recruiter of high-tech talent comments: "I wouldn't recruit at a funeral. But I would at a wedding." Having said that, this chapter takes you on a whirlwind tour of the world of recruiters and what they can do for you.

Court Royalty Makers

Executive recruiters can change your life. If they spot your talents and bring you into the spotlight of a client's attention, you can be paired up with some of the best jobs in your career. Make a pile of money, be showered with stock options — all things are possible with executive recruiters.

How do you attract recruiters?

Running ahead of the crowd — doing excellent work and being professionally visible for it — is the obvious place to start. You'll probably hear from headhunters without ever initiating a contact. Get noticed, and they'll find you.

But you can select outstanding recruiters and begin building a relationship using techniques described in numerous guides, such as *Kennedy's Pocket Guide to Working With Executive Recruiters* (Kennedy Information).

When you make the first contact, send your resume with a RedHot cover letter that attracts the eye of the recruiter or the recruiter's researcher. If you're a strong candidate, you'll be categorized in a database by industry, specialty, location, and compensation level, kept on ice until a suitable job opening occurs, and then you'll be contacted — but probably not before then.

Third-party recruiters

How can you tell the difference between an executive recruiter, an employment agency, a personnel service, or other recruiting organization? With great difficulty. The lines of distinction have become blurred.

Virtually all recruiting organizations reach out with advertising (both print and online), conduct research to find candidates, and maintain electronic databases of talented individuals. The exception: Retained recruiters say they don't advertise.

The main thing to remember is don't pay a third-party recruiter to find you a job. That's not how it should work.

How can you find recruiters? The best directory in print is *The Directory of Executive Recruiters*, an annual publication of Kennedy Information (www.kennedyinfo.com).

If you're cyber-seeking, you'll find plenty of recruiters online. Use Web search engines, such as Direct Hit (www.directhit.com) and Google (www.google.com) to identify recruiter sites. Additionally, most major career hubs have content relating to recruiters.

The largest association of recruiters, executive search firms, employment agencies, and other employment professionals is Recruiters Online Network (www.ipa.com). Look for specialists in your career field. Most are pay-for-performance firms.

The most prominent retainer executive search firms belong to the Association of Executive Search Consultants (www.aesc.org).

When a recruiter calls you at work, arrange an appointment to call back on your own time. Do not say that you aren't interested. Even if you genuinely do not consider yourself on the market, you're always open to an exceptional opportunity — and the job you love may disappear tomorrow. Always talk. If the job isn't for you, offer to suggest other candidates — doing so keeps your lines open for the future.

Generally, recruiters are not interested in anyone earning less than $75,000 a year. More typically, they seek out those earning $100,000 and up, like a $250,000-a-year-job as a marketing VP. Because recruiters are paid high fees to pirate employees in competitive companies, only in shortage labor markets are they interested in spending time with new college graduates. Joblessness is no longer a stigma, so recruiters will now consider the unemployed as well as employed individuals — but they'd still rather entice you from a competitor (*somebody else wants you so you must be good* is the thought).

What about all the community and charity work that once was razzle-dazzle on a resume? Unfortunately, in this materialistic society, good works don't count for much when a headhunter calls.

With this backdrop on the topic of executive recruiters, try these ten tips for working with people who can raise you to the aristocracy of American business.

Understand the Financial Motives of Third-Party Recruiters

Of considerable importance is whether the basic type of recruiting firm you are dealing with is on contingency or retainer. Both handle high-end people, although the retainer is better known for finding major corporate chieftains.

A *pay-for-performance*, or *contingency*, recruiting firm is paid only if its candidate is hired. No play, no pay. Contingency recruiters can be extremely useful in opening employers' doors. They push hard for their recruits and can circulate your resume to more than one company at the same time.

By contrast, like a retained legal firm, a *retainer* recruiting firm is paid merely to search for candidates for a job opening. The firm is paid an agreed-upon fee regardless of how many candidates they produce or whether their candidates are hired.

Both contingency and retainer firms offer pros and cons for you.

In the first third of your career, and sometimes later, a contingency firm may create more action for you. Contingency recruiters can offer you advocacy, quick action, and wide exposure to many employers. The contingency employer pushes hard for his or her team — you and perhaps one or two others. You won't have to wait for Company A to make a decision before being submitted to Company B. This method is like an auction — the employer who hires first wins you as a prize.

Retainer firms will not recruit from one client to fill a position at another client for at least two years. Employees of these client companies are off-limits. If you work for a client company, no matter how perfect the job at another company, the retained recruiter will not call your name. To do so would be unethical, and the firm would lose future business.

Further, a retained firm can slow down a job move because the firm only shows you one job opening at a time. Recruiting for Company A must be concluded before you are presented to Company B. If you are unemployed, you risk being presented for a *lesser job opening*. Why? Suppose a retained firm has an important client that every now and then has a marginal job to fill: one that pays a little less or is likely to sunset in a year or two or maybe is located in western Siberia. The recruiter's thinking is, "Why 'waste' a blue-chip employed candidate on a lesser position?" The unemployed candidate may be desperate enough to accept a position of lesser promise.

Nevertheless, when you begin to move up, recruitment dynamics change. Retained recruiters are likely to offer a golden bridge to your future. Because retained recruiters are paid win, lose, or draw, they do not carry a "price tag," as top-flight New York executive recruiter John Lucht explains in his excellent book, *Rites of Passage at $100,000+* (Viceroy/Holt).

If you're moving up but are not quite ready for the retained recruiter level, one way you can protect yourself in an era of declining recruitment prices brought about by technology (company resume databases, for instance) is to personally submit your resume with a cover letter bodyguard to every company where you may like to work. Ask the company to keep your resume on file or in the database for future openings and note that you'll keep it updated periodically.

Save your money

Phony enterprises, masquerading as legitimate executive search firms, scam the unwary. Never pay a "registration fee" or other advance fee to one who claims to be an executive recruiter.

Legitimate recruiters are paid by the client organization for which they are conducting a search. They *never* charge the job seeker.

Give recruiters — both contingency and retained — a list of your favorite companies where your resume is on file. Contingency recruiters will not submit you to these off-limits companies, because they will not earn a fee by doing so — the company already knows about you. Retained recruiters, who have nothing to lose, very well may recommend you, just as they would recommend an outstanding internal candidate.

When dealing with contingency recruiters, insist that your resume is never to be submitted to any employer without your specific permission. The reason for this is that you come with a price tag that can be considerable — say, $30,000 or more. As companies cut costs across the board, another candidate may be found in their database — or on the Internet — for a lot less money. You then are priced out of the running, and you'll probably never know why.

Match Your Background to the Recruiter's Specialty

Recruiters specialize. Find out which firms recruit in your career area. Most recruiter directories list specialties. Additionally, talk to others in your industry to ask if they've ever been contacted and get the names of specific recruiters to whom you can send your cover letter and resume. Sending your self-marketing materials to a tax lawyer recruiter when you're a marketer wastes everyone's time.

Ask Recruiters for Position's Job Description

Ring, ring! A recruiter is on the telephone saying that you sound like a candidate for a terrific opportunity. If you currently have a good job that you're reasonably happy with, play it safe. Make sure that a better job is available before you send your resume.

When a recruiter hands your resume and cover letter to a client, the general assumption may be that you are available. Consequently, if your resume is sent to too many businesses, this assumption could become widespread. Overexposing your resume in this manner can have serious consequences, especially if your resume gets back to your employer, who may not be amused by your itchiness.

Make sure that a recruiting firm asking you for personal information (as in willingness to move, salary, and so on) has a specific job in mind. Find out such details as information about the hiring company, the responsibilities of the position, its place in the company organization, and the relationship between the recruiter and the company. Ask for the position's job description. (You may not get one, but ask! You need the description to devise a compatible cover letter and resume.)

If possible, get these details in writing. If the recruiter is unwilling to give this information, you may want to end the conversation right then and there.

Answer All Questions Honestly

You and the recruiter share this one objective: to avoid a bad fit. Both of you have much to lose by mispackaging your qualifications. If the recruiter regularly scouts employees for a given company, the recruiter is likely to know if the new position is one that could blow up in your face. You're going to lay out your goals, ambitions, heart's desires, and other private matters; in return, grill the recruiter to find out what you want to know.

Write Computer-Friendly Cover Letters and Resumes

Increasingly, cover letters and resumes are sent to recruiters by e-mail. Computer viruses are becoming ho-hum — another week, another virus. Recruiters are wary of opening attachments from strangers. So unless you're told to send one or both as an attachment, send your cover letter and resume in plain text (ASCII). The recruiter's candidate tracking system will categorize your materials automatically and place them in a database.

In addition to a text version, you can attach your letter and resume in two documents as an option.

When you do send your letter and resume on paper, make sure that a computer can scan it. If you don't know how to prepare your materials for document imaging technology, details are given on the Resumix Web site (www.resumix.com). The main things to remember are to use clean, crisp printing on white paper and to avoid fancy graphics like underlining, italics, shadows, and design boxes. Bold and capital letters are fine.

Be Concise and Call-Free

Help a recruiter save time and improve your chances of being remembered. Keep your cover letter on track without too many baggage facts and words.

An example of excess would be to reprise the industry trends about an industry in which the recruiter specializes.

What about telephone calls? Calling with the old dodge, "Did you get my resume?" is discouraged by most recruiters. Some get hundreds of resumes a week, and the workload is crushing. Almost all recruiters cringe at the monthly telephone call that asks: "Got anything for me yet?" You'll be put in the overeager, near-miss file. (Remember, recruiters are paid to find the best people.)

Once you've been able to build a relationship with recruiters, update your resume periodically and send it along with a cover note: "Knowing you like to keep your database fresh, here's my most recent resume. My current compensation is a base of $82,000 plus a bonus paid two months ago of $23,500. I continue to be interested in relocating to the Southeastern seaboard."

Willing to Relocate? Say So

This tip may seem pretty basic, but emphasizing your geographical flexibility helps — if you mean it. If you decide you really don't want to live in Upper Icebox, find another reason to turn down the job a recruiter has just spent three weeks trying to make happen for you.

Reveal Your Salary History

Unlike your general strategy to duck salary history and requirements until you've been offered a job, be candid with bona fide executive recruiters — and if you are asked to send in tax statement proof of your earnings, say clearly that you expect the earnings history to be kept confidential between the recruiter and the employer.

Like Middle East peace, salary is always a difficult subject to negotiate. Suppose the recruiter asks that you send a marketing package, including your salary history or requirements.

With history, state the cash compensation as a separate item, adding your benefit package as a second figure. Recruiters are too sophisticated to buy the "total compensation" statement in which you combine your salary, bonus, benefits, anticipated salary, and anything else you can think of to swell the figure.

As for salary requirements, if you avoid giving any figure at all when requested in your cover letter, you probably won't be considered by the recruiter. (This probability is not true when you are dealing directly with employers.) Giving a single figure can make you look inflexible. By stating a range of salary expectations, you can give the recruiter a good gauge of your market value, while allowing room to negotiate. See Chapter 18 for more about the salary issue.

Keep a Record of All Contacts with Recruiters

Keep copies of all written correspondence and telephone conversations with recruiters. You never know when you'll need to have a record of the negotiations that took place.

Don't Depend on Recruiters for Your Job Search

This fact can't be emphasized enough: *A recruiter's responsibility is to the employer, not to you.* A recruiter is not in business to find you a job, but, rather, to find new employees for client companies.

Once you submit your resume to a recruiter, do not make independent contacts with the client without the recruiter's knowledge. Not only will this tactic probably backfire on the particular job, but it may also cause you to be blacklisted by the recruiting firm in the long run.

Once you submit your resume to a recruiter, do not make independent contact with the recruiter's client on the job the recruiter has told you about. Not only will this tactic probably backfire on the particular job, but it may also cause you to be blacklisted by the recruiting firm in the long run.

Despite their best efforts to protect your confidential status, fumbles by recruiting organizations sometimes occur. A good predefense: Tell your managers that recruiters often contact you although you're not looking.

Once a recruiter has helped you to take a new position, stay in touch. Throw the recruiter some business if you can. Refer good candidates. E-mail is a wonderful way to cultivate the right headhunters — a wise investment.

Chapter 17

Ten Hints for Answering Job Ads

In This Chapter

▶ Sleuthing the Internet and other resources

▶ Reflecting the ad in your cover letter

▶ Opening the box on blind ads

*T*oday's recruitment ads are a gold mine of information about jobs *immediately available.*

Job ads appear on the Internet, as well as in newspapers and professional trade journals. Employers are rushing online to post jobs on their own sites, on professional organization sites, and on commercial career sites.

Do cover letters relate in the same way to printed advertisements and online job postings? Most of the time, yes.

Always enclose a cover letter when you answer a printed job advertisement. Usually enclose a cover letter when you answer an online job posting, but read the instructions on the posting. Sometimes the job posting says "resumes only" or "no cover letter required." Or you'll merely be asked to fill in an online job application form. Unless the instructions ask you to omit a cover letter, send the best one you can write. On the Internet, the world is your competition.

Even if you do not find a job in the help-wanted ads so picture perfect you could frame it, looking over these ads can help you determine the characteristics of the current job market so that you get fresh ammunition for the cover letters you do write.

Repeated advertising for applicants with certain technical experience indicates the current level of training that's in demand. Many companies that advertise are expanding — if they ask for environmental engineers, they may also want mechanical engineers and administrative assistants. You can also determine which professions are searching for applicants from advertisements. For example, if you're a secretary and you find ten openings for legal secretaries and only two for medical secretaries, you may want to learn more about legal terminology before you write your cover letters.

Take these hints to heart as you respond to recruitment advertising.

Let Your Letter Reflect the Ad's Keywords or Skill Phrases

For an office position, an employer may require knowledge of *word processing*, and even specific programs like Microsoft Word or WordPerfect. Engineers may need experience with certain *computer-aided drafting and design software.* When an advertisement mentions specific qualifications — and you have them — showcase the qualifications in your letter. If the ad mentions general keywords such as *professional* or *creative,* describe yourself and your record with these exact terms.

Mine the Ad for Information about the Employer

Perhaps you hadn't thought of job ads in this way, but an advertisement acts as the employer's cover letter. Advertisements accentuate the positive, attracting attention with strong points while ignoring potential weaknesses.

Checking the ad itself is revealing. The following tips do not apply to Internet ads, but are important for printed ads.

- ✔ Is the ad large? This company may be flush with money and pay its people well — or it may be such a poor place to work that high turnover requires constant recruiting.

- ✔ Is the ad small? Maybe the firm is new and has a low advertising budget, in which case you could get a jump on the competition by getting in early. Or, if the company is small but undergoing expansion, maybe you should respond to the contact named in the ad, but at the same time, directly contact the hiring manager for whom you would work.

- ✔ A blind ad could indicate that a huge response is expected or that a senior-level position is about to open up.

Now that the Internet has made communication within a community much easier, join a Net discussion group and ask if any members have heard of the company and what they can tell you about it. Soon you'll have strong clues about which is the most powerful information to put in your cover letter.

Refer to the Advertisement Early

Telling the employer how you learned of an opening is always good. Doing so immediately establishes that you are applying for a position the company intends to fill in the near future. A convenient place to put this information is to the right of the inside address in a "RE[garding]" statement.

Customize Your Letter for Each Employer

You are responding to a particular ad for a particular job opening, so tailor your letter to the requirements the employer lists. A customized letter has a much higher chance of a positive response.

Use a Linear Format When You're a Good Match

If you possess a substantial number of the qualifications the ad requests, show those qualifications line by line. This concept is illustrated in a number of Chapter 14's model cover letters.

Use a Paragraph Format When You're a Marginal Match

Organize your letter in the literary, or paragraph, format if you lack a few qualifications or experience pertinent to the job. Paragraphing allows you to emphasize your strengths at the beginning of paragraphs, sending readers on an archaeological dig to find your weaknesses buried deep inside the text — if they can find them at all. An advertisement lists qualifications for the ideal candidate, but the ideal candidate is not always available.

Address Your Letter to a Specific Individual

Dear Somebody beats *Dear Nobody*. When the advertisement lists no name, call and scout it out. You may need to be resourceful, as companies are often closemouthed. Be persistent. Chapter 5 has some tips for tracking down hard-to-find names.

Be Resourceful in Replying to Blind Ads

Play detective to find out the employer's name when you respond to a blind recruitment ad with no clue as to the employer's identity.

- ✔ For recruitment ads that direct you to send a response to a U.S. post office box, you should be able to find out the name of the box holder (see Chapter 5). You can forget about it if the box is at a newspaper or trade journal.

- ✔ If you know only the street address, you can use a reverse directory (library copy) or one of the Internet telephone directory resources. If all else fails, drive by. Then call the company and say, "The word's out that you're looking for a _____. Who should I talk to about that?" Get the name and write a cover letter to go with your resume.

- ✔ Don't waste time trying to discover an advertiser's identity in a blind ad posted on a commercial Internet site such as JobOptions or Monster.com. The commercial services use confidential logs to protect the advertiser's preference for anonymity.

Focus on Experience Directly Related to the Job

Just as you would in any RedHot cover letter, shine a spotlight on just the benefits you have that the employer wants. No extras.

Mail Your Letters on Sunday or Monday

Some advisers suggest that your letter gets more attention if you wait until the initial flood of replies has subsided before responding to an advertisement. They may be right. But my advice is to move on a job you want right away. Get a jump on the competition. Get something out the same day you see the ad, or, at the latest, the next day.

Chapter 18

Ten Tips for Handling the Salary Issue

*W*hen you pick up a job ad that asks for your salary history and/or your salary requirements, you probably know that the advertiser is fishing for advance intelligence:

✔ Are you too experienced and rich for their budget — or too low level and inexperienced to handle the position?

✔ Will you be happy with the pay offered, or will it take more hard cash to bring you aboard? (How cheap can they get you?)

No matter why employers want to know your monetary information, don't blurt out private data in your cover letter. You may start the bidding too high or too low and be screened out before the interview. Equally to your disadvantage, divulging your pricing data prematurely seriously undermines your ability to get your best pay. It's like letting your opponent see your cards in a poker game. As the old Chinese proverb says: *To guess is cheap. To guess wrong is expensive.*

Here are some tips for dealing with up-front salary requests. This advice could enlarge your annual paycheck by thousands of dollars. You are selling a part of your life to an employer, and you deserve to make all that you're qualified to earn.

Don't Give Away Salary Issues in Your Cover Letter

If you don't "follow orders" in a job ad and spill your earnings record and expectations in your cover letter or screening telephone interview, what happens? Are you put in the don't-call stack of applicants because you were "disobedient"?

Some employers do disqualify applicants for failing to provide private financial information. That's the risk you take to gain a bigger compensation reward. (See Chapter 1.)

But most employers you'd like to work for — because they've got a brain not of the dinosaur variety — don't discard your cover letter and resume if you look good enough to interview. If your marketing materials are outstanding, leaving off the salary information is unlikely to screen you out of good places to work.

When you receive a premature request to disclose how much you've been earning and how much you expect to earn, stall the salary talk until the interview when you get a job offer. At the earliest, stall the salary talk until you've had a chance to make them want you. (See my book, *Job Interviews For Dummies*, 2nd Edition.)

Until you have an offer, the employer holds all the cards. Once you have an offer, you know you have something the employer wants, and the dynamics change. You become equals negotiating a business proposition.

Listing salary information in your cover letter weakens your bargaining position. A salary too low devalues your abilities; a salary too high looks like you're too big for the company. Both scenarios leave you out of luck.

Tell Recruiters Your Salary Information

The only time you should answer a salary question before you're offered a job is when asked by third-party employment specialists — executive or technical recruiters and employment consultants, for instance. These professionals are paid for their time, just like lawyers and physicians. They are too busy to waste precious hours with you if you don't make recommending you to clients easy for them.

Don't Inflate Your Salary History

Suppose that despite my strong urging to resist revealing your salary history in your cover letter, you decide you must do so. Tell it like it was — neither inflating nor deflating your previous income. Why not fudge a little? Employers making background checks increasingly use credit reports that reveal your past salary.

In writing about salary issues, remember three broad areas of compensation:

> ✔ **Base pay:** The basic specified salary or hourly wage.

> ✔ **Variable pay:** This is the bonus concept — the pay for performance and meeting goals. It is also overtime pay for hourly work. Although increases in base pay have been modest, and actually slowing down, variable pay has shot up because employers want to lure the best workers without locking in higher fixed costs that will trouble them in a downturn.

> America faces the tightest labor market in a generation. These conditions have spawned the use of variables such as signing bonuses, new cars, and the wildly popular stock options, which employees hope will make them rich.

> Stock options are without doubt the perk of choice. A Hewitt Associates study says that some 70 percent of companies offer stock options and bonuses. Looking at the other side of the measurement, a Watson Wyatt Worldwide study shows that almost 19 percent of employees are eligible for stock option grants.

> ✔ **Indirect pay:** This type of pay used to be called employee fringe benefits: vacations, holiday retirement funds, company lunchrooms, and so on. It often accounts for one-third of a total compensation package, sometimes more.

Show compensation in modules. List base pay and variable pay in one figure; give another figure for indirect pay; and then add the figures together for the total compensation package.

What to Do If You Have to Spill the Beans Early

Even if you have to tell, you don't have to be specific. State your figures in wide ranges so that you're not excluded from consideration for positions for which you are qualified.

Include figures slightly above and below the market value for the position to cover all your bases. (See the section "Find Out Your Market Value," later in this chapter.)

Analyze Requests for Proof of Salary

You thought the fact that your prospective employer asked what you're currently making was enough, but what do you do about requests for *proof* — asking that you enclose a copy of your W-2 form in your application?

 An employer can legally ask for your W-2 form. That's the only thing career insiders agree on. Proponents insist that the employer — especially those who hire sales personnel working on commission — is entitled to see your proof of earnings. Others, including myself, see such requests as an invasion of privacy and a presumption that you are a liar.

At the cover letter stage, as I've said, I can't imagine you would want to release your earnings information, especially in response to a blind box ad. Negotiation whiz Jack Chapman put it well in his book, *Negotiating Your Salary: How to Make $1000 a Minute* (Ten Speed Press; $11.95). Write something like the following in your cover letter:

> *I understand you've requested a salary history; I'm paid roughly the market-value of a (job title) with (#) years' experience, and while I'm not willing to publish my compensation package, I'd be happy to discuss it with you during an interview.*

(If the employer calls to say no interview until you "follow instructions" and cough up your salary history, ask for a mutual exchange: *I'll show you mine if you show me yours!* — just kidding.)

The exception to deflecting a too-early request for earnings history is when it comes from a recruiter (see Chapter 16). But third-party recruiters should be denied tax papers, partly because there's lots of turnover in recruiting offices. Documents that include your social security number and other private facts are proprietary information; just tell a recruiter that you'll be glad to show proof of income directly to an employer who is serious about making you an offer.

My conclusion: Focus your efforts on employers who trust you more, meaning those who don't request your W-2.

Write Lines that Skirt the Salary Issue

Here are some suggestions to dodge the salary issue until you're in the interview.

Remember, these statements and others like them won't advance you to the candidate pool unless your cover letter and resume are superb. Your self-marketing package must establish you as a RedHot candidate.

- ✔ *What I've learned so far about the position suggests that it really fits me, so if you pay a fair market value, I don't foresee any problems with salary. Why don't we arrange an interview, and we can discuss salary then?*

- ✔ *Assuming that your position is appropriately compensated, we'll surely be able to agree on a figure.*

- ✔ *I'll be happy to discuss my salary information when we meet to review my skills and your needs.*

- ✔ *Once we discuss some of the successes I've achieved in handling this sort of position, there should be no problem. All I require is a fair market value for the position, and I'm sure that you pay that, so let's meet to discuss the position; salary will take care of itself later.*

- ✔ *When we've had a chance to discuss what I can contribute to your position, then I'm sure that we'll be able to work out appropriate compensation that we both feel good about.*

- ✔ *After we've taken a look at how closely my skills and experience fit your needs, I'll be glad to provide complete salary information.*

- ✔ *You should know that my total compensation has ranged between ($) and ($) in recent years.*

- ✔ *If your compensation is based on performance, we'll find agreement easy when you see the benefits I bring to the job.*

- ✔ *Salary history is a personal matter, as I'm sure you understand. I'd like to speak about it in person. I can do that during our interview.*

- ✔ *Back in 1996, I started in the industry as a cashier earning minimum wage. Now I'm a company director, and I'm very proud of that growth.*

- ✔ *I'm always willing to interact with prospective employers to work out compensation questions.*

When to Say Nothing at All about Salary

If you are writing to a line manager to whom you would report, a good strategy is to say nothing at all about money, even if you were asked to do so. The hiring manager is interested in solving the job vacancy problem, while the human resources manager is interested in fulfilling instructions to recruit candidates within a specific budget range.

Balance Your Impression

If the job ad requires salary information and you use one of the lines suggested earlier in this chapter to ignore the demand, you'll come across as a savvy negotiator. That perception could be intimidating to someone who is a poor negotiator. Try to incorporate in your letter information suggesting you are also flexible and work well with people. *(When I was an editor at IDG Books, I enjoyed working with authors in situations that accommodated their needs.)*

Find Out Your Market Value

Although you really don't want to get into the topic before your job interview, you should know what's the going rate for people in your industry with skills similar to yours who are doing virtually the same job as you.

Look online at such Web sites as JobStar (jobstar.org), which lists hundreds of salary studies, and at sites maintained by professional organizations and staffing companies. Also read recruitment ads.

Some career advisers suggest networking to get salary data. Good luck. People tend to treat their earnings and your request like a national security issue about which you don't have a high enough clearance to be asking.

Don't Be Cavalier about Money

Despite all the media hoopla about Silicon Valley elite employees who expect perks like "smart-dress" allowances and free flying lessons, as well as a chance to get their "two commas" ($1,000,000) and retirement at 40, your cover letter is the absolute worst place to state your gimme-list. Keep it simple: A red company convertible every two years will do nicely. (Don't you wish?)

Chapter 19

Ten Burned-Out Words and Phrases

. . . .

In This Chapter

▶ Avoiding all-too-familiar phrases

▶ Using words that turn your letter into a hot property

. . . .

*O*ut of the frying pan and into the fire. When it rains, it pours. The acid test. Eyeball it (as a verb). Feedback. Hands-on. Meaningful. Point in time. Richly deserved. State of the art. Once these phrases had significance, but they've been penalized for their popularity. Now these tired words need a nap. Potential employers will probably yawn if you succumb to Burned-Out phrases like these:

✔ **I am very interested in —**

This phrase is usually followed by a mention of your occupation or career field — either the one you're in or the one you want to be in. If you weren't interested, you wouldn't be writing in the first place. Let this phrase rest in peace.

✔ **I am forwarding the enclosed resume for your consideration —**

Why else would you send a resume? To light a fire to keep out the winter cold?

✔ **I feel that I have —**

Feelings. Nice song — no business meaning. Nothing more than feelings.

✔ **I am energetic.**

Who would say "I am lethargic"? If you make this kind of statement, don't let the statement stand alone — back it up with details.

✔ **Please find the enclosed resume . . .**

Is the resume lost? Finding your enclosed resume is not quite like searching for the Lost City of the Incas. Your resume is right there in the same envelope you sent the cover letter in. Or is it? You did remember to *enclose* the resume, didn't you?

- **Salary requirements are negotiable.**

  Avoid using this phrase as a stand-alone statement. When you're asked to reveal your salary requirements, try to avoid doing so, but add the richness of detail described in Chapter 18.

- **I am responding to your advertisement.**

  Nothing is really wrong with this line, except that it has tire tracks all over it. This phrase comes complete with all the excitement of watching grass grow. Use the line if you must, but put as much effort as you can into coming up with something fresher.

- **I look forward to hearing from you.**

  Why do you assume the hiring authority will contact you? You may end up looking forward for a long time. Hang onto control — you make the follow-up contact.

- **Please accept the enclosed resume.**

  What does this phrase mean — please accept the resume and make a paper airplane out of it, file it away, read it, burn it, what? Do you expect your resume to be marked "Return to sender"?

- **Utilize my expertise in —**

  Don't just claim to have proficiency in a particular subject. *Prove* your expertise. Show your accomplishments. Explain what you did.

Ten overweight clichés

First priority

Priority says the same thing.

Go ahead and take action

Take action spells out your meaning.

Honest truth

Truth is enough.

Mixed together

Mixed will do.

Open up

Open is plenty.

Past history

History suffices.

Point in time

Time covers the thought.

Reason why

Reason explains fully.

Refer back to

Refer to handles the question.

This particular job

This job is all you need.

Are you a glutton for more? Eyeball 3,300 clichés on an amusing site: the Cliché finder (westegg.com/cliche).

Chapter 20

Ten Hot Tips from Hiring Pros

- -

In This Chapter

▶ Employment Management Association members share their pet peeves, weird
experiences, and best cover letter hints

- -

*T*his information-active book closes with comments by ten people who
professionally review cover letters and resumes before deciding if they
should be passed on to hiring managers.

These outstanding human resource (HR) professionals are members of the
Employment Management Association (`www.shrm.org/ema`), an arm of the
Society for Human Resource Management (`www.shrm.org`). Both groups are
topflight membership, nonprofit organizations in the employment industry.

Get ready to learn, be surprised, and maybe smile. Here's what the pros have
to say.

High Tech Requires More Than Technical Skills

Misspelled or poorly written letters: In the high-tech arena, there is no excuse
for errors in spelling and grammar. These errors only show that the individual does not know the software's capability to check spelling and grammar,
and we are not interested in technically inept applicants. Technology is our
business.

Gimmicks: Depending on the position applied for and the gimmick itself, gimmicks are sometimes helpful and a good indication of the person's creativity,
innovation, and interest. I once hired a graphics illustrator who submitted his
resume in the form of a short storybook. He was a talented, witty artist who
turned out to be an excellent addition to our publishing group.

Too much material: Unfortunately, the higher the education, the more excessive the number of attachments. Ph.D.s, for some reason, think they have to attach every article they have had printed. A simple listing of the articles would tell the reviewer if the articles are pertinent to the job opening.

Cynthia Miner, Manager, HR
Lockheed Martin Management & Data Systems
Employment Management Association Area Vice President
Goodyear, Arizona

When Gimmicks Are Way Too Far Out

I look for brief, concise information in a cover letter that gives me insight into the individual that I might not otherwise glean from their resume. The operative words are "brief and concise." I don't want to or have the time to read a book when reviewing numerous resume responses from an ad, a job fair, the Internet, or another source.

However, one cover letter I received several years ago remains in my file as the longest and most unusual I have seen. It is a five-page script — a conversation — between the applicant and an alien. It seems the applicant was "transported" off the highway late one night into an alien spaceship as the applicant was headed to another city for a series of interviews. As the conversation unfolds, some of the applicant's attributes are described, as well as recent accomplishments in his technical field of expertise. (Though little information was revealed that was not included in his resume, other than a vivid imagination.)

I have to admit that I took the time to read this one. However, professionalism, concise information, and no gimmicks are high on the list for effective cover letters. We did not pursue the applicant.

Joe Sommers, Managing Director
HRAlliance, LLC
Employment Management Association Vice President at Large
Plano, Texas

Sometimes Pictures Are Not Worth 1,000 Words

In the 25 years I have worked in human resources, I have seen some strange cover letters and resumes. But the most unusual was an 8 x 10-inch glossy photo with "To Barbara" written in the upper-left corner and "Best wishes, Tony" in the bottom right.

This was the entire cover letter — just the photo. There was a resume attached but, trust me, the sender did not get interviewed!

Recruiters don't want pictures for lots of reasons, including the fact that they're totally inappropriate. No applicant should provide the interviewer with any reason to reject them before they get the interview. An applicant who sends a photo stands a very good chance of never hearing from that organization again.

Barbara A. Mitchell, Principal
The Millennium Group International
Employment Management Association President
Vienna, Virginia

Capitalization and Complete Contact Info Count

Word capitalization abuse sets my teeth chattering. I receive many e-mails with some words capitalized and others (including proper names, beginning of sentences) not capitalized — with no pattern. And I have received e-mails with no capitalization whatsoever. As a recruiter, I expect applicants to do a professional job of writing and submitting e-mails using proper punctuation, spelling, and grammar.

Another problem: Receiving multiple e-mails, cover letters, and resumes without adequate contact information. We have many offices, and it's irritating when candidates only give a "Yahoo" address.

Karen Bloom, Principal
Bloom, Gross & Associates, Inc.
Employment Management Association Area Vice President
Chicago, Illinois

Tell Me If You'll Really Relocate

With Web searching so easy now, I appreciate it if applicants responding to a job posting outside their state specify in the cover letter if they seriously wish to relocate. I don't like wasting time if they don't at least acknowledge the geographic distance and pass on their intentions.

Lynn S. Nemser, SPHR, President
Partners in Performance Inc.
Employment Management Association Vice President at Large
Pittsburgh, Pennsylvania

Don't Get Too Personal with Me, Bub

Candidates sometimes include personal details such as clubs or hobbies to show the type of person they are or how well rounded they are. Two risks attach to this approach. First, personal details are not relevant to the job decision and make the candidate appear "fluffy," instead of professional. Second, certain personal details may lead to intentional/unintentional bias on the part of the hiring manager.

Bradford Taft, Sr. Vice President
Right Management Consultants
Employment Management Association Vice President at Large
Phoenix, Arizona

But Impersonalization Is Not Inviting Either

I cool when I receive a cover letter that is not customized but obviously written with another job in mind. It's insulting.

Letters addressed to "Dear Sir:" are off-putting to women reviewers. If you seek but do not find a name, a better salutation to eliminate the gender issue is "Dear Sir or Madam:" Worst action: "To Whom It May Concern." Best: Identify the name of the person to whom the letter is sent through research about the company.

Jeffrey E. Struve, SPHR
Consultant
Employment Management Association Immediate Past President
St. Louis, Missouri

Handwritten Corrections Are Like Spilled Ink

Since the cover letter is an organization's first impression of a candidate, there's no excuse for handwritten corrections. Marking up a cover letter is not only discourteous but also raises questions about judgment. Proof the letter — and get a friend to proof it, too.

Kathleen Kleffel, HR Consultant
Hewitt Associates
Employment Management Association Member
Chicago, Illinois

Keep It Short and On Message

What I'm looking for in a cover letter is a brief message describing your unique style, ability and past performance with an example of the specific contributions to the organizations where you worked. I look for things that wouldn't necessarily be indicated on the resume because it should reflect on the position for which you are applying (because you've done your research).

P.S. If you hate to write cover letters, get one of your employees to tell me about how great you are and hand me your phone number and say, "You've got to call this person who is a great fit for our company."

Steve LaMotta, SPHR, Vice President Business Development
People Solutions Inc.
Employment Management Association, Area Vice President
Irving, Texas

Stop! You Forgot a Cover Letter

The first thing I review, before the resume, is the cover letter — or note the lack thereof. If the cover letter is as general and as nonspecific as the generic resume, then the candidate is on a hunting expedition and has no particular interest in my company except as one of 50 submittals sent out this week. That does not cancel the candidate out — but in ranking "things to do today," I may not rank this candidate as my No. 1 call.

A good cover letter, developed to point out key matching skills to requirements, showing knowledge of my organization and industry, indicates a candidate who is conducting a thoughtful and directed career search — and who *will* be my No. 1 call.

Creating an effective cover letter for each resume submission is not a courtesy of a bygone era. It is still the trademark of the true professional.

Ken Gaffey
HR & Staffing Consultant
Employment Management Association Member
Melrose, Massachusetts

Dear Readers of *Cover Letters For Dummies*,

Thanks a million for reading my book. If you like it, perhaps you'll want to check out its companions: *Resumes For Dummies* and *Job Interviews For Dummies*. Until we meet again . . .

Sunnies,

Joyce

Joyce Lain Kennedy
jlk@sunfeatures.com

Appendix

Problem Words

● ●

In This Chapter

▶ Commonly confused words

▶ Misused phrases

▶ Avoiding redundancy

● ●

*W*hat's the difference between *its* and *it's*? When do you use *among* instead of *between*? Can you remember how many *c*'s and *m*'s are in the word *recommend* without dashing to the nearest dictionary?

If you can't answer these questions, join the crowd! (If you can, give yourself a prize and enjoy your relative freedom from dictionary dementia.) The English language creates problems for everyone. Whether dealing with spelling, commonly confused words, or strict definitions that get loosened in everyday conversation, everybody needs a little help now and then.

Don't let your cover letter fall prey to embarrassing mistakes in word usage or spelling. At worst, creative spelling or unique usage will spiral your missive into the Bermuda Triangle of cover letters. At best, you'll provide the recipient with a gaggle of giggles at your expense.

I can't promise to turn you into a word-wielding impresario, but using this guide will clear up confusing and misused language so that you can craft a credible cover letter. Look up the words you've chosen for your cover letter (don't skip the *a*'s and *an*'s — you may be surprised) and master their meanings. And if you don't remember later, no problem! Just look them up again.

a/an: The use of these two words has nothing to do with how a word is spelled but rather with how it sounds. Use *a* with words that begin with a consonant sound and *an* with words that begin with a vowel sound.

ability: See *capacity/ability*.

-able/-ible: These suffixes are a doozy when it comes to spelling. Look the words up in a dictionary because no hard and fast rules exist for determining the correct spelling. Be alert to words that are spelled alike except for the suffix ending.

able: Use this word only with active verbs. If you've used it with a passive, or being, verb, replace it with *can*. Ex: Write "I *can* do it" not "I am *able* to do it."

about: *About* is commonly used in place of *almost*. Be more accurate.

about/approximately: *Approximately* is a better word choice because it's more formal and implies greater accuracy. Using *about* may sound like you're guessing or hedging.

above: A term that tends toward the pretentious. Phrases like "Pay attention to *the above*" sound really stuffy. Use *this* or *that* with a reference. See also *aforementioned*.

absolutely: People often use this adverb to intensify their pronouncements. If you want to impress someone, use tangible experiences rather than flimsy adverbs.

absolutes: Absolutes are words that allow for no degree or comparison, such as *perfect*, *unanimous*, *always*, and *absolute*. Use these words only if you know that you can back them up with documented information. Otherwise, qualify them with *almost* or *nearly*.

accent marks: When spelling foreign words that have been adopted into English, omitting the accent marks is OK, although many people still use them to aid pronunciation.

accompanied: When used in reference to people, use the preposition *by*. If referring to things, use *with*.

accompanied by: When you use this phrase coupled with the subject, the verb remains the same. Ex: The manager, *accompanied by* his associates, *is* (not *are*) going to lunch.

according to: This phrase implies that the person to whom you're referring may not know — or be telling — the truth. If you don't want to give that impression, dump *according to* and use *said*.

active voice/passive voice: Active verbs require motion while passive verbs relate a state of existence. Active words energize your writing while passive verbs can sound wordy or indecisive. Ex: "My proposal *was* the best ever" sounds flat next to "I *proposed* a dynamite plan."

actually: See *virtually/actually*.

acumen: Means "keenness of mind" or "shrewdness."

ad: *Ad* is an abbreviation for *advertisement*. In formal language, use the entire word. If you abbreviate the word, don't use a period unless it's the end of the sentence.

adhere/cohere: *Adhere* refers to sticking together by gluing or grasping and *cohere* refers to parts of the same thing sticking together. Ex: Water molecules *cohere*. If you're referring to a cause or philosophy, use *adhere*.

adjacent/contiguous: In formal usage, *adjacent* means "lying near but not touching" while *contiguous* means "touching."

admission/admittance: *Admittance* refers only to the actual physical entry into a place. *Admission* has the extended meaning of acceptance into a group or organization.

advance/advanced: Anything in *advance* means that it is positioned in front or ahead, while someone or something that is *advanced* is higher in quality or caliber than the average.

advanced planning: See *plan ahead/advanced planning*.

advise/inform/write: In cover letters, a*dvise* is a pretentious way of saying *inform* or *write*. A cover letter is no place to offer advice to a prospective employer.

affect/effect: *Affect* means "to influence" and *effect* means "to make happen." Ex: The performance review *affected* my feelings; the *effect* was a joyous response.

aforementioned: Sounds pretentious. Use *this* or *that* instead.

agenda: Refers to a list of things to do. Use *agendas* for several lists.

ago/since: *Ago* means "earlier than the present time" and *since* means "from a definite past time to now." Never use these words together. Write "Ten years *ago* I . . ." or "It has been ten years *since* I . . ." not "It was ten years *ago since* I . . ."

ahold: This word is an inappropriate colloquialism. Use *get hold of, reach, contact,* or *obtain*.

aid/aide: *Aid* refers to an action. Ex: My job is to *aid* Mike with the acquisition of new accounts. *Aide* refers to a person. Ex: Has my *aide* gone to lunch?

all ready/already: *All ready* means "completely ready" or "totally prepared." *Already* means "by this time" or "previously." Ex: "Are they *all ready* to go? They've *already* gone." Hint: Just write *ready* instead of *all ready*.

all right: Is spelled correctly. *Alright* is alwrong.

all-round: If you want to exhibit versatility, use *all-round*. If you're referring to "everywhere," *all-around* is more appropriate.

all the better: Is all the nicer when you know that using *all* with a superlative is perfectly OK.

allude/elude/refer: *Allude* implies an indirect relationship, while *refer* implies a direct relationship. Be careful to get this distinction right. *Elude* is unrelated to either *allude* or *refer*; it means to escape or avoid someone or something.

allusion/illusion: An *allusion* is a reference, usually indirect, to something else. *Illusion* is a false impression.

along: Commonly used to mean "approximately." Avoid this usage in formal correspondence and be more accurate. Ex: "I'll be there *along* about two" sounds foolish in comparison to "I'll be there at two."

along the lines of: Space waster. Substitute *like* instead.

along with: Means "as well as." When using this phrase, match the verb to the subject. Ex: Mike, along with his secretaries, *decides* (not decide) the weekly budget.

alot: Wrong! Write *a lot*.

a lot of: Used to mean "a great deal of," *a lot of* should be avoided in formal English. If you do use this phrase, make sure that the verb agrees with the word that follows. Ex: *A lot of* job seekers *write* cover letters, or *A lot of* time *is* spent looking for a job.

American: All too frequently, we use this phrase when we mean to say that an individual is a citizen of the United States. Remember that, when writing an international cover letter, saying what you really mean is better. You also avoid possibly alienating your Mexican or Canadian readers.

among/between: This distinction is an easy one to remember: use *among* when referencing three or more and *between* when discussing two.

another/additional: You can't use these words interchangeably. *Another* means "one more" and is specific to that meaning.

anxious/eager: Another pair that you should be careful of. *Anxious* has a sense of fear, doubt, or worry; *eager* means anticipating a joyous occasion.

arbitrate/mediate: In *arbitration* one person hears both sides of an issue and gives a binding decision. *Mediation* occurs when a person hears all information and tries to persuade the parties to come to a decision. A *mediator* has no binding power, though.

arrived at the conclusion that: Another wordy phrase that gets in your way. Go with, "I *concluded*." This phrase says what you mean and saves time.

as/because: In the sense of "due to the fact," *as* and *because* can be used interchangeably, but *as* tends to sound stuffy. You can confuse your reader, though, because *as* also refers to a point in time. Writing *because* is often better and also avoids potential problems.

as to whether: The *as to* is unnecessary. Just write *whether.*

at a later date: Save your reader time and write *later.*

at the present time/at the present writing: Both are stuffy ways of saying *now.* Say what you mean.

attached hereto/herein: The redundancy police are on their way to arrest you for this one. Say *attached* and save your record.

bachelor's: See *master's/bachelor's.*

bad: Too informal. Grab your thesaurus and replace *bad* with a good word.

become/get: Same meaning, different tone. *Become* has more class. Ex: "I *got* angry" sounds rash compared to "I *became* angry."

better than/more than: Both terms are used to mean *more than*, but *better than* is illogical. Ex: "She wrote *better than* 50 cover letters." *More than* is more accurate.

between/among: See *among/between.*

between every/between each: "A garage is *between each* office" literally means that a garage is situated in the middle of every office. Instead write, "a garage is *between every* two offices," or, "a garage is *beside each* office."

between you and me: *Between you and I* is not grammatically correct. Without explaining all the confusing rules, try this quick trick: When in doubt, reverse the order of the objects — *between I and you* sounds ridiculous.

bit (with an adjective): Meaning "a small amount of," this word sounds immature in a cover letter. Ex: "Please spend a *bit* of time reading my resume."

bottom line: This near-cliché literally refers to the final line of a financial report, but it has evolved into a broader meaning of "the final result."

but: When used in place of "except," *but* is a preposition. If followed by a pronoun, use *me, her, him, us,* or *them.* Ex: "Nobody likes my cover letter *but me.*"

but/however, nevertheless: Using *but* may smooth your sentences. Using *however* or *nevertheless* formalizes your writing, but they may sound pretentious. If you're connecting two complete sentences, use a comma with *but* and a semicolon with the others. Never write *but however* — it's redundant.

but that/but what: While these terms are commonly used, they're unnecessarily wordy. Either use *that* alone or rework your sentence. Ex: Rather than writing "I don't doubt *but that* I can do the job," write "I don't doubt *that* I can do the job," or "I know I can do the job."

but (with a negative): Using *but* to mean *only* is awkward. Ex: "I received *but* four interviews." Replace *but* with *only* or revise the sentence.

can/may: *May* asks permission, while *can* expresses ability. A quick trick that helps is to rephrase the sentence using "have the ability." Ex: "*Can* I call you on Monday?" would read "Do I have the ability to call you on Monday?" I hope you do — what you need here is permission: "*May* I call you?"

cannot: Only separate this word (*can not*) when you want greater emphasis. Otherwise, "cannot" is all one word.

cannot but: "I *cannot but* be sorry." This phrase is too easily misunderstood. Can it but for everyday speech.

can't hardly: The correct form is *can hardly*. *Can't hardly* is not only grammatically incorrect, but it also has become associated with poor education in many regions.

can't help but: Dreaded double negative. Instead of saying, "You *can't help but* be impressed with me," write, "You *will* be impressed with me." See also *cannot but* and *can't hardly*.

capacity/ability: Where *ability* means competence in doing, *capacity* refers either to a position or duty or to the potential for storing. Don't use *capacity* to describe your skills. Ex: "I have the *capacity* to juggle many tasks at once" is incorrect.

capital/capitol: The only time to use *capitol* is when you are referring to the building that houses government, be it state or federal. Any other use should be *capital*.

cause/reason: A *cause* brings about an effect or result. A *reason* explains something.

city of . . . : Just name the city. "*City of* New Orleans" would be better as "New Orleans." Sorry, Arlo.

classy: An informal, but acceptable word for "stylish or elegant."

clever/ingenious/inventive: All mean varying degrees of "skillful or resourceful." *Clever* implies mentally quick but lacking depth, *ingenious* refers to an ability to discover new solutions, and *inventive* requires imagination to produce something for the first time.

close proximity: Redundant. If something's *close*, it's in *proximity*. Use one or the other, never both.

close to the point of: Write *close to* and you'll be better off.

coach: Perfectly acceptable as a verb. Ex: "I *coached* her about interviews." Alternative words to use are *teach* or *instruct*.

cohere: See *adhere/cohere*.

cohese: Informal corruption of *cohere*. Do not use.

college: See *university/college*.

commend/praise: Another pair to be careful of. *Commend* should be used when you are talking about a specific action; *praise* is appropriate for generalities.

concerning the matter of: Hopeless bureaucrat speak. Write *concerning* or *about*.

consequent: See *subsequent/consequent*.

contiguous: See *adjacent/contiguous*.

continue on: Probably the most hated and annoying redundancy possible. If you want to make your reader's eyes bulge, *continue on* with this phrase. Otherwise, just say *continue*.

decided/decisive: While both mean "unquestionable or unmistakable," *decided* has the connotation of "definite," while *decisive* connotes "conclusive." Ex: "The company team won a *decisive* victory" or "A *decided* change has occurred in company policy."

definite/definitive: Both mean "unquestionable or decided" but *definitive* connotes "authority or finality."

despite/in spite of: Both are acceptable but *despite* is slightly more formal and eliminates wordiness. Using either word with *but* is unnecessary.

different from/than: Either form is acceptable, but *different from* is more accepted.

disclose/reveal: Should be used only when referring to confidential information that is being reported. Both mean "to make known," but if you want to connote a *sudden* disclosure, use *reveal* instead of *disclose*. Ex: "He opened the file and *revealed* that all of the cover letters had been stolen!"

discover/invent: *Discover* means to find something that already exists while *invent* means to produce something that has never existed before. These terms are not interchangeable.

discrete/discreet: These two may look like variations of each other, but they have separate meanings. *Discrete* means "distinct, unattached, unrelated," while *discreet* means "careful, considered."

discriminate/distinguish: While both words mean to discern or note difference, *discriminate* more specifically means to note difference and make a judgment accordingly.

disinterested/uninterested: These will get you in real trouble! *Disinterested* means "impartial"; while the person might be interested, she is unbiased. *Uninterested* means that the person is not at all concerned with what is going on. Say what you mean.

disregardless: Disregard this word. Use *regardless* instead.

divided into/composed of: These have almost opposite meanings. *Divided into* means that something that was originally together has been broken apart, and *composed of* means that the thing has been created out of separate parts.

double negatives: Use these and people will question your educational background. Ex: "I *didn't* send *no* cover letter." Make the sentence "I *didn't* send *a* cover letter." Words such as *scarcely, barely,* and *hardly* have negative connotations also, so don't pair them with a negative word.

double possessive: Although technically incorrect, double possessives are widely used and help to clarify possession. Ex: "We met through a friend of my father's" is clearer than "We met through a friend of my father."

double superlative: Using double superlatives (*most best, most fastest*), no matter how excited you are, is most unacceptable.

due to the fact that: Why all the extra words? Use *because* instead.

each: When *each* precedes a singular noun or is the subject of the sentence, use a singular verb. Ex: "*Each* cover letter *describes* my abilities perfectly" or "*Each is* perfect." When *each* follows a plural subject, use a plural verb. "They *each read* my cover letters for me."

each and every: Redundant and unnecessarily wordy. Avoid using this phrase unless you need the extra emphasis.

effect: See *affect/effect.*

e.g.: See *i.e./e.g.*

either/or: Look at the noun which follows *or*. If the noun is singular, use a singular verb, and if it's plural, use a plural verb. Ex: "Either my cover letters or my *resume needs* to be revised."

element/factor: An *element* is "a constituent part" of something else, while a *factor* is "something which actively contributes to the production of a result."

eliminate: To remove or eradicate. Do not use this word in place of *prevent*. Remember, you must have something to remove in order to eliminate it. Ex: I *eliminated* all wasteful expenditures.

else: Does not mean *or*. Ex: "You must send a resume *else* the employer won't know your qualifications" is wrong. Replace *else* with *or*. Watch for redundancy when using *else* with such words as *nobody* or *nothing*. In most cases, *else* can be omitted.

enclose/inclose: *Enclose* is more commonly used, but both words mean "to surround" and can be used interchangeably.

end result: A symptom of Redundancy Disease. Write simply *result*, omitting *end*.

enough: Commonly used for emphasis, *enough* is often redundant. Ex: I was happy *enough* that they invited me for an interview. This sentence sounds more sophisticated sans *enough*.

entirely completed: Is *entirely* redundant. *Completed* means to bring to an end — you won't find any degrees of completeness. Eliminate *entirely*.

equally as: *As* is used in comparing two or more elements to each other. Ex: I am *as* qualified *as* the other applicants. *Equally* is used when only one element of the comparison is named. Ex: My resume was *equally* good. If you have written *equally as*, delete *equally*.

especially/specially: Another important distinction. *Especially* has the sense of "particularly"; *specially* means that the event occurred for a specific reason. "I was *specially* trained for the task," but, "I am *especially* good at meeting budgets." See *more especially*.

-ess endings: In these PC days, avoid this ending to distinguish feminine subjects. Ex: *waitress, stewardess, actress*. Either use the nongender-specific term (*waiter, steward, actor*) or choose a different term (*food server, flight attendant, thespian*).

essential: Does not mean "very important," so don't write "My personality is *essential* for my success." Used correctly, *essential* means "necessary or indispensable." Ex: A well-written cover letter is *essential* for job search success. See *more essential*.

estimated at about: Once more redundancy raises its head. Leave out *about*.

every . . . and every: Even though this phrase seems to refer to many people or things, it takes a singular verb. Ex: *Every* resume *and every* cover letter *is* read with an open mind.

everybody/everyone: These words can be used interchangeably with one exception. *Every one* (two words) emphasizes each individual and cannot be replaced by *everybody*. In all cases, these words take a singular verb. Ex: *Everyone (Everybody) thinks* that my cover letter is brilliant, or *Every one* of my cover letters *is* a masterpiece.

everyday/every day: *Every day* indicates an event which occurs every 24 hours, or daily. Ex: I revise my cover letter *every day* at 5:00 pm. *Everyday* indicates a common occurrence, one which happens often, but not daily.

every other: This phrase can be confusing. I suggest you use *every day* or *every second day* to clarify your meaning.

ex-/former: Both are correct, but *former* is more formal. Ex: "She is a *former* lawyer" is more sophisticated than "she is an *ex*-lawyer."

exceed/excel: Both of these words mean "to go beyond," but they have different connotations. *Exceed* indicates that limits or expectations have been surpassed. Ex: I *exceeded* all sales expectations. *Excel* connotes superiority. Ex: I *excel* at sales performance.

extra: When used in place of "very" or "uncommonly," *extra* is too informal for a cover letter. Ex: My cover letter is *extra* long.

factor: See *element/factor*.

farther/further: When writing about a measurable distance, use *farther*. Ex: The bathroom is *farther* than the vending machines. When indicating an extension in time, use *further*. Ex: I will examine your resume *further*.

fewer in number: Keep your words fewer in number and write *fewer*.

fewer/less: When referring to individual items use *fewer*. Ex: I receive *fewer* than four interviews per month. When referring to a quantity or class of items, use *less*. Ex: *Less* jobs are available now.

figuratively/literally: These words cannot be used interchangeably. *Figuratively* means "metaphorically" while *literally* means "actually." Ex: He *figuratively* grabbed the bull by the horns and *literally* eliminated all wasteful expenditures.

file away: Don't make reading more work than it is by using two words where one will do. Write *file* and avoid finding your resume in the round file.

fiscal/monetary: *Fiscal* means "relating to financial matters" while *monetary* refers to money.

forego/forgo: *Forego* means to go before. *Forgo* (without the *e*) means to go without.

former: See *ex-/former* or *latter/former*.

for the purpose: Keep things simple and replace with *for* or *to*.

for the reason that: Overburdened way of saying *because*.

for your information: A quick and easy way to alienate the letter reader. Omit this phrase completely.

fractions: Numbers less than one should be written out. Ex: I received *two-thirds* of my sales experience overseas.

full time/full-time: When followed by a noun, hyphenate. Ex: I worked at *full-time* jobs through college. When it stands alone, do not hyphenate. Ex: I write cover letters *full time*.

gamut/gantlet/gauntlet: Often used interchangeably, these words have different meanings. *Gamut* refers to an entire range or series. Ex: My work experience covers the *gamut* from real estate to education. A *gantlet* is a flogging ordeal, and a *gauntlet* is a glove.

gather together: Redundant. If something is *gathered*, then it's *together*. Use one or the other.

get: See *become/get*.

group/team: Both words need singular verbs and pronouns, unless you've got more than one *group* or *team*. Ex: The *group/team is* aware of *its* problems.

he/she (the _____): Used as clarification, this phrasing is awkward and avoidable. Ex: The secretary told the CEO that *he* (the secretary) should get more rest. Without the clarification, the sentence is unclear as to who needs the rest, but with the clarification, the sentence is awkward. Revise it to read, The secretary told the CEO, "I need more rest."

he, him, his/she, her, hers/it, its/they, them, their, theirs: Always make sure that these *pronouns* agree with *their* subjects. As a test, replace the pronoun with the subject, then determine if the pronoun and subject agree in number. Ex: "*Everyone* took *their* places" is incorrect because *everyone* is a singular noun. The sentence should read "*Everyone* took *his* (or *her*) place".

he (she) is a man (woman) who: Ex: *He is a man who* commands respect. Why the extra words? Write "He commands respect."

he or she: Although some feminists may be angered, standard usage for a nongender-specific pronoun requires *he*. Ex: When someone sends a cover letter, *he* should follow up with a phone call. Writing *he or she* is cumbersome. If this practice really bothers you, try alternating the words *he* and *she*.

-ible: See *-able/-ible*.

idea: This word can encompass so many different meanings that choosing a more specific word, such as *design, belief, theory, hypothesis, solution, plan, objective*, is better — you get the idea?

i.e./e.g.: *i.e.* introduces a definition and *e.g.* introduces an example. Avoid these abbreviations in your cover letters and write "that is" or "for example."

if and when: Unnecessarily wordy and logically unsound. Use one or the other.

impel/induce: Because these definitions are similar, they are often used incorrectly as synonyms. *Impel* means to urge, force, or propel while *induce* means to persuade or influence. Ex: I *impel* you to read my cover letter. Hopefully, doing so will *induce* you to call me.

imply/infer: Here's an easy way to remember the distinction between these commonly confused words: The writer or speaker *implies* and the reader or listener *infers*.

important essentials: What other kind of *essentials* do you know of? Avoid this redundancy.

in accordance with your request: Cut the useless words; write *as you requested*.

in addition to: This wordy way of saying *also* does not change the verb. Ex: My resume, *in addition to* my cover letters, *positions* me as an aggressive candidate.

inasmuch as: Isspelledcorrectly. Don't separate the words. Better yet, choose a shorter alternative like *since* or *because*.

inclose: See *enclose/inclose*.

in connection with: Save ink! Write *about* or *concerning*.

in excess of: These excess words prevent concise writing. Try *more than* or *over* instead.

ingenious/inventive: See *clever/ingenious/inventive*.

in order to (that): In order to eliminate unnecessary words, just write *to, that,* or *so that.*

in respect to the matter of: You're using up too much space. Use *about* or *regarding*.

in spite of: See *despite/in spite of*.

intensives: Words such as *too*, *very*, *really*, *horribly*, *absolutely*, and *truly* are used to intensify statements. However, they've been *so* overused that instead of intensifying the interest, they now intensify the boredom. Avoid 'em.

in the amount of: When talking about money, writing *for* is clearer.

in the area of: Another roundabout way of saying *about*. Remember that specifics are better.

in the field of . . . : Name your field rather than adding nothing words. Ex: "I have excelled *in the field of banking*," would be better with just *banking*.

in this day and age: Makes you sound really outdated. Replace with *now* or *today*.

in to/into: If you're expressing motion from one place to the inside of another, use *into*. Ex: I walked confidently *into* the room. When *in* and *to* are separated, motion towards an event or action is indicated. Ex: I walked confidently *in to* the interview.

invent: See *discover/invent*.

irregardless: *Irregardless* of how many times you've heard this word, it's wrong. Using it on a cover letter announces your ignorance of correct English. Write *regardless*.

its/it's: While apostrophes usually indicate possession, the rules change with pronouns. *Its* indicates possession. Ex: The cat got *its* claws trimmed. *It's* is a contraction for *it is*. The apostrophe replaces the missing *i*.

invaluable: Means priceless or valuable beyond estimation. If the value of something can be calculated, you cannot use this term.

join together: While beautiful in wedding ceremonies, this phrase is nevertheless redundant; you cannot *join apart*. Choose one word or the other.

juncture: While this term can be used to mean a point in time, it most accurately refers to a crisis or turning point.

keep continuing: Redundant. *Keep continuing* to use this phrase and you'll *keep continuing* to waste paper space.

kindly: Because this word means "in a kind manner," it doesn't convey the sense you want. Write instead, "Would you be so kind," or even, "please." As well, "I thank you *kindly*," would be best reworded as "I thank you *very much*."

kind of: Sounds like a kindergartner. Elevate your language; use *rather* or *somewhat* instead.

know/realize: Often used interchangeably, these words have slight differences in meaning. To *know* something is to have information or understanding. To *realize* something is to *know* it clearly or completely, to understand all aspects of it.

known to be: Means *is*. Use *is*.

know-how: Experts discourage the use of this word as too informal. Try *knowledge*, *understanding*, or *expertise* instead.

large portion of/large number of: These are weighty phrases that take up more room than you need to use. Replace with *most of* or *many*. Even better, though, would be to say *much*.

last/latest: These words are close in meaning but differ in connotation. *Last* connotes final, while *latest* means most recent.

last but not least: Should be buried; this phrase is too old for retirement.

latter/former: *Latter* refers to the second of two things, while *former* refers to the first. If you are discussing more than two objects, use *last-mentioned* or repeat the noun.

lay/lie: *Lay* means to put or place. *Lie* means to recline. To test your usage of these words, replace *lay* with *place*. If the sentence makes sense, use *lay*. If it doesn't, use *lie*.

less: See *fewer/less*.

like for: *For* gets in the way of what you mean. Simply write *like*.

like to have: Almost comically slang. Avoid in formal speech.

literally: See *figuratively/literally*.

lot/lots: Informal and unspecific. Tell us how many you mean.

love: Technically, this word refers to an intense affection or devotion, something cherished. Commonly, it has been used in so many contexts it has lost its singular meaning. Ex: "I *love* Disneyland" is probably an exaggeration. Experts suggest limiting your use of this word.

magnitude: An overblown word. Words like *importance*, *significance*, and *size* are more appropriate.

major: This adjective can only be used as a comparison. You can work on "*a* major account," but not "*the* major account."

manage: See *run/operate/manage*.

masterful/masterly: While you may be tempted to boast about your accomplishments, be careful in using these words. *Masterful* has the meaning of "strong or overbearing," while *masterly* means "with skill, expert in craft." Beware the wrong impression!

master's/bachelor's: That these are degrees in education is understood, so you can drop *degree*. Also, master's and bachelor's are informal; the formal versions are Master of Arts/Science or Bachelor of Arts/Science.

maximize/minimize: *Maximize* means "to increase an object to its utmost potential," while *minimize* means the same in the other direction. Because of these extremes, you can't greatly, significantly, or vastly *maximize* or *minimize* anything.

may: See *can/may*.

memorandum: *Memorandum* is one piece of correspondence, while more than one can be either *memorandums* or *memoranda*. *Memorandas* is not accepted.

monetary: See *fiscal/monetary*.

more especially: Hopelessly redundant. Drop the *more*, and let *especially* do its job.

more essential: Face the facts: You're either *essential* or you're not, so you can't be *more essential*. Cut the redundant *more*.

more perfect: Too frequently, this phrase is another redundancy. Perfection cannot be measured in degrees.

more than/over: Use *over* when discussing large amounts as one concept: "*over* a million dollars," but *more than* in the case of things or people you have to count individually: "I wrote *more than* a thousand cover letters."

most certainly/most carefully: These phrases can show how earnest you are, but, more often than not, they sound pretentious.

mutual cooperation: Simply redundant. How else can you have cooperation? The same goes for *mutual teamwork*.

near future: Another redundancy. Conserve words and write "soon."

needless to say: This phrase is itself *needless to say*. Such a phrase suggests that you are just filling space.

neither/nor: Always use *nor* with *neither* to avoid being wrong.

never: Don't use *never* when you mean *not*. The two are not interchangeable. "The interviewer *never* mentioned salary during the interview," is not correct. Replace *never* with *not*.

new innovation: Yet another redundancy, this phrase is like writing "repeated again."

new record: Because a record is a new mark exceeding other achievements, *new record* is redundant.

nor: See *or/nor*.

not only/but also: This follow-phrasing requires that each element be comparable. "I *not only* require a comfortable working space *but also* good wages," would be better phrased, "I require *not only* a comfortable working space *but also* good wages."

nothing: *Nothing* always takes a singular verb: "My former employers may say that I am crazy, but *nothing is* further from the truth."

now pending: The redundancy disease strikes again! Now is the only time something can be *pending*.

of: This poor preposition is misused more than almost any other part of speech. The most common mistake occurs in using *of* when you really mean *have*. Should, would, could, must, and many more besides require the use of *have*. Ignore what it sounds like.

of between/of from: As far as numbers and dollar amounts are concerned, *between* and *from* are redundancies: "An increase in revenues *of between* five to eight million dollars," would be better written without the *between*.

official/officious: Another case in which you can give the wrong impression. *Official* means "one who is invested with an office," while *officious* means "overeager, meddlesome." Obviously, a mistake you don't want to make.

one of the, if not the: If you need to use this phrase, keep the elements in both: "I am *one of the* most important people, *if not the* most important." Often, you can get away with only the first part.

operate: See *run/operate/manage*.

optimize: A contender for the gold watch, *optimize* has been greatly overused in the last years. Use variants such as "increased efficiency" or "improved to maximum levels."

or/nor: If the negative quality of a sentence carries through the whole sentence, use *or.* "Don't use slang *or* profanity in cover letters." If the negative element ends or appears to end, use *nor.* "Don't use slang in an interview, nor should you arrive late for an interview."

outline in detail: See *spell out/outline in detail.*

over: See *more than/over.*

overall: This word is a candidate for retirement; it has been used too much and too often. Use words like *general, ultimate, comprehensive,* or *final.*

paramount: Another word that cannot be modified. This word means "chief" or "supreme," so you can't have something that is *more paramount* or *most paramount.*

passive voice: See *active voice/passive voice.*

past experience/past history: If you have experienced something or if something is history, it can be nowhere but past. Cut the redundancy.

per: You should only use this word within Latin phrases; otherwise, it sounds stuffy and pretentious. A good general rule is to simply avoid Latin or foreign phrases. Instead of *per diem* or *per annum,* use daily and yearly.

percent/percentage: The term *percent* is specific and requires a definite figure, while *percentage* needs some kind of modifier, like "large" or "significant."

period of: Another redundant phrase. Instead of writing, "I worked with the company for a *period of* six years," write simply, "I worked with the company *for* six years."

person/people: Use *persons* for an exact number of people: "I managed an office of eight *persons.*" The correct use of *people* is with a large crowd or an unknown amount.

personally: People too often use this word as an unnecessary introduction. Leave it out for the sake of clarity and conciseness. Anything that involves you is, by definition, personal.

perspective/prospective: *Perspective* is someone's point of view, while *prospective* is an expectation or a potentiality. An important detail in addressing a *prospective* employer.

plan ahead/advanced planning: The dreaded redundancy, once more. Wouldn't it be nice if we could plan for what has already happened?

please be advised: A pompous way of offering information or advice. A cover letter is no place to be pompous.

point in time: Another filler phrase. Write *now* instead.

practicable/practical: *Practicable* means that something can be done, while *practical* shows that something is worthwhile.

presently: This word means not only *now* but also *soon*. The best idea is to use the word that you really mean.

proceed/precede: *Proceed* means "to move forward" in any sense, not only for walking or real movement. *Precede* means "to go before," meaning something that occurred or came before something else.

proved/proven: Both are accepted, but *proved* is more common.

provided/providing: Don't use these words if you can replace them with the simple *if*.

purposely/purposefully: *Purposely* has the meaning "intentional," as in, "I *purposely* missed the board meeting." *Purposefully* has the sense of determination for reaching a goal. This is a commonly confused pair that you should be wary of.

qualified expert: Can you be an expert if you aren't qualified? Redundancy strikes again.

rather than: This phrase requires parallel verbs: "I quit *rather than* be fired" (not being fired).

real/really: *Real* means actual or true, while *really* means very. Be careful not to interchange the two.

realize: See *know/realize*.

reason: See *cause/reason*.

reason is because: Redundant. Rather than writing, "The *reason* I left the job *is because*," simplify the sentence to, "I left the job *because*." This redundancy is also true for *reason why*.

recommend/refer: A friend or contact *refers* you *to* a job offer. A firm or company is *recommended by* someone else. You would write, "Mr. A. *referred* me *to* this vacant position. Your company is highly *recommended by* the BBB."

regarding/concerning/respecting: These are all inflated words that can be replaced by the simple "about."

represent: A misleading word, *represent* can often be replaced by "composed" or "made up."

respectfully/respectively: *Respectfully* means "with respect," while *respectively* refers to objects and the order in which they occur in sentences. This error is an easy one to make, so watch out.

resume: See *vitae/resume*.

reveal: See *disclose/reveal*.

revert back: An obvious (or at least should be) redundancy. Avoid repetition.

run/operate/manage: *Run* is often used in place of *managed* or *operated*. A *manager* works for a boss, while an *operator* is usually the owner.

saving: When you use *a* with *saving*, the correct form is singular: "My programs resulted in *a saving* of millions," not *savings*.

scrutinize: Another word that is often attacked by redundancy. "A close scrutiny" and "to scrutinize closely" are both redundant.

seem: *Seem* is a wishy-washy word. Make a strong statement instead and show how determined you are.

seriously consider: If you ask a prospective employer to *seriously consider* your application, you are implying that his consideration isn't usually serious. Cut the *seriously* and lose the redundancy.

several: *Several* is ambiguous, but is pretty close to *few*. Use "many" or "numerous" for larger numbers. Even better, be specific.

since: See *ago/since*.

slanting: *Slanting* is when you intentionally avoid information that may damage your position. While slanting is not really lying, it can definitely be deceptive. You're better off to explain issues that might trip you up in a background check.

spell out/outline in detail: *Spelling out* means giving details, so this phrase is redundant. At the same time, though, *outlining* means summarizing, so this phrase is a contradiction.

state of the art: This phrase can be used either as a noun or an adjective; as an adjective, the phrase is hyphenated.

subject: When referring to people, *subject* is too vague. Spell out what you mean.

subject matter: *Subject* is usually enough. "The *subject matter* of the meeting centered on pay raises," can easily be rewritten without the *matter*.

subsequent/consequent: Easily mixed up words. *Subsequent* means "later" or "succeeding"; a *consequent* occurrence is something that naturally follows an action.

subsequent to: Inflated writing. Just use "after."

success: Because success is a positive thing, avoid writing "good success" or "beneficial success."

such: Avoid using *such* as an intensifier. In sentences like "It was *such* a hard job," rewrite using "very," or finish the comparison: "It was *such* a hard job that I needed extra money to finish it."

sufficient enough: Either word is strong enough on its own. Pairing them is redundant.

summarize: Use *summarize* only when you are giving a shortened version of a story.

summary: See above.

sure/surely: *Surely* is the adverb form; "I *sure* like working for you" is highly informal.

take for example: In most cases, *for example* is sufficient. To test, eliminate *take*. If the sentence still makes sense, you don't need *take*. Ex: *Take, for example*, cover letters are necessary in the job search. If you eliminate *take* from this sentence, it makes more sense.

take into consideration: Long-winded way of writing *consider*.

target: Is a fine word if it targets the meaning you want. However, *objective*, *goal*, or *quota* may hit the bullseye where *target* veers wide.

team: See *group/team*.

than: *Than* as a conjunction can take either "me" or "I" ("he" or "him," and so on) depending on the context. Finish the phrase to see which one to use; "The company pays Frank more than . . ." can be finished with *me*, if the rest of the sentence is "they pay me," but can also be *I*, if the rest of the sentence is "I pay Frank."

than/then: The way to remember the difference here is to think of *then* as a mark of time and *than* as a comparison: "I worked for one manager for two years, *then* switched departments, but I liked the first department more *than* the second."

thank you in advance: Rude! Send a thank-you letter if you really mean it.

that (do you need it?): For brevity, try eliminating *that*. If the sentence still makes sense, great. Use "that" only for clarity. Ex: I read (*that*) cover letters are necessary. If you eliminate *that* here, the reader may initially misread the sentence.

that/which: An easy rule to remember: If the information following the word is necessary, use *that*. If the information is not necessary, use *which*. Ex: The cover letter, *which* is one of my best, got the manager's attention. *Which* introduces extra, not necessary, information. Ex: The cover letter *that* got the manager's attention was one of my best. In this case, the information following *that* is necessary to indicate which cover letter the writer is referring to.

there is, are, was, were: Weak construction. Revise your sentence. Ex: "*There are* two cover letters in the desk" can be rewritten as "Two cover letters are in the desk."

they: *They* say the word *they* is too general to be used in formal English. If possible, identify who *they* are. If you can't, rewrite your sentence to avoid the question, "Who is 'they'?"

thing: Undoubtedly, a more specific word exists. Avoid *thing*.

this/that/these/those: *These* words cannot stand on their own; they are not nouns. Always tell what you are referring to. Ex: *This* is great. What is great? *This* cover letter is great.

true facts: If they're not *true*, they're not *facts*. Avoid this redundancy.

try: Sometimes simple is better and *try* is a terrific word — brief and specific. But if you want more formality, you can use *attempt* (suggests a onetime event), *endeavor* (very formal, possibly pompous) or *strive* (connotes serious effort or energy).

try to/try and: *Try to* remember that *try and* is wrong. Think of it this way: To try *to* do something suggests one action while to try *and* do something suggests two actions, since *and* means in addition to. Ex: "*Try and* write a good cover letter," read literally, leads one to ask "What are you trying to do in addition to writing a cover letter?"

unfinished comparisons: "I'm the best!" Of what? Unless you're not willing to commit (advertisers often use this tactic so they don't have to prove their claim), always supply the comparison. Ex: I'm the best cover letter writer in the country. Then be prepared to back up your statement.

unique: Overused to the point of being meaningless, *unique* cannot be altered by comparative terms such as *more*, *very*, or *rather*. If something is *unique*, it should be the only one of its kind; therefore, nothing should exist to which it can be compared.

university/college: A *college* awards only undergraduate degrees, whereas a *university* awards master's and/or doctoral degrees as well.

unknown: Use this word only if what you are referring to is not known by anyone anywhere. If the thing may be known, use a more accurate word: *unidentified, undisclosed, unannounced, undetermined.*

unthinkable: If you have thought of something to declare *unthinkable*, then you have thought of it; therefore, it is not *unthinkable*, but very unlikely, impossible, or un-do-able. A more accurate description is thinkable.

up to date/up-to-date: If this phrase refers to a noun which follows it, use hyphens. Ex: Only send *up-to-date* cover letters. If the phrase stands alone, don't use hyphens. Ex: Never send cover letters that are not *up to date*.

valued/valuable: *Valuable* refers to something that costs a great deal. *Valued* refers to something (or someone) that is held in high regard, whether or not it's *valuable*. People cannot be *valuable*, but they can be *valued*. Ex: I am a *valued* employee.

very: OK in "thank you *very* much" but very, very, very overused as a superlative. Avoid this word when possible.

vice: When used preceding a noun, do not use a hyphen. Ex: *vice president*, *vice chairperson*, *vice principal*.

virtually/actually: Do not mean the same thing. *Virtually* means almost entirely, while *actually* means in fact or in truth. An easy way to remember: *Actually* is and *virtually* almost is.

vis-à-vis: Although many people use this word to mean about or concerning, its correct definition is "in relation to" or "as compared with." Ex: How do you feel about your cover letters now, *vis-à-vis* the first cover letters you wrote?

vitae/resume: A *resume* is not the same as a *vitae*. A *vitae* is a brief biographical sketch whereas a *resume* is a summary of your skills and employment history. Where *resumes* typically do not run more than two pages, some curricula *vitae* run more than 50 pages. For more information see my book *Resumes For Dummies*.

want/wish: While these words are correctly used as synonyms, *wish* usually refers to a desire for something abstract or remote and *want* refers to more available, tangible desires. Ex: I *want* to work for you. I *wish* I could make two billion dollars a year.

was a former: Redundant. Either use *was* alone or write *is a former*.

way in which: Too wordy. Eliminate *in which* and use that saved space to write something brilliant.

we: How can such a little, simple word cause any problems? When we don't know who *we* refers to. Ex: In my company, *we* attend meetings weekly. Who is *we*? Everyone? Almost everyone? Everyone but the secretaries? Be specific.

whatsoever at all: *Whatsoever* means the same thing as *at all*. Why for what reason use both together?

which: See *that/which*.

while: When used in place of *although*, be alert to possible misunderstanding. Ex: *While* I received most of my education from the University of Brazil, I got my professional experience in California and Canada. Use *although* for greater clarity.

who/whom: *Who* is a subject and *whom* is an object. Doesn't help? Think of it this way: Turn the sentence in question into a question and answer it with *he* (*she, they*) or *him* (*her, them*). If the answer is *he*, then use *who* in the sentence. If the answer is *him*, use *whom*. Ex: Tell me *who/whom* she called. Rephrased as a question: *Who* did she call? The answer: She called *him*. Since the answer is *him*, the original sentence should read: Tell me *whom* she called.

whoever/whomever: See *who/whom* and follow the same procedure.

who's/whose: When in doubt, replace with *who is* or *who has*. If the sentence makes sense, use *who's*. If it doesn't, use *whose*.

wide-: In most cases, *wide-* preceding a noun needs a hyphen. Ex: *wide-awake, wide-ranging, wide-screen*. For ultimate surety, look up the word in question in a dictionary.

-wide: Behind the noun, no hyphen. Ex: *nationwide, companywide, worldwide*.

-wise: If it means smart, use a hyphen. Ex: *street-wise, money-wise*. If it means "in regard to," then drop the hyphen. Ex: *otherwise, lengthwise, crosswise*. Beware of creating *-wise* words, such as *performancewise, saleswise,* or *moneywise*. Casewise, other choices wordwise are more appropriate contextwise. Write intelligently, not -wisely.

with the exception of: *With the exception of* this sentence, this phrase is too wordy. Replace it with *except* or *except for*.

worthwhile/worth while: Here's an easy trick: Stick *your* or *one's* in between *worth* and *while*. If it makes sense, use *worth while*. If it doesn't make sense, use *worthwhile*. Better yet, choosing a more specific description is *worth while*, such as *promising* or *worth your time*.

yet: It's only three letters, yet it takes up space. Only use this word for clarity. If a sentence makes sense without *yet*, delete it. Ex: Have you written a cover letter *(yet)*?

you know: No, I don't. Why don't you tell me? Use this tired, illogical revision of *um* and you look like a hesitant teenager, you know?

your/you're: The quick rule: Replace with *you are*. If the sentence makes sense, use *you're*. If it doesn't, use *your*.

yours/your's: *Your's* does not exist. Use *yours*.

zeal/zest: *Zeal* refers to an ardent interest in pursuit of something. *Zest* refers to a keen enjoyment or gusto. Ex: I have a *zest* for writing cover letters. I *zeal*ously want to write better cover letters.

Index

FOR DUMMIES®

The easy way to get more done and have more fun

PERSONAL FINANCE

Personal Finance For DUMMIES

0-7645-5231-7

Investing For DUMMIES

0-7645-2431-3

Home Buying For DUMMIES

0-7645-5331-3

Also available:

Estate Planning For Dummies
(0-7645-5501-4)
401(k)s For Dummies
(0-7645-5468-9)
Frugal Living For Dummies
(0-7645-5403-4)
Microsoft Money "X" For Dummies
(0-7645-1689-2)
Mutual Funds For Dummies
(0-7645-5329-1)

Personal Bankruptcy For Dummies
(0-7645-5498-0)
Quicken "X" For Dummies
(0-7645-1666-3)
Stock Investing For Dummies
(0-7645-5411-5)
Taxes For Dummies 2003
(0-7645-5475-1)

BUSINESS & CAREERS

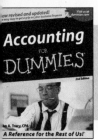

Accounting For DUMMIES

0-7645-5314-3

Grant Writing For DUMMIES

0-7645-5307-0

Resumes For DUMMIES

0-7645-5471-9

Also available:

Business Plans Kit For Dummies
(0-7645-5365-8)
Consulting For Dummies
(0-7645-5034-9)
Cool Careers For Dummies
(0-7645-5345-3)
Human Resources Kit For Dummies
(0-7645-5131-0)
Managing For Dummies
(1-5688-4858-7)

QuickBooks All-in-One Desk Reference For Dummies
(0-7645-1963-8)
Selling For Dummies
(0-7645-5363-1)
Small Business Kit For Dummies
(0-7645-5093-4)
Starting an eBay Business For Dummies
(0-7645-1547-0)

HEALTH, SPORTS & FITNESS

Fitness For DUMMIES

0-7645-5167-1

Golf For DUMMIES

0-7645-5146-9

Diabetes For DUMMIES

0-7645-5154-X

Also available:

Controlling Cholesterol For Dummies
(0-7645-5440-9)
Dieting For Dummies
(0-7645-5126-4)
High Blood Pressure For Dummies
(0-7645-5424-7)
Martial Arts For Dummies
(0-7645-5358-5)
Menopause For Dummies
(0-7645-5458-1)

Nutrition For Dummies
(0-7645-5180-9)
Power Yoga For Dummies
(0-7645-5342-9)
Thyroid For Dummies
(0-7645-5385-2)
Weight Training For Dummies
(0-7645-5168-X)
Yoga For Dummies
(0-7645-5117-5)

Available wherever books are sold.

FOR DUMMIES®

A world of resources to help you grow

HOME, GARDEN & HOBBIES

Feng Shui

0-7645-5295-3

Gardening

0-7645-5130-2

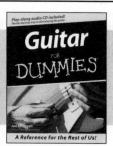

Guitar

0-7645-5106-X

Also available:

Auto Repair For Dummies
(0-7645-5089-6)

Chess For Dummies
(0-7645-5003-9)

Home Maintenance For Dummies
(0-7645-5215-5)

Organizing For Dummies
(0-7645-5300-3)

Piano For Dummies
(0-7645-5105-1)

Poker For Dummies
(0-7645-5232-5)

Quilting For Dummies
(0-7645-5118-3)

Rock Guitar For Dummies
(0-7645-5356-9)

Roses For Dummies
(0-7645-5202-3)

Sewing For Dummies
(0-7645-5137-X)

FOOD & WINE

Cooking

0-7645-5250-3

Cookies

0-7645-5390-9

Wine

0-7645-5114-0

Also available:

Bartending For Dummies
(0-7645-5051-9)

Chinese Cooking For Dummies
(0-7645-5247-3)

Christmas Cooking For Dummies
(0-7645-5407-7)

Diabetes Cookbook For Dummies
(0-7645-5230-9)

Grilling For Dummies
(0-7645-5076-4)

Low-Fat Cooking For Dummies
(0-7645-5035-7)

Slow Cookers For Dummies
(0-7645-5240-6)

TRAVEL

Italy

0-7645-5453-0

Hawaii

0-7645-5438-7

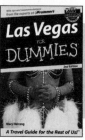

Las Vegas

0-7645-5448-4

Also available:

America's National Parks For Dummies
(0-7645-6204-5)

Caribbean For Dummies
(0-7645-5445-X)

Cruise Vacations For Dummies 2003
(0-7645-5459-X)

Europe For Dummies
(0-7645-5456-5)

Ireland For Dummies
(0-7645-6199-5)

France For Dummies
(0-7645-6292-4)

London For Dummies
(0-7645-5416-6)

Mexico's Beach Resorts For Dummies
(0-7645-6262-2)

Paris For Dummies
(0-7645-5494-8)

RV Vacations For Dummies
(0-7645-5443-3)

Walt Disney World & Orlando For Dummies
(0-7645-5444-1)

Available wherever books are sold. Go to www.dummies.com or call 1-877-762-2974 to order direct.